People Power and Protest Since 1945: A Bibliography of Nonviolent Action

**Compiled by April Carter, Howard Clark
and Michael Randle**

© April Carter, Howard Clark and Michael Randle 2006

First published 2006 by Housmans Bookshop Limited, 5 Caledonian Road,
Kings Cross, London N1 9DX
020 7837 4473; shop@housmans.com; www.housmans.com

ISBN: 0 85283 262 1

A CIP catalogue record for this bibliography is available from the British Library.

Cover design by York Publishing Services Ltd

Prepared and printed by:
York Publishing Services Ltd
64 Hallfield Road
Layerthorpe
York YO31 7ZQ
Tel: 01904 431213; Fax: 01904 430868; Website: www.yps-publishing.co.uk

Contents

Acknowledgements   viii

Foreword by Paul Rogers   ix

General Introduction   1

A. **Introduction to Nonviolent Action**   7
Introduction
1. Nonviolent action: theory, methods and examples   7
2. Gandhi and Gandhian campaigns   13
3. Nonviolent (civilian) resistance and national defence   16
4. Nonviolent intervention and accompaniment   18

B. **Elements of Nonviolent Resistance to Colonialism After 1945**   22
Africa
Introduction (including general references)
1. Central Africa to 1964   23
    a. Malawi (Nyasaland)   24
    b. Zambia (Northern Rhodesia)   25
2. Ghana (Gold Coast) to 1957   26
3. Kenya to 1963   27
4. Nigeria to 1960   28

C. **Campaigns for Rights and Democracy in Communist Regimes**   29
Introduction (including references to Bulgaria and to Mongolia, 1989/1990)
I. USSR and Central and Eastern Europe to 1991   30
1. a. Comparative studies of dissent   30
    b. Literature on the revolutions of 1989-90   31
2. Baltic States, 1944-91   32
3. Czechoslovakia, 1948-89   33
    a. The Prague Spring and resistance to occupation, 1968-69   33
    b. 'Normalization' to the Velvet Revolution, 1970-89   34
4. East Germany (GDR), 1945-89   35
    a. The 1953 uprising   36
    b. The rise of dissent to the fall of the Berlin Wall, 1960s to 1989   36
5. Hungary, 1947-89   37
    a. Destalinization and revolution, 1953-56   38
    b. Gradual growth of dissent, 1960-89   39
6. Poland, 1945-89   40
    a. Destalinization and mass resistance, 1953-56   41
    b. Reaction and developing dissent, 1960s and 1970s   41
    c. Solidarity: from opposition to government, 1980-89   43
7. Romania, 1945-89   44
8. Soviet Union, 1945-91   46

a. Growing dissent, 1965-84   47
b. The Gorbachev years and popular protest, 1985-90; and resisting
    the 1991 coup   50
9. Yugoslavia, 1945-1990   51
    a. Two stages of reform: 1950-54 and 1960s; and dissent 1960s-70s   52
    b. Post-Tito politics in the 1980s   53
II. China and Tibet, from 1947   53
1. China   53
    a. The Hundred Flowers Movement, 1956-57   54
    b. The Democracy Movement, 1976-79   55
    c. Tiananmen, The mass protests of 1989   55
    d. China since 1990   57
2. Tibet   58

D. Resisting Rigged Elections, Oppression, Dictatorship, or Military Rule 60
I. Africa   60
Introduction
1. South Africa, Resisting apartheid to 1994   60
    a. Internal resistance   61
    b. External boycotts   63
    c. Resisting South African military policies   64
2. Zimbabwe, Resisting Mugabe's autocracy since 2000   65
II. Asia   67
Introduction (including references to Nepal 1990 and Kyrgyzstan 2005)
1. Burma, Resisting military dictatorship 1988, and ongoing protest   68
2. Korea (South), Demanding democracy, 1979-80 and 1986-87   69
3. Pakistan, Resisting military rule, 1968 and 1980s   70
4. Philippines   72
    a. Resisting Marcos, 1983-86   72
    b. Challenging Estrada, 2001   74
5. Taiwan, 1970s and 1980s   75
6. Thailand, Demanding democracy 1973 and 1992   76
III. Europe   77
Introduction (including references to Portugal 1974, and to Belarus today)
1. Former Yugoslavia after 1990   79
    a. Serbia, Resisting Milosevic 1996-2000   80
    b. Kosovo, Resisting Serbian oppression 1988-98   81
2. Georgia, Challenging 'rigged' elections 2003   82
3. Greece, Resisting the Colonels, 1967-74   83
4. Spain, Resisting Franco up to 1975   85
5. Ukraine, People power and elections, 2004-2005   87
IV. Latin America   89
Introduction (including references to pre-1945 people power, Colombia,
    Guatemala and Venezuela)
1. Argentina, Resisting the military dictatorship, 1977-81   92
2. Bolivia, Resisting repression, 1964-82   93
3. Brazil, Resisting military rule, 1964-85   94

		4.	Chile	95
			a. The right mobilizes against Salvador Allende, 1972-73	95
			b. Resisting the Pinochet dictatorship, 1973-90	96
		5.	Panama, Resisting Noriega 1987-89	97
		6.	Uruguay, Resisting military rule 1973-84	98
	V.	Middle East		99

Introduction (including references to Lebanon 2005)

		1.	Iran, Overthrowing the Shah 1979-1980	100
		2.	Palestine	101
			a. Palestinian resistance after 1967 and the First Intifada, 1987-1992	102
			b. Israeli opposition to Israel's occupation	104

E. Campaigns for Cultural, Civil and Political Rights — 106

I.	Nationalist Rights or Self Determination	106
1.	Welsh Nationalism and nonviolent action	106
II.	Campaigns for Civil Rights	107
1.	The Civil Rights Movement and Black Power in the USA, 1955-68	107
2.	Northern Ireland	113
	a. The Civil Rights Movement 1967-72	114
	b. The Protestant workers' strike 1974	116
	c. The Peace People, nonviolent intervention to halt violence 1976-1979	117

F. Campaigns for Social and Economic Justice — 119

Introduction

1.	Demands for land reform and land occupations	119
2.	Protests by the unemployed	121
	a. Dolci and the reverse strike	121
3.	Factory occupations	121
	a. Britain and Europe	122
4.	Significant strikes	122
	a. California grape pickers' strike, 1965-1970	123
	b. The British miners' strike, 1984-1985	123
5.	Campaigns by homeless (squatting)	124
6.	Protests against unjust taxes and rents	124
	a. Taxes	124
	i. Poll tax protests, Britain, 1989-90	125
	ii. Fuel tax protests, 2000	125
	b. Rent Strikes	125

G. Nonviolent Action in Social Movements — 127

Introduction and references to:

	a. National/area studies	127
	b. Transnational issues and campaigns	128
1.	The New Left and student movements, 1960s	128

Introduction

| | a. General and comparative | 129 |
| | b. Britain | 130 |

	c.	France, May Events of 1968	130
	d.	Germany (West)	130
	e.	USA	130
2.	Resistance to the Vietnam War, 1961-73		131
Introduction			
	a.	General	132
	b.	Australia	133
	c.	South Vietnam (Buddhists)	133
	d.	USA	134
3.	Peace movements since 1945		137
Introduction			
	a.	General: national and transnational movements	137
	b.	Pacifist protest, conscientious objection and draft resistance	139
		i. Pacifist and nonviolent thought	140
		ii. Conscientious resistance and legal frameworks	141
	c.	Opposition to nuclear weapons since the 1950s	144
		i. Theoretical debates about nuclear weapons	145
		ii. Comparative and general studies	146
		iii. Studies of particular countries, campaigns or actions	148
	d.	Campaigns against specific wars or acts of aggression (excluding Vietnam)	151
	e.	Protests against militarism	153
4.	Feminist Protest since the 1960s		155
Introduction			
	a.	Protest for Women's Rights	157
	b.	Women's strikes	158
	c.	Feminist direct action for peace	158
5.	Green Campaigns since the 1970s		159
Introduction			
	a.	General studies and transnational protest	160
	b.	Country studies	162
	c.	Campaigns against nuclear power	163
	d.	Campaigns against deforestation	163
	e.	Campaigns against dams	164
	f.	Campaigns against mining and pollution	164
	g.	Campaigns against roads, airports, redevelopment etc.	165
6.	Campaigns for Indigenous Rights since the 1960s		165
Introduction			
	a.	Australia	166
	b.	Canada	166
	c.	New Zealand	167
	d.	USA	167
7.	Global Justice Movement against Global Neoliberalism and Multinational Corporations		167
Introduction			
	a.	General	168

		b.	Resistance to international economic organizations	170
			i. Opposing global summits	170
			ii. Opposing IMF policies and privatization (Argentian, Bolivia, Ecuador and South Africa)	170
			iii. Opposing the World Bank	172
		c.	Resistance to multinational corporations	172
			i. Logging, mining, etc.	172
			ii. Oil companies	172
			iii. Sweatshops	173
			iv. McDonald's	173
		d.	Resistance by small farmers	173
		e.	Zapatistas and other indigenous resistance in Mexico	174

H. Bibliographies, Websites and Library Resources — 175
    a. Bibliographies — 175
    b. Websites — 176
    c. MA and PhD Theses — 177
    d. Library sources and archives — 178
        i. Britain — 178
        ii. Netherlands — 178
        iii. USA — 178

I. Preparation and Training for Nonviolent Action — 180

Index to Bibliography — 184
    Author Index (by item numbers) — 184
    Subject Index (by page numbers) — 193

Acknowledgements

We are very grateful for advice on particular sections of this bibliography to Adam Baird, Jonathan Cohen, Fay Gadsden, Harri Pritchard-Jones, Lena Pritchard-Jones, Roseanne Reeves, and Jenny Pearce.

The Commonweal Collection, which specializes in books, journals and pamphlets related to nonviolence and radical politics and is housed at the the J.B.Priestley Library at Bradford University, was an invaluable aid in compiling this bibliography. Finally, we owe a particular debt of gratitude to the Joseph Rowntree Charitable Trust for their indispensable financial help towards the publishing and promoting of the work.

About the Compilers of the Bibliography

April Carter has lectured in politics at the universities of Lancaster, Oxford and Queensland, and was a Summer Fellow at the Stockholm International Peace Research Institute 1985-87. Her publications include The Politics of Women's Rights (Longman, 1988), Success and Failure in Arms Control Negotiations (SIPRI/Oxford University Press, 1989), Peace Movements (Longman, 1992), and The Political Theory of Global Citizenship (Routledge, 2001). Her latest book is Direct Action and Democracy Today (Polity, 2005).

Howard Clark has been a nonviolent activist since 1968, engaging in a variety of campaigns and projects at local, national and increasingly international level. He has a continuing close involvement with Peace News (co-editor 1971-76) and with War Resisters' International (coordinator 1985-97). In addition he has been a research fellow of the Albert Einstein Institution and the Coventry University Centre for Peace and Reconciliation Studies. His publications include: Making Nonviolent Revolution (Peace News pamphlet, 1978 and 1981), Preparing for Nonviolent Direct Action – with Sheryl Crown, and Angela Mckee (Peace News and CND, 1983), and Civil Resistance in Kosovo (Pluto, 2000).

Michael Randle has been involved in the anti-war movement in Britain since the 1950s and was one of the organizers of the first Aldermaston March against Britain's nuclear weapons in 1958. A former Chair of War Resisters' International, and subsequently co-ordinator of the Alternative Defence Commission, he is now a Visiting Research Fellow at the Department of Peace Studies, University of Bradford. He is Minutes Secretary of the Committee for Conflict Transformation Support and co-edits their quarterly Review. His publications include: People Power: The Building of a New European Home (Hawthorn Press, 1991), Civil Resistance (Fontana, 1994), Challenge to Nonviolence, (editor), (Department of Peace Studies, Bradford University, 2002), and Jubilee 2000: The Challenge of Coalition Campaigning (Centre for the Study of Forgiveness and Reconciliation, Coventry University, 2004).

Foreword

The great achievement of this book is the way in which it brings together an extraordinary wealth of experience in a manner that will be an eye-opener for most readers. If we talk about "people power" or "nonviolent action", most people will immediately think of Gandhi or Martin Luther King, a few will recall the end of the Marcos regime in the Philippines in the mid-1980s and some others will remember or have heard of the Prague Spring nearly two decades earlier. Even for most activists and others involved in peace action and movements for social change, there will be little knowledge of the theories of nonviolent action and still less of the huge number of actions taken in so many countries and in such different circumstances across the world.

Although the book is subtitled *A Bibliography of Nonviolent Action,* it is much more than this. In addition to an introduction that is both succinct and helpful, all the main sources have accounts of their content and relevance, frequently managing to get to the core of the books or articles in just a couple of sentences. What really comes across is the sheer range of examples contained within this bibliography. It is extraordinarily impressive, taking us through the campaigns in Eastern Europe and the Soviet Union at the end of the Cold War, the earlier actions in late colonial Africa, campaigns of nonviolent resistance in Latin America and the Middle East and the many examples of transnational social movements. Green movements, feminist protest, campaigns for indigenous rights and the global justice movement are all covered, and the book ends with a useful section on websites, archives and academic theses.

To my knowledge this is the first time that a task such as this has been attempted with this degree of thoroughness. It is long overdue and is a really powerful antidote to the pervasive and negative outlook that believes that change will only come through violence. By bringing together such a range of writings, the authors have done a real service to all those people who seek positive social change through peaceful means.

Paul Rogers
Department of Peace Studies
Bradford University
November 2005

Note to Readers

We hope to update this bibliography in the future. We would therefore be grateful for suggestions for additional references. Please write to: Bibliography, c/o Housmans Peace Resource Project, 5 Caledonian Road, Kings Cross, London N1 9DX, UK; email: worldpeace@gn.apc.org

General Introduction

The spectacle of large crowds assembling, camping in the centre of capital cities and entering parliamentary and government buildings in order to demand greater democracy has become common on television screens in the last few years. But 'people power' is only one facet of the increasingly frequent use of predominantly nonviolent action round the world in campaigns for human rights, peace, social justice or the preservation of the environment.

One reason for bringing out a bibliography on nonviolent action now is to draw attention to the growing number of primarily nonviolent popular campaigns (some much better known in the west than others). The other is to provide an up-to-date guide for those interested in nonviolent action in general, or those who wish to study particular types of campaign or specific movements.

The bibliography is organized to indicate the historical evolution of nonviolent action, the different contexts in which it has been used and the varying types of campaign. Introductory comments elaborate on the reasons for classification, sketch in the background and political context of campaigns and also note some controversial issues.

Nonviolent Action: Definition and Scope

Some nonviolent protests are influenced by specific adherence to the ideal of nonviolence, usually by the leaders or key groups within the movement. More often people turn to methods such as strikes, boycotts, sit downs or civil disobedience because these are ways in which people can confront those with economic, political or military might. This type of protest is also associated with the concept of 'direct action'. Now direct action often denotes nonviolent protest, but has historic links to the syndicalist tradition and is open to interpretations sanctioning sabotage and violent resistance.

Popular resistance using nonviolent means, now often summed up in the phrase 'people power', was in the past sometimes labelled 'passive resistance'. The term 'passive resistance' may now be used to denote hidden resistance, such as go-slows, as opposed to more open nonviolent defiance.

The focus here is on protest and resistance, rather than on nonviolence as a philosophy, a social, economic and political theory or as a personal way of life. These wider issues often have relevance for nonviolent protest – the life, thought and nonviolent campaigns of Mahatma Gandhi exemplify this interconnectedness – and some of the references we cite explore these links. But a primary focus on nonviolence would result in a rather different bibliography.

This bibliography covers both nonviolent campaigns guided by a philosophy of nonviolence (though not all participants necessarily share this philosophy) and the larger number of pragmatic uses of nonviolent protest or resistance. The latter may involve minor sabotage, and some protesters may engage in spontaneous violence, for example in confrontations with the police. But if the primary emphasis is on use of nonviolent (though potentially coercive) methods, these campaigns are included here as significant examples of nonviolent action.

The alternative to nonviolent resistance, which can be adopted as a strategy by the weak against the strong, is guerrilla warfare. Many guerrilla campaigns include use of mass civilian protest, such as marches or strikes, to promote their goals, as the IRA did in Northern Ireland. Whilst there are interesting comparisons to be made between guerrilla and nonviolent struggle, the only campaigns covered in this bibliography are those which are predominantly nonviolent. However, major nonviolent campaigns which are followed by resort to guerrilla tactics, as in Kosovo in the 1990s, are included. So are campaigns devised on the basis of a nonviolent strategy but which over time become increasingly associated with violent confrontation – notably the Palestinian Intifada launched in 1987.

There is an impressive history of use of nonviolent methods in movements for civil and political rights in most parts of the world. In Britain this stretches from the tax refusal and protests in the early seventeenth century to the mass 'Wilkes and Liberty' protests of the late eighteenth century and to the Chartists in the nineteenth century. The movement for women's rights involved major protests in the early twentieth century. Demands for economic rights have been closely associated with the use of strikes and boycotts by the labour movement. Mass noncooperation and boycotts were also used as tactics in some nineteenth and early twentieth century movements for national independence, as in Hungary 1849-67 (after the defeat of an armed uprising), Finland 1899-1906 and Ireland in the nineteenth and early twentieth century (prior to and to some extent after the 1916 Easter Uprising). These national campaigns of tactical nonviolence against militarily superior occupying powers are often presented as examples of nonviolent resistance.

Nonviolent action as a deliberate political strategy received greater prominence with the impact of Gandhi's campaigns in South Africa from 1894-1914 (mass civil disobedience to protest against the discrimination against Indians was launched in 1906) and his role in the Indian independence movement from 1917 to 1947. Gandhi was influenced by earlier theorists and practitioners of nonviolent resistance and civil disobedience, such as Thoreau and, particularly, Tolstoy. But he developed a much more comprehensive and sophisticated philosophy of nonviolence and its political implications.

His campaigns also gave nonviolent methods much greater credibility, although many have argued that his success depended on the nature of his opponents. Debate about the potential for resisting a totally ruthless regime continues. But the possibility of using nonviolent resistance even against a totalitarian regime was demonstrated in parts of occupied Europe during World War II, especially in Norway and Denmark.

Despite the importance of the historical legacy of nonviolent action and developments in the first half of the twentieth century, this bibliography focuses almost entirely on campaigns launched since 1945. To include all the historical material would make this book unmanageably large and expensive. Historical case studies have also been well covered in earlier bibliographies (see Section H).

But for the guidance of those unfamiliar with the literature on nonviolent action, we have included an introductory section (A.1.), which lists some classic works on nonviolent action and quite a few more recent studies, many of which do cite earlier historical examples and include bibliographical references. Some of this literature illustrates or examines the distinction between Gandhian satyagraha (sometimes translated as 'truth force'), in which moral elements are central, and more pragmatic political and strategic interpretations of nonviolence emphasized by Gene Sharp.

Secondly, it is impossible to ignore the absolutely central role played by Gandhi in developing the theory of nonviolent resistance and in influencing later campaigns. So, although Gandhi's major resistance campaigns occurred before 1945, we have included a subsection of introductory literature on Gandhian thought and action (A.2.).

One outcome of the increasing awareness of the potential of mass nonviolent action has been a growing literature on the possibility of nonviolent (or civilian) resistance as a basis for a defence policy. This literature (A.3.) covers examples of earlier campaigns, notably World War II resistance to Nazi Germany, and also introduces the strategic debate.

Although most earlier examples of nonviolent protest took place within nation states, there has been a growing tendency towards transnational action (exemplified in many recent social movements). Activists committed to nonviolence have also increasingly explored the possibility of organized intervention to express solidarity and offer aid and publicity to those struggling against draconian regimes or a particular threat. A number of comparative studies of different types of nonviolent intervention are included in section A.4.

Nonviolent Methods: Achievements and Limits

Some campaigns of nonviolent resistance have had positive results – for example the use of people power in the Philippines in 1986. But others, like some violent campaigns, have failed to achieve their goals for a range of reasons. These 'failures' may however have featured significant examples of nonviolent action and are still instructive. Success is also often hard to define: campaigns may achieve immediate goals but fail to alter the wider context. The US Civil Rights Movement, for example, contributed to ending official segregation in the Deep South, but did not fundamentally change the economic and social discrimination suffered by African Americans. Even if campaigns can claim victory, it may be partially attributable to the wider political and economic context – as was true of the demonstrations of people power in Central and Eastern Europe in 1989. In general campaigns which count as successful have been better covered by the literature, but success is not a criterion for inclusion in this bibliography.

Campaigns which use nonviolent methods (especially if the great majority adopt them for purely tactical reasons) do not guarantee that a spirit of nonviolence will obtain once the cause is won. The decolonization of the Indian subcontinent, with the massacres arising out of partition to create a separate Muslim Pakistan, and the increasing corruption associated with Congress Party rule, illustrate this point dramatically. Gandhi's anguish in 1947-48 about the massacres, which he did his utmost to stop, and his doubts about future Congress Party rule, underline the problems of political victory not accompanied by wider social and attitudinal change.

Indeed, tactical nonviolence does not necessarily mean that the goals are 'nonviolent' in a broader sense. The great majority of the campaigns covered have been undertaken by those suffering oppression, injustice or discrimination. But nonviolent methods can be, and have been, used by groups supporting what liberals and the left regard as illiberal or right wing causes – two obvious examples are the Protestant workers' strike in Northern Ireland to overthrow power sharing with Catholics, and the truckers' strike against nationalization which immobilized Chile under Allende before the military coup. Where large sections of the population engage in major protest it suggests that there are serious political questions to be addressed, though there may also be apparently irreconcilable conflicts of interests or ideology.

'People power' can also be seen as a challenge to constitutional legitimacy, and it becomes especially problematic if there are two ideologically divided 'peoples' within a state, as the mass opposing demonstrations in the Ukraine in 2004/2005 and in Lebanon in early 2005 suggested. On the other hand, popular action, despite risks that it will lead to violence, is infinitely preferable to an immediate resort to the gun. Popular protest may also reveal basic conflicts and popular discontents, which cannot always be suppressed or satisfactorily resolved by political deals at an elite level.

Some recent nonviolent campaigns have also raised questions about intervention by external governments and divided those on the left – for example the protests against election results (which demonstrators claim were rigged) in Georgia and the Ukraine have been seen as inspired by the USA, countering Russian influence on the existing governments. But few campaigns are wholly insulated from external influences – and opponents frequently allege external manipulation. So although it is important both for participants and observers to be aware of the interests and possible role of external states or parties, possible external intervention is not a sufficient reason to discount mass popular demonstrations. Although external government agencies may be able to fund and encourage protest, widespread involvement suggests genuine and deep popular grievances. There is an obvious contrast here with an elite military coup d'etat. We have therefore included all examples which reasonably count as nonviolent direct action in this bibliography.

Other Aspects of Nonviolence and this Bibliography

Nonviolence as a principle suggests an important role for reconciliation between hostile groups. But sometimes there appears to be a conflict between demands for rights or social justice and the aim of overcoming antagonism between different racial, ethnic or religious groups, since resistance can (at least in the short term) intensify hatreds and result in violence. The civil rights campaigns by African Americans in the USA and Catholics in Northern Ireland prompted this kind of debate (Martin Luther King had to respond to many prominent critics), and illustrated how protest can lead to polarization. The titles listed under these campaigns do cover some of these debates. But forms of nonviolent protest can also be used to intervene between antagonistic communities, as the Peace People in Northern Ireland illustrate. Studies of nonviolent intervention quite often include both 'partisan' and 'nonpartisan' initiatives. Reconciliation therefore features in this bibliography where it is linked to nonviolent action.

One important facet of Gandhi's nonviolent campaigns was the development of a constructive programme – the creation of alternative economic, social and sometimes political institutions. Gandhi's emphasis suggested a conscious attempt to devise a nonviolent form of society free from inequality and coercion. But the logic of resistance quite often leads to a movement promoting alternative institutions. The Kosovan Albanian resistance to Serb domination and exclusion of Albanians from mainstream life in the 1980s-90s led to the creation of independent universities and forms of self-government. Moreover, some types of direct protest encourage constructive alternatives which may include an emphasis on democratic involvement: boycotts suggest the need for alternative goods or institutions; sit-in strikes can lead naturally to taking over a workplace and running it under workers' control; land occupations can lead to cooperative farming. Indeed, spontaneous mass resistance and revolutionary upsurges often prompt the creation of forms of direct democracy, as Hannah Arendt has argued eloquently in her 1963 book On Revolution. New movements such as feminism and the greens in the 1970s and the movement for global justice since 1999 often encourage radical experiments in democratic organization. These issues are raised in some of the general literature on nonviolent action and in studies of particular campaigns and movements included in this bibliography. But we have not attempted to cover the specialized literature on cooperatives, workers' control and direct democracy.

The widespread use of nonviolent action and its increasing credibility as a form of resistance has created a need for books and pamphlets setting out possible strategic, tactical and organizational approaches. Nonviolent campaigns have also been stimulated by the distribution and translation of manuals of advice. The Albert Einstein Institution at Harvard has been prominent in producing such pamphlets and making them available on the net – a few of these pamphlets which include some historical background and analysis are included in this bibliography under section A.

Particular campaigns and demonstrations also prompt ad hoc briefings on tactics, organization and legal issues, and may involve advance training sessions. Since the 1970s a number of individuals and groups have offered training for nonviolent action. We have drawn attention to websites and organizations relevant to planning or training for nonviolent action in Section I.

Scope and Format of Entries

This bibliography is produced primarily for activists, students and peace researchers based in Britain, so availability in British libraries has been one consideration in selection of titles. But we hope it will also be helpful to those in other parts of the world with an interest in nonviolent action. For practical reasons we have confined ourselves to English language sources and reluctantly omit various important works not yet translated into English.

We have aimed at transnational coverage of major examples of civil resistance and other significant nonviolent protest. But given the compilers' own experience, and the focus on sources generally available in Britain, there is a particular emphasis on British examples in some subsections of F (campaigns for social justice) and G (social movements). The exclusion of non-English language sources also inevitably creates some bias in the coverage.

When indicating the increased use of nonviolent action since 1945 we have included major books and articles covering the campaigns and some literature which elaborates on the ideas of key protesters or sets the wider political context. We have tried to cite useful and reasonably accessible books, pamphlets and periodical articles, which cover central personalities, different social and political groups involved, and varying ideological perspectives (including critical assessments). There is often a mix of academic assessments, journalistic accounts and movement sources. We have deliberately been selective.

Short 1-2 page articles in mainstream dailies or weeklies, or in movement periodicals, are not normally listed (unless there is a dearth of literature on a campaign). But we try to indicate which periodicals (general, movement-based or academic) might be helpful to those wanting to do further research. In some cases websites are also included, especially where they provide information not otherwise available, but general websites on nonviolence are listed in Section H.

Brief introductory summaries explain the political context of the relevant campaign, and may end with references to introductory literature. There are also brief introductions to each main section and, where relevant (as under D), to regions of the world encompassing a number of campaigns. These introductions sometimes note and give brief references to campaigns not listed separately: for example under C we refer to the people power protests in Mongolia in 1990; and under D.II to the 1990 Movement for the Restoration of Democracy in Nepal, as well as the 2005 demonstrations against rigged elections and nepotism in Kyrgyzstan.

Entries are annotated where it seems helpful, either to explain a title or draw attention to aspects of a book or article which are particularly relevant. But some titles are self-explanatory. In a few cases additional titles are included under one entry – either referring to other works by the same author, supplementary works or direct critiques of a key thesis. (All titles are then indexed under the same item number). Relevant sources in other parts of the bibliography are cross-referenced at the end of sections or sub-sections.

A. Introduction to Nonviolent Action

1. Nonviolent Action: Theory, Methods and Examples

The aim here is to indicate some classic works on the theory and practice of nonviolent action/resistance, introduce authors contributing to the literature from a variety of ideological perspectives, and to note recent studies of people power.

Theoretical writings analyse the nature and dynamics of nonviolent action and discuss political, sociological and psychological explanations for the impact of nonviolent protest. The interpretation of power is a key issue, and a few of the titles listed are chosen partly for this reason; some of them have also inspired those engaging in resistance.

Nonviolent action has (as noted in the Introduction) become closely associated with the concept of 'direct action' since the 1950s, although direct action with its syndicalist roots is still open to interpretations which endorse some forms of violence. Several titles on direct action are therefore included.

Nonviolent action is even more closely associated with the concept of 'civil disobedience'. The justification for disobeying unjust laws, or illegally challenging unjust regimes, has been elaborated (with different emphases) by key practitioners of civil disobedience such as Henry Thoreau, who went to jail for refusing to pay tax which would support slavery and the war on Mexico, Gandhi and Martin Luther King. These classic statements are frequently reprinted in various collections on nonviolent action or on civil disobedience listed below. The US Civil Rights Movement, civil disobedience against nuclear weapons and draft resistance to the Vietnam war sparked an academic debate among jurists and political theorists (referred to in some of the titles below). The most notable examination of the circumstances in which civil disobedience is justified within parliamentary democracies was provided by John Rawls, who in his landmark book <u>A Theory of Justice</u> (1972) explored the issue in depth in Chapter Six. Briefer summaries of Rawls' position (which is similar to Gandhi's) are available elsewhere, perhaps most accessibly in H.A. Bedau (ed.), <u>Civil Disobedience</u> (see below).

There is now a growing literature on nonviolent action and people power, so although the movements of the 1950s and 1960s prompted a number of books, many titles are quite recent and reflect the manifold examples of people power in the last 30 years. There are also quite a few edited collections which introduce key texts and/or provide a wide range of examples of the use of nonviolent action, and many of these are listed below. See also A.2, A.3, and A.4.

1. Ackerman, Peter and Jack Duvall, <u>A Force More Powerful: A Century of Nonviolent Conflict</u>, New York and Basingstoke, Palgrave, 2000, pp. 544. Analysis of a selection of predominantly nonviolent struggles from Russia 1905 to Serbia 2000, arguing against the 'mythology of violence'. Some of the case studies are standard in books on

nonviolence; but others – for example the 1990 movement in Mongolia – are less familiar. Each chapter has a useful bibliography. The book arose out of a 1999 US documentary television series 'A Force More Powerful'.

2.Ackerman, Peter and Christopher Kruegler, Strategic Nonviolent Conflict: The Dynamics of People Power in the Twentieth Century, Westport CT, Praeger, 1993, pp. 366.

Traces the emergence of strategic nonviolent conflict, discusses the principles involved and relates these to some of the major nonviolent struggles in the 20th century.

3.Arendt, Hannah, On Violence, London, Allen Lane, 1970, pp. 106.

A critical examination by major political theorist of the nature of power and violence (with examples from contemporary movements), in which Arendt concludes that violence is not only different from power, as she defines it, but its opposite.

4.Bedau, Hugo Adam (ed.), Civil Disobedience: Theory and Practice, Indianapolis, Bobbs Merrill, 1969, pp. 282.

Provides wide range of contributions on the case for and against civil disobedience, including classic essays by Henry Thoreau and Martin Luther King, Bertrand Russell on civil disobedience against nuclear weapons, and Noam Chomsky and others on draft resistance to the Vietnam war and John Rawls' 'Justification for civil disobedience'.

5.Benewick, Robert and Trevor Smith (eds.), Direct Action and Democratic Politics, London, Allen and Unwin, 1972, pp. 324.

Part 1 surveys historical and theoretical issues related to direct action and role of political violence – Benewick stresses that they are distinct, but most contributors do not. There is no specific discussion of nonviolence. Part 2 provides descriptive analyses of particular campaigns in Britain, and Part 3 includes reflections on the role of the state, political parties and the media.

6.Bleiker, Roland, Popular Dissent, Human Agency and Global Politics, Cambridge, Cambridge University Press, 2000, pp. 289.

Theorizes transnational ('transversal') dissent, looking back to De Boetie's renaissance theory of power and tracing evolution of modern collective action, and draws on Foucault to explore a 'discursive' concept of power. Provides a critique of Sharp's 'consent' theory of power, illustrated by analysis of East German political and cultural dissent culminating in the collapse of the Berlin Wall.

7.Carter, April, Direct Action and Democracy Today, Cambridge, Polity, 2005, pp. 298.

Focuses on links between democracy and nonviolent direct action; chapters 1 & 3 in particular refer to a wide range of predominantly nonviolent campaigns and chapter 4 covers the recent resistance to multinationals and global neoliberalism. The second part of the book raises theoretical issues and refers inter alia to liberal debates about civil disobedience. Her earlier book, Direct Action and Liberal Democracy (London, Routledge, 1973, pp. 169) made a case for nonviolent direct action in parliamentary systems.

8.Case, Clarence Marsh, <u>Non-Violent Coercion: A Study in Methods of Social Pressure</u> [1923] New York, Garland, 1972, pp. 423.

Early sociological study of nonviolent action in social movements and of Gandhian strategy.

9.Cohen, Carl, <u>Civil Disobedience: Conscience, Tactics and the Law</u>, New York, Columbia University Press, 1971, pp. 222.

Considers arguments for, and objections to, the use of civil disobedience. Argues that it is important to take tactical considerations into account when deciding whether or not to engage in civil disobedience.

10.Cooney, Robert and Helen Michalowski, <u>The Power of the People: Active Nonviolence in the United States</u>, Culver City CA, Peace Press Inc, 1977, pp. 240.

Traces the nonviolent tradition from the Colonial period, with sections on women's suffrage, the labour movement, anti-conscription and anti-war campaigns during both World Wars, the Civil Rights Movement and the opposition to nuclear weapons and the war in Vietnam. Well illustrated and with thumbnail sketches of several leading activists.

11.Deming, Barbara, <u>Revolution and Equilibrium</u>, New York, Grossman, 1971, pp. 269.

Collection of essays by feminist nonviolent activist and journalist, covering wide range of protests. Includes an important theoretical essay, from which the book takes its title, in which Deming confronts the case for violence made by Frantz Fanon, in his critique of colonialism, and by many US militants in the late 1960s, and argues that radical nonviolent action can be an alternative. The title essay is available as a separate pamphlet from A.J. Muste Memorial Institute, 339 Lafayette St, New York, NY 10012, USA.

12.Epstein, Barbara, <u>Political Protest and Cultural Revolution: Nonviolent Direct Action in the 1970s and 1980s</u>, Berkeley, University of California Press, 1991, pp. 327.

Covers environmental/peace/feminist protest in the USA, analysing key ideas and organizing methods as well as evolution of some major campaigns, for example against the Seabrook nuclear energy plant and the Livermore nuclear weapons laboratory.

13.Gregg, Richard B., <u>The Power of Nonviolence</u> [1935] London, James Clark, 1960, pp. 192.

Classic analysis of 'moral jujitsu' as the basis of nonviolent resistance, and in particular of Gandhi's interpretation and strategy of nonviolent action ('satyagraha').

14.Hare, A. Paul and Herbert H. Blumberg (eds.) <u>Nonviolent Direct Action: American Cases: Social-Psychological Analyses</u>, Washington DC, Corpus Books, 1968, pp. 575.

Combines earlier and contemporary theoretical analyses of nonviolence (with a social-psychological emphasis) with examples of nonviolent action in Civil Rights and peace campaigns in the USA.

15.Havel, Vaclav, 'The power of the powerless' in Jan Vadislav (ed.), <u>Vaclav Havel: Living in Truth</u>, London, Faber, 1987, pp. 36-122. (Also available in several other collections of Havel's essays.)

Influential analysis of 'post-totalitarian' society in the Soviet bloc in the 1970s, and eloquent argument for individual integrity and acts of dissent, by leading Czechoslovak playwright and dissident who became President after 1989. This text inspired many activists in Eastern Europe at the time and others around the world, including Aung San Suu Kyi, key figure in nonviolent resistance in Burma.

16.Helvey, Robert L., <u>On Strategic Nonviolent Conflict: Thinking about Fundamentals</u>, Boston MA, The Albert Einstein Institution, 2004, pp. 178. Downloadable from: http://www.aeinstein.org/organizations/org/OSNC.pdf

Written by a retired Colonel with the US army, this study, in the Gene Sharp school of thought, examines the basis of political power, and the methods and strategy of nonviolent struggle.

17.Holmes, Robert L (ed.), <u>Nonviolence in Theory and Practice</u>, Belmont, Wadsworth, 1990, pp. 208.

Reader with excerpts on religious roots of nonviolence, and classic essays on nonviolence and pacifism – including Thoreau, Tolstoy, Gandhi and King, and William James on 'The moral equivalent of war'. The final sections give examples of nonviolent resistance in Occupied Europe, India, the USA, the Middle East and the Philippines. (Some essays also noted in relevant sections.)

18.Lakey, George, <u>Powerful Peacemaking: A Strategy for a Living Revolution</u>, Philadelphia PA, New Society Publishers, 1987, pp. 246. Revised edition of <u>Strategy for a Living Revolution</u>, New York, Grossman and San Francisco, W.H. Freeman, 1973.

Lakey analyses revolutionary popular movements (such as El Salvador and Guatemala 1944 and France 1968) and issues of cultural preparation, organization, leadership and tactics from a committed nonviolent standpoint. He also discusses how to develop and defend revolution by decentralizing power and use of nonviolent civilian defence.

19.De Ligt, Bartelemy, <u>The Conquest of Violence: An Essay on War and Revolution</u> [1935], New York, Garland 1972, pp. 306, and London, Pluto Press, 1989 (with introduction by Peter van den Dungen), pp. 306.

Classic anarchist argument for nonviolent resistance.

20.Lynd, Staughton and Alice Lynd (eds.), <u>Nonviolence in America: A Documentary History</u>, Maryknoll,NY, Orbis Books, 1995, pp. 530.

(This is a revised and extended edition of Staughton Lynd, (ed.), <u>Nonviolence in America</u>, Indianapolis, Bobbs Merrill, 1966.)

Anthology includes writings by opponents of slavery, anarchists and 'progressives' in the 19th century, and trade unionists, conscientious objectors and peace campaigners in the 20th century. Includes the Civil Rights campaign and anti-Vietnam War protests. The revised edition covers radical Catholic resistance, nonviolent trade unionism, resistance to US imperialism in Central America in the 1980s and assistance to Central American refugees, opposition to the 1991 Gulf War and environmental protests.

21.McAllister, Pam (ed.), <u>Reweaving the Web of Life: Feminism and Nonviolence</u>, Philadelphia PA, New Society, 1982, pp. 440.

Examines feminism, pacifism and nonviolence and anti-nuclear protests in the US.

22.Martin, Brian, and others, <u>Nonviolent Struggle and Social Defence</u>, ed. Shelley Anderson and Janet Larmore, London, War Resisters International, 1991, pp. 141.

Analysis of nonviolent action, and case studies of people power in Asia, Eastern Europe, Middle East, Central and South America and South Africa. (Based on a conference at the Bradford School of Peace Studies.) See also: Brian Martin, Wendy Varney and Adrian Vickers, 'Political jiu-jitsu against Indonesian repression: Studying lower profile resistance', <u>Pacifica Review</u>, vol. 13 no. 2 (June 2001), pp. 143-56.

23.Miller, William Robert, <u>Nonviolence: A Christian Interpretation</u>, London, Allen and Unwin, 1965, 380pp.

Discusses the nature and dynamics of nonviolent action and several nonviolent campaigns.

24.Powers, Roger S, William B. Vogele, Christopher Kruegler and Ronald M. McCarthy (eds.), <u>Protest, Power and Change: An Encyclopaedia of Nonviolent Action from ACT-Up to Women's Suffrage</u>, New York, Garland, 1997, pp. 610.

Valuable guide to both the theory and practice of nonviolence, summarizing 104 nonviolent campaigns or actions, listing methods of protest, and examining relevant organizations and personalities.

25.Randle, Michael, <u>Civil Resistance</u>, London, Fontana, 1994, pp. 259.

Chapters 1-4 focus on the history and dynamics of nonviolent resistance and its increasing use in recent decades, with an emphasis on national resistance to oppressive regimes. The second half of the book analyses civilian (nonviolent) defence. The author deals specifically with issues of nonviolent direct action in a democracy in his monograph: <u>Direct Action: A Threat to Democracy?</u>, University of Bradford, Dept of Peace Studies, Peace Studies Papers Fourth Series, Working Paper 5 (May 2002.)

26.Schell, Jonathan, <u>The Unconquerable World: Power, Nonviolence and the Will of the People</u>, Allen Lane/Penguin, London, 2004, pp. 435.

An argument by leading US intellectual on historical trends promoting nonviolence as a potential alternative to war. Part 2 'Nonviolence', pp. 103-231, focuses in particular on Gandhi and dissent in Eastern Europe.

27.Schock, Kurt, <u>Unarmed Insurrections: People Power Movements in Nondemocracies</u>, Minneapolis, University of Minnesota Press, 2005, pp. 228.

Seeks to address lack of explicitly comparative analysis of how nonviolent methods promote political transformation. Examines success of the anti-apartheid movement in South Africa (1983-90), and pro-democracy movements in the Philippines (1983-86), Nepal (1990) and Thailand (1991-92), and explores failure of such movements in

China (1989) and Burma (1988). Useful tables list major actions in each movement. Includes analysis and criticisms of 'consent' theory of power.

28.Scott, James C. Domination and the Arts of Resistance: Hidden Transcripts, New Haven, Yale University Press, 1990, pp. 251.

Study of the more or less clandestine 'discourse' of subordinate groups subjected to structural domination, noting 'hidden transcripts' often expressed in disguised forms, e.g. rumours, songs, gesture or jokes. Argues most insubordination occurs at the level of 'infrapolitics', but that there are occasions when 'the hidden transcript is spoken directly and publicly in the teeth of power', which can lead to open protest or rebellion, as in Romania December 1989 or Chile June 1988. Chapter 8 explores these breakthroughs.

29.Sharp, Gene, The Politics of Nonviolent Action, Boston, Porter Sargent, 1973, 3 volumes, pp. 902.

Now classic analysis of theory and dynamics of nonviolent action and exhaustive list of methods with examples. Includes extensive bibliographical references. Sharp's consent theory of power has been debated and criticized: see Brian Martin, 'Gene Sharp's theory of power', Journal of Peace Research, vol. 26, no 2 (May 1989), pp. 213-222; and Kate McGuinness, 'Gene Sharp's theory of power: A feminist critique of consent', Journal of Peace Research, vol. 30, no 1 (1993), pp. 101-15.

30.Sharp, Gene (with collaboration of Joshua Paulson and assistance of Christopher A. Miller and Hardy Merriman), Waging Nonviolent Struggle: 20th Century Practice and 21st Century Potential, Boston, Porter Sargent, 2005, pp. 598.

This volume draws on Sharp's extensive earlier work on both the theory and practice of nonviolent action. It includes 23 brief case studies of campaigns from the Russian revolution of 1905 to the Serbian people power of 2000, many well known but some (for example 'Saving Jewish husbands in Berlin in 1943') less so. Some of these case studies are based on research by Sharp's collaborators. The final section looks to the future, discussing strategic guidelines and the applications of nonviolent struggle to today's world.

31.Sibley, Mulford Q (ed.), The Quiet Battle: Writings on the Theory and Practice of Nonviolent Resistance, New York, Doubleday, 1963, pp. 390.

Includes extracts from variety of writings on nonviolence and accounts of nonviolent campaigns, together with a bibliography.

32.Solnit, Rebecca, Hope in the Dark: The Untold History of People Power, London, Cannongate Books, 2005, pp. 181.

Brief personal reflections on activism and the potential for change, touching on Zapatistas, the social justice movement, indigenous peoples' action and the transnational opposition to war in Iraq. No index.

33.Thompson, Mark R., Democratic Revolutions: Asia and Eastern Europe, London, Routledge, 2004, pp. 180.

Examines popular uprisings which overthrow authoritarian regimes, assessing what conditions make popular revolt possible and are conducive to success. Includes examples from China, East Germany, the Philippines and Serbia.

34.United Reformed Church, <u>Nonviolent Action: A Report Commissioned for the United Reformed Church</u>, London, SCM Press, 1973, pp. 84.

Report by an ecumenical group whose brief was to consider whether civil and international tensions could be resolved by nonviolent methods. The report looks at the problem of violence from a Christian perspective, summarizes some of the better known historical examples of nonviolent action, and considers related issues. Includes a chapter on 'Nonviolent methods and international conflict' where the possibilities of nonviolent defence are mentioned.

35.Wehr, Paul, Heidi Burgess and Guy Burgess (eds.), <u>Justice Without Violence</u>, Boulder CO, Lynne Rienner Publishers, 1994, pp. 301.

This book arises out of the US Conflict Resolution Consortium's 'Justice Without Violence' project. Starts with four theoretical chapters analysing literature on nonviolence and approaches to power. There are also eight varied case studies (not all of nonviolent action campaigns) exploring relations between violence and nonviolence (which is broadly defined).

36.Zinn, Howard, <u>Disobedience and Democracy: Nine Fallacies on Law and Order</u>, New York, Vintage Books, 1968. Reissued by London, Pluto, 2003, pp. 148.

Zinn is a well known radical historian and contributor to the literature on nonviolence and civil disobedience.

37.Zunes, Stephen, Lester R. Kurtz, and Sarah Beth Asher (eds.), <u>Nonviolent Social Movements: A Geographical Perspective</u>, Oxford, Blackwell, 1999, pp. 330.

Starts with brief essay on power by Kenneth Boulding and a discussion by Pam McAllister of women and nonviolent action, which critiques the masculinist bias of many works on nonviolence. The rest of the book contains well documented accounts of nonviolent action around the world, mostly focusing on the period since 1970s, though a few essays look back to earlier 20th century examples. (Individual chapters are also cited in the appropriate sections.)

2. Gandhi and Gandhian Campaigns

Gandhi is the best known theorist and practitioner of nonviolent action, who developed his distinctive theory of 'satyagraha' (truth force); and the success of the movement for Indian independence has enhanced the prestige of nonviolent resistance (though not all the resistance remained nonviolent). There is a huge literature by and about Gandhi and his campaigns both in South Africa up to 1914 and in India from 1917 to 1948. M.K. Gandhi, <u>Collected Works</u> run to 90 chronologically arranged volumes and 10 supplementary volumes. Here a few key sources only are listed, including some well known critical assessments. (See also bibliographies under H.)

38.Bondurant, Joan V., The Gandhian Philosophy of Conflict, London, Oxford University Press, 1958, pp. 269. (Revised edition University of California Press, 1969.)

Analysis of Gandhi's approach and three campaigns in India: the 1918 Ahmedabad textile workers' dispute, the 1919 resistance to the Rowlatt Bills and the 1930-31 Salt March.

39.Brown, Judith M. Gandhi and Civil Disobedience: The Mahatma in Indian Politics, 1928-1934, Cambridge, Cambridge Univesity Press, 1977, pp. 414.

Leading Gandhi scholar examines crucial phase of independence struggle from standpoint of both Congress Party and British Government.

40.Brown, Judith M. Gandhi: Prisoner of Hope, New Haven, Yale University Press, 1989, pp. 440.

Sympathetic but objective biography with an emphasis on political tactics and organization.

41.Brown, Judith M. Gandhi's Rise to Power: Indian Politics 1915-1922, Cambridge, Cambridge University Press, 1972, pp. 382.

42.Chatfield, Charles, The Americanisation of Gandhi: Images of the Mahatma, New York, Garland, 1976, pp. 802.

Contemporaneous reports and assessments of Gandhi and his campaigns published in US newspapers and political and religious journals at various periods of his life. Final sections deal with Gandhi's impact on US society, including notably his influence on the struggle for racial justice.

43.Copley, Antony, Gandhi: Against the Tide, Oxford, Blackwell, 1987, pp. 118.

Brief Historical Association study giving historical context and referring to historiographical debates, noting 'Cambridge school' argument that internal weaknesses of British Administration main cause of independence, and 'subaltern studies' school which stresses autonomous resistance of peasants and workers.

44.Dalton, Dennis, Mahatma Gandhi: Nonviolent Power in Action, New York, Columbia University Press, 1993, pp. 279.

Analysis of Gandhi's concept of satyagraha, political leadership and of the 1931 Salt Satyagraha and 1947 fast, as well as covering critiques by contemporaries and making comparisons with Martin Luther King and Malcolm X.

45.Fischer, Louis, The Life of Mahatma Gandhi, London, Jonathan Cape 1950, pp. 593. Reissued by Granada (London) 1983.

Lively sympathetic biography used as the basis for Richard Attenborough's 1982 film 'Gandhi'.

46.Gandhi, Mohandas K. Satyagraha in South Africa, Ahmedabad, Navajivan, [1928] 1950, pp. 348.

His own account of the seminal civil disobedience campaigns against legislation discriminating against the Indian population, and the evolution of his strategy and theory of 'satyagraha'.

47.Gandhi, Mohandas K. Selected Works of Mahatma Gandhi, ed. Shriman Narayan, Ahmedabad, Navajivan, 1968, 6 volumes: pp. 375, 379-794, 471, 464, 514, 555.

Includes Satyagraha in South Africa (vol. 3) as well as Gandhi's highly personal Autobiography published 1927 (vols 1-2), important pamphlets, such as his translation of Ruskin's Unto This Last (vol. 4), letters on key issues (vol. 5) and speeches on historic occasions (vol. 6).

48.Hardiman, David, Gandhi in his Time and Ours: The Global Legacy of his Ideas, London, Hurst, 2003, pp. 356.

Sympathetic but not uncritical assessment of Gandhi's style of politics, his conflicts with the Raj and with opposing groups and critics within India, and his impact on later movements. The author has studied Gandhi, and also 'subaltern' movements in India, for many years.

49.Moore, Barrington, Jr. The Social Origins of Dicatorship and Democracy: Lord and Peasant in the Making of the Modern World, London, Allen Lane, 1967.

Chapter 6 'Democracy in Asia: India and the price of peaceful change' argues Gandhi 'was the spokesman of the Indian peasant and village artisan' (p. 378) and comments critically on Gandhi's desire to return to an 'idealized past' of the village community purged of untouchability, and failure to challenge interests of landed aristocracy.

50.Nanda, Bal R., Gandhi and His Critics, Delhi, Oxford University Press, 1985, pp. 178.

Nanda, who has also written a balanced biography of Gandhi, and studies of other Indian leaders close to Gandhi (including Gandhi's mentor Gokhale), here examines controversial aspects of Gandhi's life and thought.

51.Orwell, George, 'Reflections on Gandhi', Partisan Review, 16 (January 1949), pp. 85-92. Reprinted in A Collection of Essays, New York, Harcourt, 1953.

A frequently cited critical view of many aspects of Gandhi's philosophy and life, which nevertheless recognizes his positive contribution as a politician.

52.Overy, Bob, 'Gandhi as a political organiser' in Michael Randle (ed.), Challenge to Nonviolence, Department of Peace Studies, University of Bradford, 2002, pp. 132-62.

This is a chapter from his unpublished PhD thesis (see H.c.).

53.Parekh, Bhikhu, Gandhi, Oxford, Oxford University Press, 1997, pp. 111. (Past Masters series.)

Brief account of Gandhi's life and work and critical assessment of his ideas by political theorist and Gandhi scholar.

54.Parekh, Bhikhu, Gandhi's Political Philosophy: A Critical Examination, Notre Dame IN, University of Notre Dame Press, 1989, pp. 284.

55.Sharp, Gene, <u>Gandhi Wields the Weapon of Moral Power: Three Case Histories,</u> Ahmedabad, Navajivan, 1960, pp. 316.

Analyses Champaran 1917-1918, the 1930-31 Salt Satyagraha and independence campaign, and Gandhi's last fast against Hindu-Muslim rioting, in Delhi in 1948.

56.Shridharani, Krishnalal, <u>War Without Violence: A Study of Gandhi's Method and its Accomplishments,</u> London, Gollancz, 1939, pp. 288. Reprinted by New York, Garland, 1972, pp. 351.

Respected analysis of satyagraha. Includes final comments on role of nonviolent action in democratic states in resisting an invasion.

57.Woodcock, George, <u>Gandhi,</u> London, Fontana/Collins, 1972, pp. 108. (Fontana Modern Masters Series.)

3. Nonviolent (Civilian) Resistance and National Defence

Nonviolent action has been primarily a means of protest or of popular resistance to unjust and repressive regimes. But the effectiveness of some national campaigns of nonviolent resistance seeking national independence suggested the possibility of planning for mass noncooperation and resistance to deter aggression or undermine an occupying power. Proposals for nonviolent or 'civilian' defence go back to the 1920s and 1930s, but it became a subject of more thorough political and academic debate from the 1950s in the light of the new strategic situation posed by nuclear weapons. Commander Sir Stephen King Hall proposed a nonviolent defence policy for Britain in his book <u>Defence in the Nuclear Age,</u> London, Gollancz, 1958. Later studies drew on earlier historical campaigns, in particularly the movement for Indian independence, and examples of nonviolent resistance to Nazism (especially in Norway and Denmark), and elaborated the strategic implications of nonviolent defence. Academic analyses of nonviolent defence were commissioned in the 1970s by the Danish, Dutch, Norwegian and Swedish governments, and it was discussed by Baltic governments after they achieved independence from the Soviet Union. Radical pacifists have also debated this approach using the concept of 'social defence'.

Advocates of civilian resistance have in addition stressed its relevance as a means of countering the threat quite often posed by the military to democracy in their own countries – that of a coup d'etat. The literature often notes the general strike against the Kapp Putsch in Germany in 1922, French civil resistance to the generals in Algeria in 1961, and (more recently) the popular opposition to the attempted Moscow coup in 1991. A less well known, and less successful, example of gradually emerging nonviolent resistance to coups occurred in Fiji after the two coups in 1987.

58.Alternative Defence Commission, <u>Defence Without the Bomb,</u> London, Taylor and Francis, 1983. Chapter 7, 'Strategies against occupation: 2. Defence by civil resistance', pp. 208-48, analyses the meaning and implications of nonviolent defence and considers it applicability to Britain.

59.Boserup, Anders and Andrew Mack, <u>War Without Weapons: Nonviolence in National Defence,</u> London, Frances Pinter, 1974, pp. 194.

Originally published in Danish and commissioned by the Danish government, this study examines the theory of nonviolent defence, strategic and organizational issues, historical examples and the possibility of combining nonviolent and military forms of defence.

60.Bulletin of Peace Proposals, vol. 9, no 4 (1978).

Issue devoted to reconsideration of nonviolent defence with contributions by leading exponents, including Sharp, Roberts and Galtung, and articles on its role in Sweden's Total Defence strategy and on the Dutch government research project.

61.Burrowes, Robert, The Strategy of Nonviolent Defense: A Gandhian Approach, Albany NY, State University of New York Press, 1996, pp. 367.

Draws on a reinterpretation of Clausewitz's classic work on war and discusses nature of power underlying nonviolent strategy and potential for social change.

62.Galtung, Johan, 'On the strategy of nonmilitary defense' in Peace, War and Defence: Essays in Peace Research, vol. 2, Copenhagen, Christian Ejlers, 1976, pp. 378-426.

63.Keyes, Gene, 'Strategic non-violent defense: The construct of an option', Journal of Strategic Studies, vol. 4, no 2 (June 1981), pp. 125 -51.

64.Martin, Brian, Social Defence, Social Change, London, Freedom Press, 1993, pp. 157.

Anarchist perspective on civilian (nonviolent) defence. Chapter 5 is an abbreviated version of: Brian Martin, 'Lessons in nonviolence from the Fiji coups', Gandhi Marg., vol. 10 no. 2 (Sept. 1988), pp. 326-39.

65.Roberts, Adam, 'Civil resistance to military coups', Journal of Peace Research, vol. 12 no. 1 (1975), pp. 19-36.

Discusses resistance to Kapp Putsch in Germany 1922 and attempted coup in France by generals based in Algeria 1961.

66.Roberts, Adam (ed.), Civilian Resistance as a National Defence, Hardmondsworth, Penguin, 1969. (Originally published as The Strategy of Civilian Defence, London, Faber and Faber, 1967.)

Chapters 4-8 cover the technique of nonviolent action and campaigns of national nonviolent resistance to occupation and to Nazi or Communist regimes, the Introduction discusses the Czechoslovak resistance to Soviet occupation in 1968, and Chapter 9 by Basil Liddell Hart compares guerrilla and nonviolent resistance.

67.Schmid, Alex P, Social Defence and Soviet Military Power: An Inquiry into the Relevance of an Alternative Defence Concept, Leiden, Centre for the Study of Social Conflict, State University of Leiden, 1985, pp. 469.

A generally sceptical assessment of social (nonviolent) defence as an alternative to military preparations against putative Soviet aggression. Concludes that it is not a substitute for nuclear deterrence or military defence, but could supplement them. Useful discussion of 10 conditions favourable to (or crucial for) success of social defence.

See also Howard Clark, <u>Civil Resistance in Kosovo</u> (D III 1.b.) who discusses Schmid's conditions.

68.Semelin, Jacques, <u>Unarmed Against Hitler: Civilian Resistance in Europe, 1939-1943</u>, Westport CT, Praeger, 1993, pp. 198. (Translation of <u>Sans armes face a Hitler</u>, Paris, editions Payot, 1989.)

Examines the main traits of Nazi occupation in Europe, the complexities of noncooperation, and the role of social cohesion and public opinion in mounting an effective opposition. Includes a chapter on civilian resistance to genocide and considers why the Final Solution was hampered or even prevented in certain countries. Final chapter on 'The new field of civilian-based defence strategies'.

69.Sharp, Gene and Bruce Jenkins, <u>The Anti-Coup</u>, Boston MA, The Albert Einstein Institution, 2003, pp. 64.

Sets out in short accessible form a nonviolent strategy for defeating or deterring military coups.

70.Sharp, Gene, <u>Civilian-Based Defense: A Post-Military Weapons System</u>, Princeton NJ, Princeton University Press, 1990, pp. 166.

A strategic analysis by leading exponent of civilian defence.

71.Summy, Ralph, 'Nonviolence and the case of the extremely ruthless opponent', <u>Pacifica Review</u> (May/June 1994), pp. 1-29. Also available in M. Kumar and P. Low (eds.), <u>Legacy and Future of Nonviolence</u>, New Delhi, Gandhi Peace Foundation, 1996, pp. 141-57.

72. Varney, Wendy and Brian Martin, 'Lessons from the 1991 Soviet coup', <u>Peace Research</u>, vol. 32 no 1 (Feb 2000), pp. 52-68.

See also: de Ligt, <u>Conquest of Violence</u>, chapter 12; Martin et al, <u>Nonviolent Struggle and Social Defence</u> (esp. Griffen, Vanessa, 'Social defence against coups: The case of Fiji', pp. 59-67); and Randle, <u>Civil Resistance</u>, chapters 5 and 6 and Appendix listing sources on civilian defence (A.1.) A further reference on resistance to the attempted 1961 general's coup in France is: Talbott, <u>The War Without a Name</u>, chapter 9 (see G.3.d.) For analysis of mass popular resistance thwarting right wing coup attempt in 2002 in Venezuela, see section D.IV. Introduction.

An important website for research on nonviolent resistance to military coups, occupation or dictatorship is: www.aeinstein.org

(<u>The Anti-Coup</u> and two other pamphlets by Gene Sharp, <u>There Are Realistic Alternatives</u> and <u>From Dictatorship to Democracy</u> are all available on this site.)

4. Nonviolent Intervention and Accompaniment

Peace movement activists have frequently tried to intervene either to resist particular forms of militarism, injustice or oppression, or to express solidarity with those suffering. Some acts of protest (for example sailing into nuclear test areas, see G.3.) have resulted in widespread publicity. Intervention to demonstrate transnational solidarity (for example with Palestinians resisting Israeli military action – see section D.V.2.) has also sometimes increased international awareness of the issue.

Intervening to prevent war – Maude Royden's proposal for a 'Peace Army' to create a barrier against Japanese aggression in China in the 1930s is an early example – has proved difficult to implement for political, strategic and practical reasons. But there are some interesting examples. Interventions with more limited objectives, such as monitoring conflict or protective accompaniment of individuals under threat, have yielded rather more promising results. The 'non-partisan' interventions organized by Peace Brigades International, and now also envisaged by the Nonviolent Peace Force, are intended to 'create space' for civil society actors. While raising human rights concerns with the local authorities, and also internationally, those intervening avoid making condemnatory statements.

This section includes a number of comparative studies of intervention, and accounts of some specific cases.

A major source only available in electronic form is:

Schweitzer, Christine with Donna Howard, Mareike Junge, Corey Levine, Carl Stieren and Tim Wallis, Nonviolent Peace Force Feasibility Study 2002, available at www.nvpf.org

This study provides the most thorough record of the practices of existing and recent peace teams in the field, as well as of the selection, training and support of personnel. Christine Schweitzer, the first coordinator of the Balkan Peace Team and later director of the Nonviolent Peace Force, has written widely on this subject, including: Christine Schweitzer and Howard Clark, Balkan Peace Team Final Evaluation (BPT, Bund fur Soziale Verteidigung, 2002), downloadable from www.Soziale-verteidigung.de

73.Blincoe, Nicholas and others, Peace Under Fire: Israel, Palestine and the International Solidarity Movement, London, Verso, 2004, pp. 240.

Collection of news reports, web-logs and diaries of International Solidarity Movement activists engaged in peaceful resistance to Israeli military action in the occupied territories, including contributions relating to Rachel Corrie and Tom Hurndall, who were both killed.

74.Boardman, Elizabeth F., Taking a Stand: A Guide to Peace Teams and Accompaniment Projects, Philadephia PA, New Society Publishers, 2005, pp. 177.

Description by participants of work done by peace and accompaniment groups, who runs them and what is involved in joining them. Chapters on Christian Peacemaker Team, Voices in the Wilderness project in Iraq, Peace Brigades International and the International Solidarity Movement (involved in Palestine).

75.Bhatia, Bela, Jean Dreze and Kathy Kelly, War and Peace in the Gulf: Testimonies of the Gulf Peace Team, Nottingham, Spokesman Books, 2001, pp. 181.

Account by participants of transnational team which went to Iraq to try to intervene between the two sides in the 1991 Gulf War. (See also Robert J. Burrowes 'The Persian Gulf War and the Gulf Peace Team' in Moser-Puangsuwan and Weber, Nonviolent Intervention Across Borders, pp. 305-18 – see below in this section.)

76.Griffin-Nolan, Ed., <u>Witness for Peace: A Story of Resistance</u>, Westminster, John Knox Press, 1991, pp. 237.

Account of border and conflict monitoring in Nicaragua in 1980s (in attempt to restrain the US-backed Contras and gather evidence on impact of US foreign policy), and also of accompaniment of Guatemalan refugees returning home in 1989. (Extracts from this book available in Moser-Puangsuwan and Weber, <u>Nonviolent Intervention Across Borders</u>, pp. 279-304 – see below in this section.) The approach adopted in Nicaragua was extended to other parts of Central America and to Colombia in the 1990s. See also: Witness for Peace, <u>Ten Years of Accompaniment</u>, Washington DC, Witness for Peace, 1994.

77.Hare, A. Paul and Herbert H. Blumberg, (eds.), <u>Liberation Without Violence: A Third Party Approach</u>, London, Rex Collings, 1977, pp. 368.

Covers both 'partisan' nonviolent resistance, for example resistance to extension of a military camp on the Larzac plateau in France, and 'nonpartisan' nonviolent intervention to try to prevent violent conflict, for example the role of the Gandhian peace brigade (Shanti Sena) in the Ahmedabad riots of 1969. Parts 3 and 4 analyse examples of partisan and nonpartisan intervention by international teams at a transnational level. Several chapters are listed in later sections. Part 5 analyses processes of change and applying the third-party approach. There is an extensive bibliographic guide, pp. 288-341.

78.Mahoney, Liam and Enrique Eguren, <u>Unarmed Bodyguards: International Accompaniment for the Protection of Human Rights</u>, West Harford CT, Kumarian, 1997, pp. 288.

Authoritative account of work of Peace Brigades International in a number of countries in both Central and South America and in Asia by former volunteers. The authors interviewed generals connected with Guatemalan death squads to discover how far Peace Brigades International had inhibited the squads. See also: Coy, Patrick G., 'Cooperative accompaniment in Sri Lanka with Peace Brigades International' in Charles Chatfield, Ron Pagnucco and Jackie Smith (eds.), <u>Solidarity Beyond the State: The Dynamic of Social Movements</u>, Syracuse NJ, Syracuse University Press, 1997.

79.Moser-Puangsuwan, Yoshua and Thomas Weber, (eds.), <u>Nonviolent Intervention Across Borders: A Recurrent Vision</u>, Honolulu, Spark M. Matsunaga Institute for Peace, 2000, pp. 369.

Analyses different kind of 'intervention' and notes history of earlier 20th century attempts. It provides accounts of transnational actions around the world designed to mobilize protest, provide assistance, promote reconciliation and development, witness human rights violations and 'accompany' endangered individuals, highlight danger (e.g. of nuclear testing), demonstrate solidarity, or to prevent or halt war. Includes chronology and summary of actions with suggestions for further reading, pp. 343-56.

80.Olson, Theodore, 'The World Peace Brigade: Vision and failure', <u>Our Generation Against Nuclear War</u>, vol.3, no. 1 (1964), pp. 34-41.

The World Peace Brigade was founded in 1962 to develop the potential of transnational action. Its first project in Central Africa was planning a march in support of Zambian claims to independence (the march became unnecessary); the second was the Delhi Peking Friendship March to promote understanding at the time of the brief border war between India and China. For more on World Peace Brigade, see Prasad, War is a Crime Against Humanity (G.3.a.), pp. 325-331.

81.Peace News, no. 2441 (December 2000-February 2001) Special issue on 'Interventions' examines different types of intervention, including nonviolent direct action, and reviews some relevant books.

82.Rigby, Andrew, 'Unofficial nonviolent intervention: Examples from the Israeli-Palestinian conflict', Journal of Peace Research, vol. 32, no.4 (November 1995), pp. 453-67. Also available (with discussion of issues raised) as 'Nonviolent intervention' in Michael Randle (ed.), Challenge to Nonviolence, Department of Peace Studies, University of Bradford, 2002, pp. 51-74.

83.Weber, Thomas, 'From Maude Royden's Peace Army to the Gulf Peace Team: An assessment of unarmed interpositionary peace forces', Journal of Peace Research, vol. 30, no. 1 (1993), pp. 45-64. See also: Keyes, Gene, 'Peacekeeping by unarmed buffer forces: Precedents and proposals', Peace and Change, vol. 5, no 2/3 (1978), pp. 3-10.

84.Weber, Thomas, Gandhi's Peace Army: The Shanti Sena and Unarmed Peacekeeping, Syracuse NY, Syracuse University Press, 1996, pp. 293. Foreword Elise Boulding.

Examines how the Gandhian movement in India developed Gandhi's idea that nonviolent volunteers should act in place of armed police (for example to quell riots) and provide a nonviolent alternative to the army. Includes substantial bibliography pp. 267-84.

See also Arrowsmith, To Asia in Peace (G.2.a), and section G.3.d.

B. Elements of Nonviolent Resistance to Colonialism After 1945

Africa

Most anti-colonial struggles in Africa took place after India had become independent, and movements in British colonies were often influenced by the Indian example. The fact that Britain had in principle indicated willingness to dismantle its empire also created a context relatively favourable to nonviolent struggle (compared for example to Portugal, ruled internally by a dictatorship and committed – until after the 1974 internal revolution – to keeping its colonies). But Britain, until brought under pressure from both nonviolent and violent popular movements, expected to grant independence in stages, gradually increasing African representation in government. Moreover, where there were large numbers of white settlers there was counter-pressure to enshrine white dominance. The process of decolonization was, therefore, by no means always smooth. Britain responded to the (limited) anti-settler violence in the Mau Mau rebellion of the 1950s with ruthless military force and detained over 70,000 suspects in appalling conditions.

The nature of African resistance to colonial policies varied between countries, even within the British imperial sphere. In Uganda, for example, the opposition to British plans for a federation of East African countries was led by the traditional ruler of Baganda, Kabaka Mutesa II, who was deported by the Governor. In Tanganyika, however, a modernizing nationalist movement was created by TANU, supported by up to a million members by 1960 and with an extensive network of local organizations and youth and women's groups. Because of British government responses to events in neighbouring countries, TANU, led by Julius Nyerere, did not need to launch a major independence struggle. It won all but one seat in the 1960 elections and Tanganyika became independent in 1961. There was however earlier peasant resistance in the 1940s-50s to attempts at agricultural reform, land seizures and local government reorganization. See:

85. Spear, Thomas, <u>Mountain Farmers: Moral Economics of Land and Agricultural Development in Arusha and Meru</u>, Oxford, Nairobi and Berkeley, James Currey, Mkuku na Nyota and University of California Press, 1997, Chapter 11.

For useful brief surveys of decolonization see:

Birmingham, David, <u>The Decolonisation of Africa</u>, London, UCL Press, 1995, pp. 109 (Introductions to History series).

Charts the processes of nationalism, liberation and independence in the various countries of Africa between 1922, when self-government was restored to Egypt, and 1994, when a non-racial democracy was established in South Africa.

Hargreaves, John, <u>Decolonization in Africa</u>, London, Longman, [1988] 1996, pp. 298, 2nd edition.

There was a lively debate in Africa about the case for violence or nonviolence and some movements chose predominantly nonviolent tactics. There was also a close link between anti-colonialism and resistance to apartheid in South Africa, where Gandhi's influence was still significant (see section D.I.1). A survey of the debates and of some of the movements can be found in:

86.Sutherland, Bill and Matt Meyer (eds.), Guns and Gandhi in Africa: Pan African Insights on Nonviolence and Armed Struggle and Liberation in Africa, Trenton NJ, Africa World Press, 2000, pp. 279.

Reflects range of views of those actively involved in the anti-colonial struggle and resistance.

See also:

87.Kaunda, Kenneth, On Violence, ed. Colin Morris, London. Collins, 1980, pp. 184.

Kaunda, President of Zambia and an advocate of nonviolence, wrestles with problems of violence and nonviolence, giving his reasons for ultimately accepting the case for armed struggle in neighbouring Zimbabwe.

1. Central Africa to 1964

The Central African Federation, embracing Nyasaland, Northern and Southern Rhodesia, was created in 1953, and its chief architect, Roy Welensky, was Prime Minister until 1963. Africans feared that this move was intended to cement the permanent dominance of the 250,000 white settlers in Southern Rhodesia (Africans were to be allotted only one third of the seats in the new Federal Assembly) and bitterly opposed federation from the outset. Further concessions to the white settlers by the British, such as the promise in 1957 not to amend Federal Acts, and the 1958 Electoral Act ensuring white supremacy, together with rumours that the Federation would be granted Dominion status, prompted major unrest in Nyasaland. But British governments became increasingly uneasy after 1959 about imposing white rule in the face of African resistance and settler repression. Malawi and Zambia gained their right to secede and become independent African states in 1964.

In Southern Rhodesia there was also an upsurge of mass politics in the 1940s-50s, intensified in 1960-61, including strikes, marches and rural resistance to destocking policies. See:

88.Ranger, Terence, 'African politics in twentieth-century Southern Rhodesia', in Ranger (ed.), Aspects of Central African History, London, Heinemann, 1968, pp. 210-45.

However, Zimbabwean leaders looked to British government intervention and tried compromise policies until the banning of the African National Congress in 1959. Its successors, the National Democratic Party, and subsequently the Zimbabwe African People's Union, both led by Joshua Nkomo, were banned in 1961 and 1962 respectively. A more militant breakaway party, the Zimbabwe African National Union was formed in 1963 under Ndabaningi Sithole and Robert Mugabe. After the intransigent white government of Ian Smith declared unilateral independence from Britain in November

1965, and the British Labour government failed to quell the rebellion, both ZAPU and ZANU resorted to bitter guerrilla warfare (ZAPU assisted by independent Zambia). The two parties came together as the Patriotic Front, under pressure from the Frontline states, to negotiate with Ian Smith's regime in 1979, but split up again before the national elections in 1980, when Robert Mugabe became the first President.

89.Alport, Baron Charles James MacCall, The Sudden Assignment, London, Hodder and Stoughton, 1965, pp. 255.

Alport was appointed High Commisioner to the Federation from 1961-63, and gives an official British perspective on these contentious years.

90.Rotberg, Robert I, The Rise of Nationalism in Central Africa: The Making of Malawi and Zambia: 1873-1964, Cambridge MA, Harvard University Press, 1967, pp. 360.

Chapter 8 'Discovering their voice: the formation of national political movements' (pp. 179-213) goes up to 1948; chapter 10 'The Federal dream and African reality' (pp. 253-302) charts growing resistance from 1953; and chapter 11 traces 'The triumph of nationalism' (pp. 303-16). Gives some detail on protests and indexes 'non-violent resistance'. Includes detailed bibliography.

91.Wood, J.R.T., The Welensky Papers: A History of the Federation of Rhodesia and Nyasaland, Durban, Graham Publishing, 1983, pp. 1329.

Account based on Welensky's perspective, stressing top level negotiations and relations with successive British colonial secretaries.

a. Malawi (Nyasaland)

The Nyasaland African Congress, led by Dr.Hastings Banda, launched in 1958 a major campaign of nonviolent resistance, including tax refusal, against the Central African Federation, prompting fears among white settlers and repressive measures by the Federal government: 1300 Africans were detained and 51 killed. The British government appointed the Devlin Commission to look into the situation. Devlin (Report of the Nyasaland Commission of Enquiry, London, Her Majesty's Stationery Office, 16 July 1959, pp. 147) criticized the police state measures and reported majority African opposition to Federation. His report led to the Monckton Commission, set up in July 1959, to review the Federation, signalling its likely demise.

92.Baker, Colin, State of Emergency: Crisis in Central Africa, Nyasaland, 1959-1960, London, Tauris Academic Studies, 1997, pp. 299.

Detailed account of period.

93.Clutton Brock, Guy, Dawn in Nyasaland: The Test Case in Africa, London, Hodder and Stoughton, 1959, pp. 192.

Clutton Brock, a member of the African National Congress, worked with a village cooperative in Southern Rhodesia. His book puts the political and economic case against the Federation. Clutton Brock justifies strikes and 'disorderly conduct' in Nyasaland, because 20 years of constitutional tactics had been unsuccessful. Postscript on Devlin

Report, and includes chronology of political events in Nyasaland from 1859 (coming of Livingstone) to proposed conference on constitution of Federation in 1960.

94.Short, Philip, <u>Banda</u>, London, Routledge and Kegan Paul, 1974, pp. 357.

Biography which includes the early years of Hastings Banda, who intended to be a medical missionary but became a central figure in Malawi's independence struggle, and later the increasingly autocratic president of his country. Banda's role in the struggle against the Federation is covered pp. 55-172.

See also: Rotberg, <u>The Rise of Nationalism in Central Africa</u>, and Wood, <u>The Welensky Papers</u> (see esp. chapter 22 on the Nyasaland emergency, chapter 27 on the Monckton Report, and chapter 34 on 'The right to secede' and the 1962 decision on Nyasaland).

b. Zambia (Northern Rhodesia)

There had been signs of resistance to white rule from the 1930s, notably growing trade union activism in the copper belt. The campaign for an end to the Central African Federation (and later for independence) included strikes, boycotts of racist shops and of beer halls imposing a colour bar, sit-ins and political noncooperation, which took place periodically from 1953 until independence. Women were prominent in the boycott campaigns. The use of nonviolent methods was influenced by Kenneth Kaunda, who emerged as the main leader of the independence struggle. Kaunda admired Gandhi and developed his own version of 'positive action', although many of those taking part in the struggle did not accept nonviolence in principle and dealt harshly with those who did not join the resistance. There was also extensive sabotage of government property during the 1961 civil disobedience campaign.

95.Hall, Richard, <u>Zambia 1890-1964: The Colonial Period</u>, London, Longman, 1976, pp. 202.

Chapter 3, 'Colonialism and the roots of African nationalism' covers early copperbelt strikes; chapter 4 'Federation – genesis and exodus', includes extensive information on developing resistance to the colour bar, to the building of the Kariba dam and eviction of local farmers, and to the Federation itself. Chapter 5 'The creation of Zambia' examines final stages of resistance and political developments. His earlier book,

<u>Zambia</u>, Pall Mall Press, 1965, pp. 375, also covered the evolving struggle in chapters 5-7.

96.Kaunda, Kenneth, <u>Zambia Shall Be Free</u>, London, Heinemann, 1962, pp. 202.

97.Macpherson, Fergus, <u>Kenneth Kaunda of Zambia: The Times and the Man</u>, Lusaka, Oxford University Press, 1974, pp. 478.

98.Makasa, Kapasa, <u>Zambia's March to Political Freedom</u>, Nairobi, Heinemann, 1985, 2nd edition, pp. 199. (Originally published as <u>March to Political Freedom</u>, 1981).

Personal account by an activist prominent in the independence struggle of political events from the 1940s to 1963.

99.Mwangilwe, Goodwin B., <u>Harry Mwaanga Nkumbula: A Biography of the Old Lion of Zambia</u>, Lusaka, Multimedia Publications, 1982, pp. 157.

Nkumbula was the first major exponent from the 1940s of African resistance to white dominance and federation, and led the Northern Rhodesian African National Congress. But in the later 1950s he moved towards gradual reform policies and stood for a seat in the 1959 elections, whilst Kapepwe and Kaunda opted for further resistance and founded their own separate party.

See also books on the Central African Federation listed above, and Olson, 'World Peace Brigade' (A.4.).

2. Ghana (Gold Coast) to 1957

Ghana was the first African country south of the Sahara to gain its independence from colonialism. Small steps towards African representation had begun in the 1920s, and under the post-World War II constitution African parties were allowed to contest elections. But the British tended to favour cooperation with conservative African chiefs, who no longer represented the people as a whole, and a small intellectual elite. Kwame Nkrumah, as leader of the Convention People's Party founded in 1949 and drawing support from the urban population, encouraged a nationalist movement demanding immediate independence. He was imprisoned after protests in 1950, won the 1951 elections from jail, and was soon after released. He became the first prime minister of newly independent Ghana in 1957. Nkrumah had led a campaign of nonviolent 'positive action' influenced by Gandhi, which was one element in the political processes which led to early independence, though its significance is disputed by some historians.

100.Agbodeka, Francis, <u>African Politics and British Policy in the Gold Coast, 1868-1960: A Study in the Forms and Forces of Protest</u>, London, Longman, 1971, pp. 206.

101.Austin, Dennis, <u>Politics in Ghana, 1946-1960</u>, London, Oxford University Press, [1964] 1970, pp. 459.

Regarded as classic account of this period.

102.James, C.L.R., <u>Nkrumah and the Ghana Revolution</u>, London, Alison and Busby, 1977, pp. 227.

Frequent references to strikes and nonviolent resistance, but see especially chapter 7, 'Positive action'.

103.Nkrumah, Kwame, <u>The Autobiography of Kwame Nkrumah</u>, Edinburgh, Thomas Nelson, 1957, pp. 310.

See especially chapters 10 and 11.

See also Miller, <u>Nonviolence</u>, chapter 19 (A.1.).

3. Kenya to 1963

A large white settler population occupying much of the best land made the transition to independence in Kenya more bitter than in other East African countries. African opposition to white rule began to emerge in Kikuyu political organizations in the 1920s. Jomo Kenyatta became leader in 1928 of the Kikuyu Central Association, which started in the 1930s to represent Africans more generally until banned in 1940. After the war the British began to allow very limited African representation on the legislative council and then the Governor's Executive Council, but settler resistance encouraged African support for the new Kenyan African National Union, which agitated on issues of representation, land and racial discrimination. The Mau Mau violent uprising began in 1952 and continued until 1956, and the British government imposed an emergency until 1959, during which Kenyatta and other Kikuyu leaders were detained (although they denied direct involvement with Mau Mau) along with 70,000 others. The shock of Mau Mau and revelations about deaths and ill treatment in the camps speeded up transfer of power to Africans, despite problems caused by the settlers and by divisions between African parties. Kenya achieved independence in December 1963.

There were nonviolent protests before independence. A major nonviolent rural campaign involving a mass march on Nairobi was waged in 1938 by the Wakamba (supported by some other tribal groups) against colonial soil erosion policies, which meant economically disastrous enforced destocking. The leaders were arrested. See: Felice V. Gadsden, 'Notes on the Kamba destocking controversy of 1938', International Journal of Historical Studies, vol. 7 no. 4 (1978). There were also frequent strikes, including the 1947 Mombasa dock strike and general strikes in Mombasa and Nairobi, and there was a debate about 'positive action' versus violent resistance.

104.Arnold, Guy, Kenyatta and the Politics of Kenya, London, Dent, 1974, pp. 226.

Study of the political figure who was central to the struggle for independence from 1928 and became head of Kenya's first African government.

105.Bennett, George and Alison Smith, 'Kenya: from "White Man's Country" to Kenyatta's state 1945-1963', in D.A. Low and Alison Smith (eds.), History of East Africa, vol. 3, Oxford, Clarendon Press, 1976, pp. 109-56.

Summary of developing African opposition, including early 'passive resistance' and land protests, attempts at unionization, and links with the East African Indian National Congress, as well as role of Mau Mau.

106.Clayton, Anthony and Donald C. Savage, Government and Labour in Kenya, 1895-1963, London, Frank Cass, 1974, pp. 481.

107.Kenyatta, Jomo, Suffering Without Bitterness: The Founding of the Kenya Nation, Nairobi, East Africa Publishing House, 1968, pp. 348.

108.Mboya, Tom, Freedom and After, London, Deutsch, 1963, pp. 288.

Mboya was a union leader and prominent in Kenya's independence struggle. His book also covers negotiations with Britain.

109.Odinga, Oginga, <u>Not Yet Uhuru</u>, London, Heinemann, [1967] 1984, pp. 323.

Autobiography of a nationalist leader, a rival of Mboya, who in the mid-1960s left the ruling Kenyan African National Union because he disagreed with land resettlement and economic policies, and argued for greater socialism. Includes references to 1938 destocking campaign and to strikes.

4. Nigeria to 1960

The British accepted the principle of African representation through direct election to the legislative council as early as 1922, though on a strictly limited franchise. Signs of African resistance also date back to the 1920s. Significant protests by women against colonial rule took place in 1929, when a local demonstration against a proposed tax sparked a mass movement of tax resistance and a longer term mobilization of women. The trade unions also engaged in politically directed strikes, notably in 1945, and continued to agitate until 1950. In the first years after the war Nigerian politics were more turbulent than in Ghana, but the Administration acted to pre-empt further trouble by proposing a review of the post-war constitution to grant Nigerians a much greater political role. The need for radical action faded as new political opportunities became available. Instead, negotiating an agreement between diverse regions of Nigeria became a central issue. Nigeria became independent in 1960.

110.Ananaba, Wogu, <u>The Trade Union Movement in Nigeria</u>, London, C. Hurst, 1969, pp. 336.

Chapter 7 covers the 1945 general strike.

111.Brown, Carolyn A. <u>'We Were All Slaves': African Miners, Culture and Resistance at the Enugu Government Colliery</u>, Portsmouth, Oxford and Cape Town, Heinemann, James Curey and David Philip, 2002, pp. 354.

Part 2 is on major miners' strike organized by the militant Zikist movement. The movement became associated with riots and an assassination attempt and was banned in April 1950.

112.Nba, Nina Emma, <u>Nigerian Women Mobilized: Women's Political Activity in Southern Nigeria, 1900-1965</u>, Berkeley, University of California Institute of International Studies, 1982, pp. 344.

113.Isichei, Elizabeth, <u>A History of Nigeria</u>, London, Longman, 1983, pp. 517.

Chapter 17 'Colonialism rejected' (pp. 396-412) examines workers' and women's protests and growing nationalism from the 1920s to 1950.

C. Campaigns for Rights and Democracy in Communist Regimes

The case for examining resistance to Communism separately from other campaigns against dictatorship or repression is that Communist Party regimes, following the pattern developed by Lenin and Stalin in the USSR, have practised very specific methods of political, economic and social control, designed to embed Party ideology and incorporate the whole population in the policies and organizations directed by the Party. At times (as under Stalinism) these controls have meant creating an atmosphere of denunciation and terror and sending huge numbers of people to execution, prison, labour camps or exile. In reaction against such terror, Communist regimes often encouraged partial liberalization. But as genuine freedom of debate and association threatened Party control, from the 1960s most Communist regimes in Europe resorted to a form of 'post-totalitarian' control, avoiding the excesses of Stalinism but maintaining Party dominance, censorship and limits on travel, and quelling signs of dissidence by expulsion from jobs, public denunciation and sometimes by arrest and imprisonment. A seminal analysis of 'post-totalitarianism' and the significance of individual dissent is Vaclav Havel's essay 'The power of the powerless' (see A.1.).

Because of the distinctive influence of Mao, China did not move towards this pattern of stable Party rule until the 1980s, and since the 1990s has developed an unusual mix of Party dominance and an increasingly privatized economy. Since 1989-1990 official Communist Party rule has crumbled throughout the former Soviet Union and Eastern Europe. Although in many countries the legacy of Party rule has significantly influenced political methods and attitudes, and many former Party leaders continued in power or rose to prominence, it is more appropriate to class these under 'authoritarian' rule.

In a Communist Party state even a critical speech or document could be a significant act of dissent, and promoting independent ideas or forms of culture a major challenge to the regime – though in periods of liberalization the range of the permissible has been blurred. Intellectual or cultural dissent could therefore be one end of a continuum leading to petitions, posters, public meetings and marches, hunger strikes, students boycotting classes or industrial workers going on strike. Whilst intellectual protest has often been quite distinct from worker or peasant unrest, in periods of major popular pressure for change, as in 1956 and 1989, they have merged.

This section covers the countries where there has been sustained organized dissent and mass popular nonviolent resistance at some stage – these are also the countries where there is a fairly substantial literature in English. It does not include Bulgaria, although there was some intellectual dissent, public protest on ecological issues, and large demonstrations in 1989. But see:

114.Ward, Philip, <u>Bulgarian Voices: Letting the People Speak</u>, Cambridge, The Oleander Press, 1992, pp. 330.

See also: Crampton, Richard, 'The intelligentsia, the ecology and the opposition in Bulgaria', World Today, vol. 46, no. 2 (1990), pp. 23-26. On growing intellectual dissent in later 1980s, focused on the environment.

This section also excludes Albania, where a semi-Stalinist regime (which from the later 1950s sided with China against the USSR in the Sino-Soviet dispute) insulated itself against Gorbachev's perestroika and avoided popular revolt in 1989, although there was a credible report of protest in one city in January 1990.

Significant, but little known, popular resistance occurred in 1989-1990 in Mongolia, but there is not enough literature to justify a separate section. See:

115.Becker, Jasper, The Lost Country: Mongolia Revealed, London, Hodder and Stoughton, 1992, pp. 325. See also: Ackerman and Duvall, A Force More Powerful, pp. 439-54 (A.1.).

Because of similarities and links between the Communist countries there are several comparative surveys of dissent and opposition in Communist states. The dramatic events surrounding the collapse of Communism in Eastern Europe also resulted in a number of books on 1989.

I. USSR and Central and Eastern Europe to 1991

1.a. Comparative Studies of Dissent

116.Bugajski, Janusz and Maxine Pollack, East European Fault Lines: Dissent, Opposition and Social Activism, Boulder Col, Westview, 1989, pp. 333.

Comparative analysis of different causes of dissent, for example religion or human rights, the tactics used and methods of repression.

117.Curry, Jane Leftwich (ed.), Dissent in Eastern Europe, New York, Praeger, 1983, pp. 277.

Essays on individual countries.

118. From Below: Independent Peace and Environment Movements in Eastern Europe and the USSR, New York, Helsinki Watch Report, 1987.

119.Jacobson, Julius (ed.), Soviet Communism and the Socialist Vision, New Brunswick NJ, Transaction Books, 1972, pp. 363.

A compilation of essays, most originally published in New Politics magazine, covering the USSR, Poland and Czechoslovakia.

120.Klippenstein, Lawrence, 'Conscientious Objectors in Eastern Europe: The quest for free choice and Alternative Service', in Sabrina Petra Ramet (ed.), Protestantism and Politics in Eastern Europe and Russia: The Communist and Postcommunist Eras, Durham, Duke University press, 1992, pp. 276-309 and 393-404.

Useful overview of pacifism and conscientious objection.

121.Schapiro, Leonard (ed.), Political Opposition in One-Party States, London, Macmillan, 1972, pp. 289.

Collection of essays originally published in the academic journal Government and Opposition discussing the concept of totalitarianism, Soviet policies, and developments in Yugoslavia, Czechoslovakia and Albania.

122.Skilling, H.Gordon, Samizdat and an Independent Society in Central and Eastern Europe, Basingstoke, Macmillan, 1989, pp. 293.

123.Tokes, Rudolf L. (ed.), Opposition in Eastern Europe, London, Macmillan, 1979, pp. 306.

Includes surveys of human rights and political change, worker and peasant opposition, and essays on Czechoslovakia, East Germany, Poland and Hungary from 1968-78.

See also: Schell, The Unconquerable World, chapter 7 'Living in truth', pp. 186-215 (A.1.).

1.b. Literature on the Revolutions of 1989-90

124.Ash, Timothy Garton, We The People: The Revolution of '89 Witnessed in Warsaw, Budapest, Berlin and Prague, Cambridge, Granta Books in association with Penguin, 1990, pp. 156. (Published in New York by Random House as The Magic Lantern)

125.Burke, Patrick, Revolution in Europe, 1989, Hove, Wayland, 1995, pp. 48.

Well illustrated account for a popular audience, factually reliable and good summary analysis.

126.Jones, Lynne,States of Change: A Central European Diary: Autumn 1989, London, Merlin Press, 1990, pp. 139.

Account by prominent peace activist.

127.Habermas, Jurgen, 'What does Socialism mean today? The rectifying revolution and the need for new thinking on the Left', New Left Review, no. 183, 1990, pp. 3-62.

Habermas reconsiders the meaning of socialism in the light of the 1989 revolutions in East Central Europe. Critically reviews six types of ideological explanation for the events: Stalinist, Leninist, reform communist, post modernist, anti-communist and liberal.

128.Hawkes, Nigel (ed.), Tearing Down the Curtain: The People's Revolution in Eastern Europe by a team from the Observer, London, Hodder and Stoughton, 1990, pp. 160.

129.Randle, Michael, People Power: The Building of a New European Home, Stroud, Glos, Hawthorn Press, 1991, pp. 224.

Chapter 1 discusses the context of the revolutions, chapter 2 the build up of protests (including in Bulgaria) and the role of international and transnational pressures, chapter 3 reflects on possible implications of people power for the future of Europe. Part II of the book is a series of interviews with key participants in the events of 1989 both about the revolutions and future possibilities.

130.Roberts, Adam, <u>Civil Resistance in the East European and Soviet Revolutions</u>, Cambridge Mass, Albert Einstein Institution (Monograph No 4), 1991, pp. 43.

131.Simpson, John, <u>Dispatches from the Barricades: An Eye-Witness Account of the Revolutions that Shook the World, 1989-90</u>, London, Hutchinson, 1990, pp. 320.

132.Stokes, Gale, <u>The Walls Came Tumbling Down: The Collapse of Communism in Eastern Europe</u>, New York and Oxford, Oxford University Press, 1993, pp. 319.

An analytical account sketching in the historical background and tracing the growing opposition during the 1980s.

See also Ackerman and Duvall, <u>A Force More Powerful</u>, chapter 12, pp. 421-54 (A.1.).

Periodical sources: a number of academic journals and movement periodicals specialized in analysis of the Soviet bloc.

<u>Problems of Communism</u>, published every two months, an official US publication, nevertheless ran informative and analytical articles by academic specialists; <u>Index on Censorship</u> covered dissent from a human rights perspective. During the late 1970s and 1980s valuable sources for oppositional thought and activities were <u>Labour Focus on Eastern Europe</u> and <u>East European Reporter</u> (founded in 1985).

2. Baltic States, 1944-91

Lithuania, Latvia and Estonia, despite distinct languages and cultural and religious differences, are closely linked not only by geography but by common interests and historical experience. All three were incorporated into the Tsarist Empire, all three enjoyed a period of independence which they won after the First World War, and all three were annexed by the Soviet Union under the 1939 Nazi-Soviet Pact, then occupied by the Germans and returned again to Stalinist domination from 1944. Russian immigration and policies of Russification began after 1945, and substantial Russian minorities complicated later moves towards independence. Because the Baltic states had been incorporated so recently into the Soviet Union, there was a degree of continuing resistance to Moscow rule from 1945 to the 1980s, at first primarily through guerrilla warfare, and from the 1960s taking the form of nonviolent dissent. When Gorbachev's political reforms opened the way to mobilization and electoral choice, all three countries moved towards renewed independence in the period 1987-91, turning to people power in Latvia and Lithuania when threatened with military repression.

133.Clemens, Walter C, Jr., <u>Baltic Independence and Russian Empire</u>, New York, St Martins Press, 1991, pp. 346.

Covers the period from 1945, including detailed discussion of moves towards independence from 1988-90 (chapters 8-12), giving weight to role of nonviolent resistance.

134.Eglitis, Olgerts, <u>Nonviolent Action in the Liberation of Lativa</u>, Cambridge MA, Albert Einstein Institution (Monograph No 5) 1993, pp. 72.

Examines the moves towards independence 1987-90 and resistance to Soviet attempts in 1991 to re-impose control, plus appendices detailing guidelines prepared in 1991 for a nonviolent defence.

135.Lieven, Anatol, The Baltic Revolution: Estonia, Latvia, Lithuania and the Path to Independence, New Haven, Yale University Press, 1993 (revised edition), pp. 454.

136.Miniotaite, Grazina, Nonviolent Resistance in Lithuania, Cambridge MA, Albert Einstein Institution (Monograph No 8), 2002, pp. 98.

Includes overview of resistance to Tsarism and Soviet rule before discussing struggle for independence 1988-91, and with final chapter on prospects for civilian-based defence.

137.Senn, Alfred Erich, Lithuania Awakening, Berkeley CA, University of California Press, 1990, pp. 294.

Covers developing opposition 1987-1990.

138.Trapans, Jan Arveds (ed.), Towards Independence: The Baltic Popular Movements, Boulder CO, Westview Press, 1991, pp. 166.

Published in cooperation with Radio Free Europe/Radio Liberty.

Growing resistance in the Baltic states is also noted briefly in most studies of the Soviet Union under Gorbachev. See some of the entries under the USSR below (C.I.8).

3. Czechoslovakia, 1948-89

After the Communist seizure of power in February 1948 Czechoslovakia suffered extreme Stalinist repression. Destalinization occurred much later than in neighbouring Poland and Hungary. The revolutionary events of 1956 encouraged some pressure for change within the Party, and sparked brief dissent by intellectuals and students, which was rapidly contained. Moves towards destalinization began effectively in 1963, and gathered momentum as writers, intellectuals and students began to express dissent, culminating in the Prague Spring and widespread popular mobilization. The Soviet occupation of August 1968 prompted mass nonviolent resistance, and popular activism was not crushed until Gustav Husak took over from Alexander Dubcek as Party Secretary in 1969 and a process of 'normalization' began. From 1970, despite the efforts of a committed minority and the rise of Charter 77, opposition was strictly limited and the majority of people responded with apathy and cynicism to the new regime. Widespread popular involvement in protest did not occur again until November 1989, when (following the gradual negotiated transfer of power in both Poland and Hungary and the dramatic collapse of the Berlin Wall) the Velvet Revolution swept away Communist Party rule.

a. The Prague Spring and Resistance to Occupation, 1968-69

Studies of the Czechoslovak reform movement and resistance to Soviet occupation tend to focus on intellectuals and students. Workers only got involved late in the Prague Spring (partly because they had reason to worry about the impact of economic reforms). But the workers' council movement, which developed from December 1968 to June 1969, was a significant assertion of autonomous worker power. There was also cooperation between workers and students, for example in a strike in November 1968 against the removal of Josef Smrkovsky as President of the National Assembly.

139.Fisera, Vladimir (ed.), Workers' Councils in Czechslovakia: Documents and Essays 1968-69, London, Alison and Busby, 1978, pp. 200.

140.Golan, Galia, The Czechoslovak Reform Movement, Cambridge, Cambridge University Press, 1971, pp. 349.

Starts with brief summary of period 1956-1962 and then analyses in detail developments both within the Party and in other social spheres up to 1968, including the role of dissent and public protest.

141.Golan, Galia, Reform Rule in Czechoslovakia: The Dubcek Era 1968-1969, Cambridge, Cambridge University Press, 1973, pp. 327.

142.Mlynar, Zdenek, Night Frost in Prague: The End of Humane Socialism, London, Hurst, 1980, pp. 300.

Account by Party leader close to Dubcek of internal Party politics leading up to the Soviet invasion, personal account of the Kremlin 'negotiations' after the abduction of top leaders, and his resignation from the Party in November 1968.

143.Skilling, H. Gordon, Czechoslovakia's Interrupted Revolution, Princeton NJ, Princeton University Press, 1976, pp. 924.

Extensively researched and very detailed account of the evolution of reform in the period 1963-1968.

144.Windsor, Philip and Adam Roberts, Czechoslovakia 1968, London, Chatto and Windus (for the Institute of Strategic Studies), 1969, pp. 200.

The first half by Windsor explores the broad context and reasons for the Soviet invasion; Roberts (pp. 97-143) assesses the resistance drawing on the BBC monitoring service reports and interviews. Key documents relating to the invasion are included in appendices.

b. 'Normalization' to the Velvet Revolution, 1970-89

After initial resistance to the Husak regime, opposition focused primarily, especially after the launching of Charter 77, on human rights. But Charter 77 did engage in a dialogue with the European Nuclear Disarmament campaign: see Kavan, Jan and Zdena Tomin, Voices from Prague: Documents on Czechoslovakia and the Peace Movement, London, Palach Press, 1983, pp. 75. A small Independent Peace Association was founded in 1988, see: Sormova, Ruth, Michaela Neubarova and Jan Kavan, 'Czechoslovakia's nonviolent revolution', in Martin et al, Nonviolent Struggle and Social Defence, pp. 36-42 (see A.1.). There was also cultural dissent among some young people, symbolized by the rock band The Plastic People of the Universe, and commemoration of John Lennon was linked to peace protest.

145.Committee to Defend Czechoslovak Socialists, Voices of Czechoslovak Socialists, London, Merlin Press, 1977, pp. 134.

Selection of accounts of opposition, trials and Open Letters, including coverage of the rock musicians The Plastic People and the text of Charter 77.

146.Havel, Vaclav, <u>Open Letters: Selected Prose 1965-1990</u>, edited by Paul Wilson, London, Faber and Faber, 1991, pp. 415.

Collection of Havel's political (as opposed to dramatic) writings from his 1965 speech to the Writers Union 'On evasive thinking' to his 'New Year's Address as President of Czechoslovakia January 1990. In between there are Havel's open letters from the late 1960s to the 1980s which reflect his increasing importance as an active opponent of the regime and theorist of 'the power of the powerless'. This is one of several collections of Havel's works. <u>Living in Truth</u>, edited by Jan Vladislav (see A.1.) includes a chronology of Havel's life, writings and political activity.

147.Kusin, Vladimir V, <u>From Dubcek to Charter 77: A Study of 'Normalization' in Czechoslvakia, 1968-1978</u>, Edinburgh, Q Press, 1978, pp. 353.

148.Pelikan, Jiri, <u>Socialist Opposition in Eastern Europe: The Czechoslovak Example</u>, London, Allison Busby, 1976, pp. 220.

Focuses on the Party purges and the emergence of a 'socialist opposition' in the early 1970s and political trials in 1972.

149.Riese, Hans-Peter (ed.), <u>Since the Prague Spring: The Continuing Struggle for Human Rights in Czechoslovakia</u>, London, Allen and Unwin, 1981, pp. 208.

A collection of relevant political documents, including Charter 77, open letters to political leaders and organizations and to prominent individuals in the West.

150.Skilling, H. Gordon, <u>Charter 77 and Human Rights in Czechoslovakia</u>, London, Allen and Unwin, 1981, pp. 363.

Well researched analysis and extensive collection of documents.

151.Urban, Jan, 'Czechoslovakia: The power and politics of humiliation' in Gwyn Prins (ed.), <u>Spring in Winter: The 1989 Revolutions</u>, Manchester, Manchester University Press, 1990, pp. 99-136.

Examines November 1989 in wider context of Czechoslovak experience and problems facing new regime.

152.Wheaton, Bernard and Zdenek Kavan, <u>The Velvet Revolution: Czechoslovakia 1989-1991</u>, Boulder, CO, Westview Press, 1992, pp. 255.

See also: Ash, <u>We the People</u>, pp. 78-130, and other titles on 1989 Revolutions (C.I.1.b.).

4. East Germany (GDR), 1945-89

The German Democratic Republic was the first European Communist state to respond to the death of Stalin. A general strike, called in June 1953, was crushed by tanks. The intellectuals remained silent in June 1953, but during 1956 some responded to the ferment of ideas and activities in Poland and Hungary, though this 'revisionism' was subsequently crushed. See:

153.Croan, Melvin, 'East German Revisionism: The Spectre and the Reality' in Leopold Labedz (ed.), <u>Revisionism: Essays on the History of Marxist Ideas</u>, London, Allen and Unwin, 1962, pp. 239-56.

Until the building of the Berlin Wall in 1961, many of those opposed to the regime crossed to the West (and significant numbers attempted to escape over the Wall subsequently). Limited dissent developed gradually in the 1960s and 1970s, often fostered by the Protestant Church, and there were a few prominent Marxist dissidents. By the 1980s significant autonomous groups were campaigning for cultural freedom and peace. Responding to Gorbachev's perestroika in the Soviet Union, and to the opening of the Hungarian border in September 1989, a mass exodus of East Germans, combined with growing protests inside the country, led to the collapse of the regime. This collapse was heralded by the breaching of the Berlin Wall.

a. The 1953 Uprising

154.Brant, Stefan, <u>The East German Rising, 17th June 1953</u>, London, Thames and Hudson, 1955, pp. 202.

155.Ebert, Theodore, 'Non-violent resistance against communist regimes' in Roberts (ed.), <u>Civilian Resistance as National Defence</u>, pp. 204-27 (A.3.).

156.Hildebrandt, Rainer, <u>The Explosion: The Uprising Behind the Iron Curtain</u>, Boston, Little Brown, 1955, pp. 198.

b. The Rise of Dissent to the Fall of the Berlin Wall, 1960s to 1989

157.Allen, Bruce, <u>Germany East: Dissent and Opposition</u>, Montreal, Black Rose, 1991, pp. 171.

158.Bahro, Rudolf, <u>The Alternative in Eastern Europe</u>, London, NLB Books, 1978, pp. 463.

Bahro was a prominent Party member, who responded with shock to the 1968 Soviet invasion of Czechoslovakia, and this book proposes a Marxist-based reform programme. He was imprisoned for eight years after this book was published in West Germany in 1977.

159.Bleiker, Roland, <u>Nonviolent Struggle and the Revolution in East Germany</u>, Cambridge, Mass., Albert Einstein Institution (Monograph No. 6), 1993, pp. 53.

160.Fullbrook, Mary, <u>Anatomy of a Dictatorship: Inside the GDR 1949-1989</u>, Oxford, Oxford University Press, 1995, pp. 307.

161.Grix, Jonathan, <u>The Role of the Masses in the Collapse of the GDR</u>, Basingstoke, Macmillan, 2000, pp. 213.

162.Hirschmann, Albert O., 'Exit, voice and the fate of the German Democratic Republic', <u>World Politics</u>, vol. 45 (January 1993), pp. 173-202.

163.Joppke, Christian, <u>East German Dissidents and the Revolution of 1989: Social Movement in a Leninist Regime</u>, New York, New York University Press, 1995, pp. 277.

164.Keithly, David M., <u>The Collapse of East German Communism: The Year the Wall Came Down, 1989</u>, Westport CT, Praeger, 1992, pp. 241.

165.Kopstein, Jeffrey, 'Chipping away at the state: Workers' resistance and the demise of East Germany' in <u>World Politics</u>, vol. 48 (April 1996), pp. 391-423.

Overview of reasons for collapse of GDR, critical of emphasis on intellectuals and 'civil society', and stressing role of workers and 'everyday resistance' over four decades.

166.Opp, Karl-Dieter, Peter Voss and Christiane Gern, <u>Origins of a Spontaenous Revolution: East Germany 1989</u>, Ann Arbor MI, University of Michigan Press, 1995, pp. 280.

Study based on fieldwork interviewing various actors.

167.Philipsen, Dirk, <u>We Were the People: Voices from East German's Revolutionary Autumn of 1989</u>, Durham NC, Duke University Press, 1993, pp. 417.

168.Ramet, Pedro, 'Church and peace in the GDR', <u>Problems of Communism</u>, vol. 35 (July-August 1984), pp. 44-57.

Focuses on role of Protestant Church in dissent and autonomous peace activity.

169.Sandford, John, <u>The Sword and the Ploughshare: Autonomous Peace Initiatives in East Germany</u>, London, Merlin Press/European Nuclear Disarmament, 1983, pp. 111.

170. Thompson, Mark R, 'Why and how East Germans rebelled', <u>Theory and Society</u>, vol. 25 no. 2 (April 1996), pp. 263-99.

171.Volkmer, Werner, 'East Germany: Dissenting views during the last decade' in Tokes (ed.), <u>Opposition in Eastern Europe</u>, pp. 113-41 (C.I.1.a.).

172.Woods, Roger, <u>Opposition in the GDR under Honecker, 1971-1985: An Introduction and Documentation</u>, London, Macmillan, 1986, pp. 257.

See also: <u>From Below</u>, Helsinki Watch Report (C.I.1.a.), Ash, <u>We the People</u>, pp. 61-77, and other titles (C.I.1.b.).

5. Hungary, 1947-89

Hungary suffered under the brutal Stalinist regime of Rakosi until 1953, and after the death of Stalin sections of the Party leadership (with support from Moscow) moved towards reform. The central figure in this change of policy was Imre Nagy, who became Prime Minister in 1953 and allowed political debate to re-emerge. However, the hardliners made a comeback in 1955 and ousted Nagy, leading to a bitter struggle in 1956 between different factions of the Party. Following Khrushchev's February 1956 attack on Stalin's crimes, many Communists demanded the rehabilitation of Laszlo Rajk, executed in a Stalinist show trial as a 'Titoist' in 1949. Writers and students engaged in campaigns for change, culminating in mass demonstrations demanding greater democracy, a new government under Nagy and withdrawal of Soviet troops. Protests erupted into fighting outside the radio building after security policy fired on the crowd, and crowds also attacked the secret police stations.

The government declared martial law and called in Soviet troops (October 23-24), triggering armed defiance by many Hungarians. After heavy fighting, Soviet troops withdrew from Budapest on October 29, but after Nagy declared Hungary's withdrawal from the Warsaw Pact new troops moved into Hungary and attacked Budapest; bitter fighting continued from November 4-11 and Nagy and colleagues were arrested by Soviet troops when leaving the Yugoslav embassy on November 22 (contrary to explicit promises), and later executed. But during the period November 12 – December 13 the industrial workers, who had been at the forefront of the fighting, began to organize independent workers' councils and to call brief general strikes. (Hannah Arendt has celebrated this expression of popular nonviolent resistance and participatory democracy in the Epilogue to the second edition of her Origins of Totalitarianism, London, Allen and Unwin, 1958, pp. 492-502.)

After the suppression of the 1956 resistance there were no major protests for two decades, but from the 1960s an intellectual opposition gradually emerged, growing in strength in the late 1970s with declarations of support for Charter 77 in Czechoslovakia and a flourishing samizdat. The Hungarian regime from the 1960s-80s experimented with economic reforms and limited pluralism, and although it imprisoned a few dissidents, avoided extreme use of repression. By the 1980s Hungarians, supported by reformers within the Party, began to enjoy a greater degree of pluralism and cultural freedom, indicated by the emergence of a semi-autonomous peace organization, student activism and then in 1988 the evolution of opposition parties. The Communist regime, spurred on by mass attendance at a ceremonial reburial and rehabilitation of Imre Nagy in June that year, agreed in October 1989, to constitutional amendments and free parliamentary elections.

a. Destalinization and Revolution, 1953-56

173. Aczel, Tamas, and Tibor Meray, The Revolt of the Mind: A Case History of Intellectual Resistance behind the Iron Curtain, New York, Praeger, 1959, pp. 449.

Focuses on the Hungarian Writers' Union from 1953-59.

174. Harman, Chris, Bureaucracy and Revolution in Eastern Europe, London, Pluto Press, 1974, pp. 296.

Examines the 1956 Revolution primarily from standpoint of role of the workers, with emphasis on the workers' councils, pp. 124-87.

175. Kecskemeti, Paul, The Unexpected Revolution: Social Forces in the Hungarian Uprising, Stanford CA, Stanford University Press, 1961, pp. 178.

176. Kopacsi, Sandor, In the Name of the Working Class, London, Fontana/Collins, 1989, pp. 348.

Eyewitness account by the police chief of Budapest in 1956, who refused to obey Soviet orders to quell the uprising and was later sentenced to life imprisonment, but released in 1963 in an amnesty granted by Khrushchev.

177.Lomax, Bill, 'The Workers' Councils of Greater Budapest', in Ralph Miliband and John Saville (eds.), <u>Socialist Register 1976</u>, London, Merlin Press, 1976, pp. 89-110. Excerpt from his book <u>Hungary 1956</u>, London, Alison and Busby, 1976, pp. 222, which provides a chronology, background to the 1956 uprising and an account of the events of October/November.

178.Meray, Tibor, <u>Thirteen Days that Shook the Kremlin: Imre Nagy and the Hungarian Revolution</u>, London, Thames and Hudson, 1959, pp. 290.

179.Vali, Ferenc, <u>Rift and Revolt in Hungary</u>, Cambridge MA, Harvard University Press, 1961, pp. 590.

Detailed scholarly study of Hungary from the Communist takeover to 1956, and with a final section on the period of 1957-61 when the Kadar regime established control.

180.Zinner, Paul E., <u>Revolution in Hungary</u>, New York, Columbia University Press, 1962, pp. 380.

b. Gradual Growth of Dissent, 1960-89

181.Hankiss, Elemer, 'What the Hungarians saw first' in Gwyn Prins (ed.), <u>Spring in Winter: The 1989 Revolutions</u>, Manchester, Manchester University Press, 1990, pp. 13-36.

182.Haraszti, Miklos, <u>A Worker in a Worker's State</u>, Harmondsworth, Penguin (in association with New Left Review), 1977, pp. 175.

An inside account of conditions at the Red Star Tractor Factory by a young Marxist, who was arrested, tried and given a suspended sentence for 'grave incitement'. The trial hearings are an appendix, pp. 159-74. Haraszti had also got into trouble with the authorities for his satirical poetry and for suspected membership of a Maoist group, see pp. 11-17.

183.Kenedi, Janos, <u>Do It Yourself: Hungary's Hidden Economy</u>, London, Pluto Press, 1981, pp. 128.

Hilarious account by a leftist dissident, published in samizdat, of the corruption involved in getting materials to build a house. A brief introduction by Bill Lomax summarizes developments in the Hungarian opposition.

184.Konrad, George, <u>Anti-Politics</u>, London, Quartet, 1984, pp. 243.

Konrad was a central theorist of building civil society from below.

185.Konrad, George and Ivan Szelenyi, <u>The Intellectuals on the Road to Class Power</u>, Brighton, Harvester Press, 1979, pp. 252.

The authors were arrested in 1974 for 'subversion' for writing this samizdat work, their friends were interrogated and in one case arrested. The resulting protests in Hungary and abroad led to their release. They were allowed to emigrate, but Konrad chose to stay and became an important figure in the internal dissent of the 1980s (pp.xiii-xix). The text is an analysis of the 'socialist society' emerging in the Soviet bloc in the 1970s, arguing that former conflicts between intellectuals and the Party bureaucracy were being superseded by the increasing integration of technocratic intellectuals with the ruling bureaucracy. The main conflict was between an oppressed working class and the bureaucrats and technocrats. The role of the 'marginal' intelligentsia was to 'articulate workers interests and promote 'a critical social consciousness' (see pp. 234-52).

186.Koszegi, Ferenc and E.P. Thompson, The New Hungarian Peace Movement, London, Merlin Press/European Nuclear Disarmament, c.1983, pp. 53.

187.Schopflin, George, 'Hungary: An uneasy stability', in Archie Brown and Jack Gray (eds.), Political Culture and Political Change in Communist States, London, Macmillan, 1977, pp. 131-58.

Brief analysis of the Kadar regime.

188.Schopflin, 'Opposition and Para-Opposition: Critical currents in Hungary, 1968-78, in Tokes (ed.).

Opposition in Eastern Europe, pp. 142-86 (C.I.1.a.).

189.Tokes, Rudolf L., Hungary's Negotiated Revolution: Economic Reform, Social Change and Political Succession, Cambridge, Cambridge University Press, 1996, pp. 544.

Chapter 4, pp. 167-209, covers opposition and dissent from 1962 into the 1980s, and Chapter 7, pp. 305-56, 'Negotiated revolution: from the Opposition Roundtable to the National Roundtable'.

See also: Ash, We The People, pp. 47-60 and other titles (C.I.1.b.).

6. Poland, 1945-89

Polish history is associated with heroic armed uprisings, culminating in the Warsaw rising against the Nazi occupiers in 1944. But there was also a tradition of passive or nonviolent resistance to keep alive Polish culture under Russian and German occupation in the 19th century. Between 1945 and 1989 there were more examples of mass nonviolent action in Poland than in any other country of Eastern Europe and, although intellectuals and students played a crucial role, as did the Catholic Church, in Poland working class activism was decisive.

The movement demanding total destalinization in 1956 managed to avoid Soviet armed intervention and serious bloodshed. Major strikes in 1970-71 and 1976 were a prelude to the remarkable Solidarity movement in 1980-81. Declaration of martial law in December 1981 drove resistance underground for several years, but later in the 1980s Solidarity re-emerged, and was able (in the context of rapid change inside the USSR) to negotiate with the Communist Party a peaceful transfer of power. Solidarity won a landslide victory in the elections of June 1989. For a concise overview of Polish developments from 1945-80 by a distinguished Polish writer, see:

190. Szczypiorski, Andrzej The Polish Ordeal: The View from Within, London, Croom Helm, 1982, pp. 153.

a. Destalinization and Mass Resistance, 1953-56

Poland had suffered severely in the Stalinist period 1948-53. After 1953 there were moves within the Party for change, but Party reformers did not link up with developing pressure from below until 1956; after the June rebellion in Poznan, students, intellectuals, workers and devout Catholics joined in the ferment. Gomulka (who became Party Secretary in early October 1956) managed to negotiate with Khrushchev to prevent Soviet troops suppressing the popular movement.

191. Fejto, Francois, A History of the People's Democracies, Harmondsworth, Penguin, [1969] 1974, 2nd edition, pp. 565.

Examines destalinization in Poland and why the Polish 1956 uprising avoided bloodshed, making comparisons with Hungary and its 1956 Revolution, see pp. 79-80 and 87-123. These events are set in the wider context of Soviet and bloc politics.

192. Karol, K.S., Visa for Poland, London, MacGibbon and Kee, 1959, pp. 259.

Account by a Polish journalist (who left in 1949) of the evolution of destalinization from above and demands for democratization from below in 1955-56, and the October 1956 revolution. Karol explains the background context of Poland's wartime experiences and the Communist seizure of power and in Part Two assesses Poland a year after October 1956.

193. Hiscocks, Richard, Poland: Bridge for the Abyss?, London, Oxford University Press, 1963, pp. 359.

194. Lewis, Flora, A Case History of Hope: The Story of Poland's Peaceful Revolutions, Garden City NY, Doubleday, 1958, pp. 281.

Covers developments in 1956, especially the June and October public protests.

195. Syrop, Konrad, Spring in October: The Story of the Polish Revolution 1956, London, Weidenfeld and Nicholson, 1957, pp. 219.

b. Reaction and Developing Dissent, 1960s and 1970s

Gomulka presided over an increasingly reactionary regime, and in his last years, when he was losing his control over events, advocated the invasion of Czechoslovakia and condoned a virulent anti-semitic campaign launched by a group within the Party. There was very limited dissent in the early 1960s, but in March 1968 there were mass student demonstrations, sparked by banning of a play, in which students called for a Polish Dubcek. Gomulka was ousted in December 1970, the excuse being created by the major shipyard strikes of that year, and was replaced by Edvard Gierek.

196.Bernhard, Michael H., <u>The Origins of Democratization in Poland: Workers, Intellectuals and Opposition Politics, 1976-1980</u>, New York, Columbia University Press, 1994, pp. 298.

Covers the 1976 strikes, the founding of KOR (the Workers' Defence Committee) by intellectuals to support workers and the subsequent development of opposition.

197.Bethell, Nicholas, <u>Gomulka</u>, Harmondsworth, Penguin, 1972, pp. 307.

Gomulka, who was labelled a 'nationalist' Communist and imprisoned during the Stalinist period in Poland, played a key role in October 1956 and became the new Party Secretary. But hopes for radical reform were soon dashed. See chapters 13-15 (pp. 194-252). His loss of power is charted in chapters 16-17 (pp. 225-84).

198.Bromke, Adam, <u>Poland: The Last Decade</u>, Ontario, Mosaic Press, 1981, pp. 189.

This book, which reprints the author's articles in a variety of academic journals, includes some material on 1980, but is mostly valuable for its coverage of the preceding decade. See especially pp. 56-62 'Gomulka's legacy: Two vantage points', extracts from tape of meeting between striking workers at Szczecin and Gierek Jan 1971. and statements made at Polish Party's Central Committee meeting in Feb 1971; and pp. 94-111 'The opposition in Poland' (both also available in <u>Problems of Communism</u>, Sept-Oct 1978).

199.Brumberg, Abraham (ed.), <u>Poland, Genesis of a Revolution</u>, New York, Vintage Books, 1983, pp. 336.

Gives background on strikes.

200.<u>Dissent in Poland: December 1975-July 1977</u>, London, Association of Polish Students in Exile, 1977, pp. 200.

Collection of documents relating to demands for human rights, worker rights and political change, including accounts of trials and an eyewitness account of the 1976 strike.

201.Green, Peter, 'Third round in Poland', <u>New Left Review</u>, no. 101-102, Feb-April 1977, pp. 69-108.

Analysis of the successful June 1976 strikes against price rises.

202.Lipski, Jan Jozef, <u>KOR: A History of the Workers' Defense Committee in Poland, 1976-1981</u>, Berkeley CA, University of California Press, 1985, pp. 561.

203.Michnik, Adam, <u>Letters from Prison and Other Essays</u>, Berkeley CA, University of California Press, 1985, pp. 354.

Michnik was a leading intellectual and activist in the opposition that developed after 1968.

204.Raina, Peter, <u>Political Opposition in Poland 1954-1977</u>, London, Poets and Painters Press, 1978, pp. 551.

History of intellectual dissent including documents.

205.Rupnik, Jacques, 'Dissent in Poland, 1968-78: The end of revisionism and the rebirth of civil society', in Tokes (ed.), <u>Opposition in Eastern Europe</u>, pp. 60-112 (C.I.1.a.).

See also: Harman, <u>Bureaucracy and Revolution in Eastern Europe</u>, pp. 242-53 for account of the 1970 strikes in Gdansk and Szczecin shipyards (see C.5.a.).

c. Solidarity: from Opposition to Government, 1980-89

The sit-in strike in the Gdansk shipyard in August 1980 launched Solidarity: a mass movement and alternative trade union, which soon had branches in almost all sectors of society. The dramatic role of Solidarity up to the end of 1981, followed by its brutal suppression when General Jaruzelski declared martial law, attracted widespread attention in the west. So did its re-emergence in the late 1980s. Solidarity – as a predominantly worker movement, demonstration of nonviolent people power and a challenge to the Soviet bloc – stimulated a large literature from different ideological perspectives.

206.Ash, Timothy Garton, <u>The Polish Revolution: Solidarity 1980-82</u>, London, Jonathan Cape, 1983, pp. 386.

Account by academic expert on Eastern Europe who witnessed many of the events

207.Ascherson, Neal, <u>The Polish August: The Self-Limiting Revolution</u>, Harmondsworth, Penguin, 1981, pp. 320.

Account of Solidarity to mid-1981 by British journalist familiar with Eastern Europe, with text of Gdansk and Szczecin Agreements and postscript on December 1981.

208.Kemp-Welch, A. <u>The Birth of Solidarity: The Gdansk Negotiations, 1980</u>, London, Macmillan, 1983, pp. 213.

Translation of the Gdansk negotiations between the strikers and the Party.

209.MacShane, Denis, <u>Solidarity: Poland's Independent Trade Union</u>, Nottingham, Spokesman Books, 1981, pp. 172.

Stresses working class and trade union nature of Solidarity in contrast to nationalist and religious aspects – based on interviews with Solidarity leaders and advisers and rank and file members.

210.Myant, Martin, <u>Poland: A Crisis for Socialism</u>, London, Lawrence and Wishart, 1982, pp. 254.

Examines Solidarity and the imposition of martial law against background of Polish post-war history and the Gomulka and Gierek regimes.

211.Polet, Robert, <u>Polish Summer</u>, London, War Resisters'International, 1981, pp. 43.

212.Potel, Jean-Yves, <u>The Summer Before the Frost: Solidarity in Poland</u>, London, Pluto Press, 1982, pp. 229.

Eye-witness account of early stages of revolution combined with broader analysis. Includes notes on key individuals and organizations and an overall chronology.

213.Rosenberg, Tina, <u>The Haunted Land: Facing Europe's Ghosts After Communism</u>, New York and London, Random House/Vintage, 1995.

Part 2 is on Poland and chapter 6, pp. 223-58, 'The prisoner' includes material on resistance to the imposition of martial law, political developments after martial law was lifted in July 1983, and negotiations between Solidarity and the Party, as well as 1993 trial of Jaruzelski for crimes he had committed.

214.Singer, Daniel, <u>The Road to Gdansk: Poland and the USSR</u>, New York, Monthly Review Press, 1981, pp. 290.

The first half of the book examines changes in the USSR, pp. 157-285 cover Polish developments from 1970.

215.Touraine, Alain and others, <u>Solidarity: The Analysis of a Social Movement: Poland 1980-1981</u>, Cambridge, Cambridge University Press, 1983, pp. 203.

Analysis by leading theorist of social movements with emphasis on research into opinion of ordinary members of Solidarity, and examination of strategic decisions.

216.Zielonka, Jan, 'Strengths and weaknesses of nonviolent action: The Polish case', <u>Orbis</u>, vol. 30 (Spring 1986), pp. 91-110.

217.Walesa, Lech, <u>A Way of Hope</u>, New York, Henry Holt, 1987, pp. 325; London, Pan Books, 1988.

Memoir by central (but increasingly controversial) figure in Solidarity giving his perspective on his role and developments.

See also: <u>From Below</u>, Helsinki Watch Report, on Polish Freedom and Peace group (C.I.1.a.); Ash, <u>We the People</u>, pp. 25-46; and other titles (C.I.1.b.).

7. Romania, 1945-89

The role of nonviolent resistance in Romania (Rumania in earlier spelling) has been fairly limited. The Stalinist Romanian leadership engaged in largely token revisionism after 1953. But the Hungarian revolt of 1956 did have popular repercussions, especially among the significant Hungarian minority inside Romania, and some intellectuals formulated demands for reform. These intellectuals were purged in 1958 (after the execution of Imre Nagy in Hungary). An authoritative source for this period is:

218.Ionescu, Ghita, <u>Communism in Rumania: 1944-1962</u>, London, Oxford University Press, 1964, pp. 378.

Under the new leadership of Ceausescu in the 1960s Romania asserted a degree of independence in its relations with the USSR and in its foreign policy. It blocked closer East European economic integration under the USSR and became an uncooperative member of the Warsaw Pact, refusing to take part in the invasion of Czechoslovakia in 1968. The Romanian government's 'neutralist' foreign policy was welcomed in the West, but this communist nationalism did not result in significant reforms inside

Romania. Indeed, it led to greater suppression of the Hungarian minority in Transylvania. From the 1970s Ceausescu and his wife fostered Maoist-style adulation, in the context of an omnipresent security police and increasing poverty and misery among the population as a whole. These conditions minimized intellectual dissent until the late 1980s – though a small group of writers led by Paul Goma published an 'open letter' against the cult of personality in 1977. There were a number of protests by miners and other workers, some brutally suppressed. When popular revolution broke out in Romania in December 1989, starting among the Hungarian minority, it did not maintain the disciplined nonviolence of East Germany and Czechoslovakia, but rapidly evolved into violent fighting. This violence was encouraged both by security police firing on the crowds and by the murky role of sections of the security services in the overthrow of Ceausescu.

Thus studying developments in Romania is partly of interest in suggesting both the limits of dissent and the limits of nonviolence. Nevertheless, the worker strikes and elements in the 1989 popular uprising are examples of nonviolent action in very adverse conditions.

219.Antal, Dan, Out of Romania, London, Faber and Faber, 1994, pp. 226.

Personal account of life as a conscript and rebellious student throws light on Romanian conditions and the first chapter discusses the 1989 protests and toppling of the Ceausescus.

220.McPherson, William, 'In Romania', in The Best of Granta Reportage, London, Granta Books, 1993, pp. 291-326.

The author was in Romania from January-June 1990, and provides insights on the earlier uprising and the confused nature of politics in the immediate aftermath.

221.Rady, Martyn, Romania in Turmoil: A Contemporary History, London, I.B. Tauris, 1992, pp. 216.

Analyses Ceausescu's regime and outlines the emerging resistance in the later 1980s, including the mass worker demonstrations in Brasov in November 1987, the uprisings in Timisoara and Bucharest, the execution of the Ceausescus and subsequent confused politics and violence. Includes a survey of sources.

222.Ratesh, Nestor, Romania: The Entangled Revolution, New York, Praeger, 1991, pp. 179. Introduction by Edward Luttwack.

223.Tokes, Laszlo, With God for the People as told to David Porter, London, Hodder and Stoughton, 1990, pp. 226.

Account by Reformed Church minister who resisted oppression of the Hungarian minority, and whose defiance sparked the December 1989 revolt in Timisoara, which spread to Bucharest.

See also: Fraudendorfer in Randle, People Power, pp. 108-22, (C.I.1.b); Skilling, Samizdat and an Independent Society in Eastern Europe, pp. 191-95 for intellectual dissent (C.I.1.a.); Simpson, Dispatches from the Barricades, which has a chapter on the Romanian uprising (C.I.1.b.).

8. Soviet Union, 1945-91

The revolutionary tradition in Russia included both violent peasant revolts and the growth of organized strikes with the spread of industrialization. The revolutions of 1905 and February 1917, despite some acts of violence, were both notable examples of people power. After the Bolsheviks seized control in late 1917, however, the Communist Party (after fighting a prolonged civil war) increasingly repressed all political opposition. There was some spontaneous resistance to the brutalities of collectivization, but during the Stalinist terror of the 1930s dissent was almost totally quashed.

After 1945 Soviet politics falls into four main periods: repression and renewed terror from 1945-March 1953, when Stalin died; uneven destalinization from 1953 to the ousting of Khruschev in 1964; rejection of liberalization and a long period of inertia under Brezhnev and his immediate successors from 1964-1984; and the rapid moves towards glasnost and perestroika launched after 1985 by Gorbachev, which created the possibility for popular activism and led to the dissolution first of Soviet control over Eastern Europe and then of the Soviet Union itself.

During 1945-1953 there was guerrilla resistance in some areas newly annexed by the Soviet Union, such as the western Ukraine, but no other significant signs of opposition. After the death of Stalin, conflict at the top of the Party, release of many labour camp inmates, and the (officially secret) denunciation of Stalinist crimes by Khrushchev in 1956, and again in 1961, allowed for a degree of liberalization. This 'thaw' was promoted in literature and the arts, and initially in the churches, but was limited by fears of mass unrest (especially in the non-Russian republics) and by pressure from hardline Party members. Khrushchev's own agenda was to promote socialism, so his policies on national cultural autonomy and religious practice tended to be repressive: for example, thousands of religious institutions were closed between 1959 and 1964.

In 1953 the death of Stalin prompted uprisings in several camps, the best known in Vorkuta, see:

224.Scholmer, Joseph, <u>Vorkuta</u>, London, Weidenfeld and Nicholson, 1954, pp. 204 (chapter 11).

There were later open protests by national minorities such as the Crimean Tatars and Meskhetians, who had been forcibly transported to distant areas of the USSR during the war and were demanding return to their homelands, and by the Baptists who were subject to particular persecution. But in general between 1953 and 1964 those seeking greater freedom tried to manoeuvre within the boundaries of uncertain official tolerance. There were signs of worker dissent in go-slows and occasional strikes, but the regime managed for a long time to prevent news of any major strikes and worker demonstrations from leaking out. For example, the strike in June 1962 in Novocherkassk against wage cuts and prices rises, crushed when the army turned machine guns on demonstrators (described by Alexander Solzhenitsyn in volume 3 of <u>The Gulag Archipelago</u> – pp. 506-14 of London Fontana edition 1978 – and later documented from KGB archives) was hidden from both the Soviet public and western academics for many years.

So it is the two later periods which are covered in this bibliography, although the discussion of dissent from 1965 often includes some material on earlier periods, particularly the Khrushchev era.

a. Growing Dissent, 1965-84

Ironically, it was the attempted repression under Brezhnev of all signs of opposition to the official party line that sparked the widespread emergence of organized dissent in the USSR. Dissent occurred among national minorities, religious groups, intellectuals, scientists and writers; and repression of diverse groups encouraged the emergence of a small human rights movement. Samizdat (the clandestine circulation of information, essays and banned novels) flourished and much of it was published in the West. The impact of repression was partially counteracted by the emergence of an official policy of detente in the 1970s, which eased communications between East and West, especially for privileged groups like scientists, and enabled western organizations to campaign more effectively on human rights issues inside the Soviet bloc. By the early 1980s there were even signs of opposition based on environmental and peace issues. The small Moscow Trust Group, which was wholly independent of the Party-sponsored official Peace Committee, was founded in 1982 and replicated in other major cities.

During the Cold War there was widespread approval in the West of dissenters inside the Soviet Union and often official support for them, for example for Jews trying to emigrate to Israel. There is therefore an extensive literature in English, both translations of samizdat and of works by prominent dissidents, and western academic surveys. A highly selective list of sources, covering the range of dissent and ideological differences among dissenters, is given below.

225.Bourdeaux, Michael, 'Religion' in Archie Brown and Michael Kaser (eds.), The Soviet Union Since the Fall of Khrushchev, 2nd edition, London, Macmillan, 1978, pp. 157-80.

Useful brief survey of Soviet policy towards and reactions by all religious groups in the USSR: the Orthodox Church, Catholics, Protestants, Jews, Muslims and Buddhists. The responses range from conformity and cooperation through passive resistance to open opposition. For more detail on latter see: Bourdeaux, Michael, Religious Ferment in Russia: Protestant Opposition to Soviet Religious Policy, London, Macmillan, 1968, pp. 266.

226.Browne, Michael (ed.), Ferment in the Ukraine: Documents by V. Chornovil, I. Kandybam L. Lukyanendo, V. Moroz, and Others, London, Macmillan, 1971, pp. 285.

227.Bukovksy, Vladimir, To Build a Castle: My Life as a Dissenter, New York, Viking Press, 1979, pp. 438.

Memoir covering public protests in 1965 and 1967, trials, experiences of prison including noncooperation and hunger strikes and use of psychiatric treatment.

228.A Chronicle of Current Events, London, Amnesty International, 1971 to 1983. Published sporadically due to the problems of compiling and distributing it within the Soviet Union; The Chronicle was closed down altogether for a while after 1973. An invaluable primary source of documents collected by the internal human rights movement and translated from the Russian.

Includes protest statements, accounts of demonstrations and hunger strikes, trials of dissidents and their condemnation to exile, psychiatric hospitals or prison, and the conditions they suffered.

229.Cohen, Stephen F. (ed.), An End to Silence: Uncensored Opinion in the Soviet Union from Roy Medvedev's Underground Magazine Political Diary, New York, W.W. Norton, pp. 375.

Roy Medvedev was the most prominent dissident intellectual committed to Marxism (most were anti-Communist) and condemned Stalinism and 'neo-Stalinism' from that perspective. See also his critical history of Stalinism, Let History Judge, London, Macmillan, 1972; and On Socialist Democracy, London, Macmillan, 1975; and Samizdat Register 1 and 2, edited by Roy Medvedev, London Merlin Press, 1977 and 1981, featuring 'Voices of the Socialist Opposition in the Soviet Union'.

230.Gorbanevskaya, Natalia, Red Square at Noon, London, Andre Deutsch, 1972, pp. 285.

On the demonstration in Red Square against the Soviet invasion of Czechoslovakia in August 1968 and subsequent trial and sentences.

231.Haynes, Viktor and Olga Semyonova, Workers Against the Gulag, London, Pluto Press, 1979, pp. 129.

Covers worker protest (omitted from much of the literature on dissent), including the founding of an independent trade union in the Donbass coal mining area, most of whose members were jailed and its leader sent to a psychiatric hospital.

232.Kontinent 1: The Alternative Voice of Russia and Eastern Europe. and Kontinent 2, London, Andre Deutsch, 1976 and 1977, pp. 180 and 246.

Translated selections from new Russian opposition journal based abroad, committed to 'absolute religious idealism', 'absolute anti-totalitarianism', 'absolute democratism' and 'absolute non-partisanship'. Kontinent 1 includes the dialogue between Sakharov and Solzhenitsyn, arising out of the latter's 'Letter to the Soviet leaders' attacking the ruling ideology.

233.Mamonova, Tatyana, Women and Russia: Feminist Writings from the Soviet Union, Boston, Beacon Press, 1984, pp. 273.

Mamonova was forced into exile by the KGB.

234.Medvedev, Zhores, Soviet Science, Oxford, Oxford University Press, 1979, pp. 262.

Medvedev, himself a distinguished geneticist, charts the history of Soviet science at different stages, the beginnings of dissent under Khrushchev (pp. 88-102) including Sakharov's opposition to a renewal of nuclear testing, and measures to discipline dissident scientists after 1971 (pp. 180-96). Medvedev wrote a samizdat attack in 1962 on the theories of T.D. Lysenko (Stalin's protege) in an attempt to rescue Soviet biology from the influence of Lysenko, then still dominant. This attack was later published in the West, and for this and other dissident activities Zhores was incarcerated in a psychiatric hospital until released through the intervention of his brother Roy, Tvardovsky and others (see Roy and Zhores Medvedev, A Question of Madness, London, Macmillan, 1970).

235.Medvedev, Zhores, 10 Years After Ivan Denisovitch, London and Basingstoke, Macmillan, 1973, pp. 202.

Inside account of the role of the literary magazine Novy Mir under its editor Tvardovsky, which published Solzhenitsyn's novel on the labour camps. It also details the moves to ban Solzhenitsyn's later novels and expel him from the Soviet Writers' Union, and Solzhenitsyn's protests, as well as the closure of Novy Mir, and Tvardovsky's funeral in late 1971.

236.Reddaway, Peter, 'The development of dissent and opposition', in Brown and Kaiser (eds.) The Soviet Union Since the Fall of Khrushchev, pp. 121-56.

Concise informative overall survey of emerging dissent since 1965.

237.Rubenstein, Joshua, Soviet Dissidents: Their Struggle for Human Rights, Boston, Beacon Press, 1980, pp. 304.

Covers dissent from the 'Thaw' of the 1950s to the Helsinki Watch Groups, but focusing mainly on period since 1965.

238.Sakharov, Andrei, Memoirs, London, Hutchinson, 1990, pp. 773.

Sakharov, who worked on development of the Soviet H Bomb, gradually became the most distinguished Soviet dissident, who supported detente and disarmament and human rights inside the USSR. His political ideas, which evolved towards liberalism, were elaborated in Progress, Coexistence and Intellectual Freedom, Harmondsworth, Penguin, 1969, and Sakharov Speaks, London, Collins, 1974, pp. 251 (which includes the earlier essay). Partly protected by his eminence as a scientist, and the award of the Nobel Peace prize in 1975, he was eventually exiled to Gorky in 1980, and released by Gorbachev in 1986.

239.Stead, Jean and Danielle Grunberg (eds.), Moscow Independent Peace Group, London, Merlin Press/European Nuclear Disarmament, 1982, pp. 44.

Selected documents and press reports, plus reports on 1982 peace march by Stead and Grunberg.

240.Tokes, Rudolf L. (ed.), Dissent in the USSR: Politics, Ideology and People, Baltimore, John Hopkins University Press, 1975, pp. 453.

Includes analysis of the nature, strategy and tactics of dissent, as well as the role of samizdat, dissenting songs and a discussion of why many alienated intellectuals do not protest. The main focus is on political dissent, and it includes a chapter on Sakharov, but religious dissent is examined in chapter 6.

See also: From Below, Helsinki Watch Report, pp. 107-35 for detailed history of Moscow Trust Group (C.I.1.a.).

b. The Gorbachev Years and Popular Protest, 1985-90; and Resisting the 1991 Coup

Moves to sanction greater freedom of speech and association and promote choice in the elections of 1989 encouraged popular participation, which began to manifest itself in public demonstrations about specific grievances and (especially in some non-Russian republics) political initiatives hostile to Communist Party dominance. Fearing an end to Party control, and especially the dissolution of the Soviet Union, Party hardliners combined with members of the security forces and military to stage a coup against Gorbachev in August 1991. This coup was defeated by inefficiency, by a display of people power encouraged by Boris Yeltsin, the elected President of Russia, and by divisions in the security and military forces. It also ironically hastened the end of the USSR.

241.Brown, Archie, The Gorbachev Factor, Oxford, Oxford University Press, 1996, pp. 406.

Analysis of perestroika primarily in terms of change and political manoeuvring at the top, including the conflict with Yeltsin. Chapter 8 (pp. 252-305) covers Gorbachev's mixed responses to demands for national autonomy, the abortive coup attempt and its aftermath.

242.Gorbachev, Mikhail, The August Coup: The Truth and the Lessons, London and New York, Harper Collins, 1991, pp. 127.

Gorbachev's own brief account with some appended documents.

243.Hosking, Geoffrey, The Awakening of the Soviet Union, London, Heinemann, 1990; revised 2nd edition, Mandarin Paperbacks 1991. pp. 246.

A study of the Gorbachev period with a particular emphasis on pressure from below. Chapter 3 'the return of the repressed' summarizes the earlier dissent which laid the basis for activism from 1985. Chapter 4, 'A civil society in embryo' discusses early environmental campaigns, the rising protests against nuclear power after Chernobyl, the unofficial peace movement and the rapid increase in informal groups including the Leningrad 'Cultural Democratic Movement' and the Moscow 'Club for Social Initiatives'. Chapter 5, 'The flawed melting pot', covers the evolution of national movements in Armenia, Georgia, the Ukraine and Baltic republics.

244.Khasbulatov, Ruslan, The Struggle for Russia: Power and Change in the Democratic Revolution, London, Routledge, 1993, pp. 270.

Khasbulatov was Yeltsin's ally in the Russian Soviet (parliament) in pressing for more radical change in the late 1980s and was also prominent in resisting the attempted coup. Later he became the defender of the Russian parliament against Yeltsin's autocratic policies. On the coup attempt see pp. 139-69.

245.Remnick, David, Lenin's Tomb: The Last Days of the Soviet Empire, Harmondsworth, Penguin, 1994, pp. 586.

Lively and comprehensive account by a Washington Post reporter, who was in the USSR from 1988 to 1991. Chapter 27, 'Citizens', discusses the coal miners' strikes of

1989 and 1991 in Siberia and a demonstration by Democratic Russia in Moscow in March 1991. Part 4, 'First as tragedy, then as farce', pp. 433-90, covers the August coup, emphasizing popular support for the resistance to the coup as well as the mistakes of the plotters.

246. Steele, Jonathan, <u>Eternal Russia: Yeltsin, Gorbachev and the Mirage of Democracy</u>, London, Faber and Faber, 1994, pp. 429.

Chapter 1 summarizes the beginnings of civil society under Gorbachev and Chapter 4 (pp. 59-79) gives an eyewitness account of the coup, stressing the inefficiency of the coup plotters and the limited popular response to Yeltsin's call for popular defiance and a general strike.

247. White, Stephen, Alex Pravda and Zvi Gitelman (eds.) <u>Developments in Soviet and Post-Soviet Politics</u>, revised 2nd edition, Basingstoke, Macmillan, 1992, pp. 347.

This book is primarily a survey of the Gorbachev era focusing on the changes in the Party and the state, economic policy and foreign policy. But several chapters cover the 1991 coup with differing emphases: pp. 3-7, 147-49, 294-95. Chapters by Thomas F. Remington, 'Towards a participatory politics?' (pp. 147-73) and David Mandel, 'Post-Perestroika: Revolution from above v. revolution from below' (pp. 278-99) raise questions about popular activism and protest.

9. Yugoslavia, 1945-1990

The Yugoslav government, as a result of its break with Moscow in 1948, became the first East European country to embark on a serious attempt at destalinization and political reform, focusing especially on worker 'self management', and became a model for many reform Communists during the 1950s. The popular upsurge experienced across much of Eastern Europe in 1956 did not therefore occur in Yugoslavia. There were, however, strict limits to liberalization – Milovan Djilas became the most prominent Yugoslav dissident after 1954 for challenging Party control and was jailed for his book <u>The New Class</u> – and the security police exercised considerable power until 1966.

In the early 1960s reformers within the Party pressed for further liberalization and democratization, launching the 'second reform movement', and in the second half of the decade there was increasing political debate and popular activism testing the limits of the new relaxation of controls. Worker strikes became common and student protests culminated in the mass demonstrations of 1968. Nationalist movements were, however, potentially a greater threat to the federation. Major constitutional reforms increased the autonomy of the individual republics and provinces, and Belgrade tried to meet what were seen as legitimate grievances (for example of Albanians in Kosovo up to 1966). But the revived nationalist movement in Croatia in 1970-71 (with echoes of Croatian nationalism during the War years) was seen by Tito as unacceptable and crushed. The purge of the Croatian Party brought an end to the democratization encouraged since the mid-1960s. There was, however, some scope for autonomous action and dissent in the 1970s, the final phase of Titoism.

After Tito's death in 1980 there was a fragile compromise between the constituent republics, undermined in the late 1980s by Serbia's growing intransigence. There was a rise of environmental and peace activism and student protest, especially in Slovenia. The success of the growing popular movement in Slovenia (resisting Serbian military dominance) eventually, however, precipitated the dissolution of the Yugoslav federation.

a. Two Stages of Reform: 1950-54 and 1960s; and Dissent 1960s-70s

248.Carter, April, Democratic Reform in Yugoslavia: The Changing Role of the Party, London, Frances Pinter, 1982, pp. 285.

Focuses on period 1964-72. See especially discussion of the trade unions (and worker dissent), pp. 159-68; students, pp. 172-76; dissenting periodicals, pp. 193-98 and chapter 12 'The party and political dissent', pp. 202-25.

249.Djilas, Milovan, Rise and Fall, New York,, Harcourt, Brace Jovanovic, 1985, pp. 424.

Memoirs covering his role at top of the Party and government until 1954 and his dissident role up to 1962.

250.Doder, Dusko, The Yugoslavs, London, Allen and Unwin, 1979, pp. 256.

Account by Washington Post correspondent in Belgrade 1973-76, including material on dissent and conversations with Djilas.

251.Markovic, Mihailo and Cohen. R.S., The Rise and Fall of Socialist Humanism, Nottingham, Spokesman Books, 1975, pp. 93.

Markovic was a key member of the Praxis group, espousing Marxist humanism and a critical stance, and discusses its role. (But by the 1990s he had become a leading Serb nationalist ideologist.)

252.Mihajlov, Mihajlo, 'Yugoslavia – The Approaching Storm', Dissent, 21, Summer 1974, pp. 370-72.

Mihajlov became Yugoslavia's second best known dissident for attacking the Soviet Union and calling for a multi-party system.

253.Pervan, Ralph, Tito and the Students, Nedlands WA, University of West Australia Press, 1978, pp. 239.

Analysis of 1968 student protests and Tito's role in defusing them.

254.Plamenic, D. 'The Belgrade Student Insurrection', New Left Review, no. 54, 1969, pp. 61-78.

Description and analysis of the June 1968 student unrest, culminating in march to demand reforms and occupation of the Sociology and Philosophy Faculties. Author argues that the expectations created by the democratization, which arose out economic reforms, came into conflict with the continuing reality of strict Party control.

255.Rusinow, Dennison, The Yugoslav Experiment 1948-1974, London, Hurst, 1977, pp. 410.

Highly regarded scholarly analysis of changing political developments. Rusinow discusses the student protests of 1968 (which he analysed in greater depth in 'Anatomy of a Revolt', American University Field Staff Reports, 1968), and provides illuminating analysis of the Croatian nationalist movement of 1970-71.

256.Sher, Gerson S, Praxis: Marxist Criticism and Dissent in Socialist Yugoslavia, Bloomington, IN., Indiana University Press, 1977, pp. 360.

Mostly discussion of radical reinterpretation of Marxist theory. But chapter 5 'The praxis of Praxis' (pp. 194-241) covers student protest in 1968 and the 1970s as well intellectual opposition.

257.Stojanovic, Svetozar, 'The June student movement and social revolution in Yugoslavia', Praxis International Edition, no. 3-4, 1970, pp. 394-402.

258.Wilson, Duncan, Tito's Yugoslavia, Cambridge, Cambridge University Press, 1979, pp. 269.

Clear summary by former British Ambassador of both foreign policy and internal politics of Yugoslavia up to 1978, with brief mention of forms of dissent.

b. Post-Tito Politics in the 1980s

259.Mastnak, Tomaz, 'Civil society in Slovenia: From opposition to power', in Paul G.Lewis (ed.), Democracy and Civil Society in Eastern Europe, Basingstoke, Macmillan, and New York, St Martin's Press, 1992, pp. 134-51.

See also interview with Marko Hren from Slovenia in Randle, People Power, pp. 131-48 (C.I.1.b), and From Below, Helsinki Watch Report, pp. 181-203 on Ljubljana Peace Group (C.I.1.a.); Clark, Civil Resistance in Kosovo, pp. 41-45 on the demonstrations of 1981 and subsequent repression in Kosovo, and chapter 3, pp. 46-69, 'The turn to nonviolence', starts with the miners' protests of 1988 to defend Kosovan autonomy and the developing popular resistance (D.III.1.b.).

II. China and Tibet, from 1947

1. China

Although the Communists came to power in 1949 after decades of guerrilla warfare in rural areas, there is also a significant tradition of nonviolent resistance in China. Merchants shutting down their businesses as a political protest dates back at least to the 18th century (see Sharp, Politics of Nonviolent Action, vol. 2, p. 236 (A.1.)), and national consumer boycotts against Japanese oppression took place in 1908, 1915 and 1919. Students and workers demonstrated and went on strike to demand national independence from foreign colonial intervention in 1919 (during the May the Fourth Movement) and again in 1925 (see Jean Chesneaux, The Chinese Labor Movement

1919-1927, Stanford CA, Stanford University Press, 1968, and Jeffrey N. Wasserstrom, Student Protests in Twentieth Century China, Stanford University Press, 1991). The period of Civil War from 1945-1949 also saw protests by intellectuals, students and workers against the increasingly corrupt regime of Chiang Kai-shek.

Since the Communist takeover of 1949 there have been three periods of significant dissent and protest followed by a Party crackdown on all opposition: 1956-57; 1976-79; and May-June 1989. A fourth period began in the 1990s, when the increasing emphasis on the market combined with cautious steps towards political liberalization have allowed wider dissent, which is still continuing.

Although the mass demonstrations and unrest of the Cultural Revolution, at its height from 1966-69, did involve widespread popular agitation, and provided a grounding for some later dissidents, this period does not qualify for inclusion in this bibliography for two reasons. Firstly, the 'Revolution' was deliberately fostered by Mao and a clique close to him and promoted uncritical adulation of Mao; and, secondly, the demonstrators frequently engaged in physical violence and terrorized individuals and groups seen as opponents of Maoism.

a. The Hundred Flowers Movement, 1956-57

During 1956, when mass unrest swept through parts of Eastern Europe, there were some reverberations in China, such as strikes and withdrawals from agricultural cooperatives. Perhaps to defuse unrest, or to engage intellectuals in the next stages of socialist development, the Party leadership, in particular Mao, encouraged intellectuals to speak out in this period, and many cautiously began to do so. This apparent sanctioning of dissent encouraged students also to protest and many workers to start asserting their demands through petitions, marches, hunger strikes, sit-ins and strikes. Mao and the Party responded in mid-1957 by suppressing all dissent and hundreds of thousands of intellectuals were blacklisted, students expelled, and many sentenced to manual labour or exile.

260.Doolin, Dennis, Communist China: The Politics of Student Opposition, Stanford CA, Hoover Institute, Stanford University, 1964, pp. 70.

This is Doolin's translation of a Beijing Student Union pamphlet, together with his own introduction.

261.MacFarquahar, Roderick, Contradictions Among the People 1956-1957 (vol. 1 of The Origins of the Cultural Revolution), New York, Columbia University Press, 1974, pp. 438.

Highly respected scholarly analysis.

262.Perry, Elizabeth J. 'Shanghai's strike wave of 1957', China Quarterly, 157, March 1994, pp. 1-27.

Looks at little known worker unrest accompanying intellectual dissent.

263.Wu Ningkun, A Single Tear, London, Hodder and Stoughton, 1993, pp. 367.

Wu, a university teacher of English educated in the US, returned to China in 1951. This is a personal account of his experiences. The Hundred Flowers campaign is covered pp. 47-72.

b. The Democracy Movement, 1976-79

After Mao died in September 1976 there was a struggle at the top of the Party between ardent Maoists who had instigated the Cultural Revolution and officials anxious to promote stability. The emerging new leader Deng Xiaoping also sponsored economic (market) reforms. In this context there was a groundswell of political activity from below, first manifested in April 1976 in a popular ceremony of traditional mass mourning in Tiananmen Square for Prime Minister Zhou Enlai (viewed as a moderate), which was seen as a pro-Deng demonstration. This was the first expression of the Democracy Movement that blossomed in late 1978. Although students and intellectuals were predominant there were also peasant protests. The authorities started to arrest individual dissidents early in 1979 and closed down the Democracy Wall in December that year, but underground publishing continued.

264.Goodman, David S.G. (ed.), Beijing Street Voices: The Poetry and Politics of China's Democracy Movement, London and Boston, Marion Boyars, 1981, pp. 208.

265.Index on Censorship, vol. 9, no. 1, Feburary 1980. This issue is largely dedicated to dissent in China.

266.Schell, Orville, Discos and Democracy: China in the Throes of Reform, New York, Pantheon Books, 1988, pp. 384. Includes material on 1976-79 and 1986-87.

267.Seymour, James D. (ed.), The Fifth Modernization: China's Human Rights Movement, 1978-1979, Stanfordville NY, Human Rights Publishing Group, 1980, pp. 301.

268.Wei Jingsheng, The Courage to Stand Alone: Letters from Prison and Other Writings, New York and London, Penguin, 1998, pp. 283.

Wei, a prominent advocate of 'the fifth modernization' – democracy, was arrested and jailed in 1979.

c. Tiananmen, The Mass Protests of 1989

There were signs of unrest before 1989: students in Heifei demonstrated in December 1986 against the Party's role in elections to the Peoples Congress, and student protests spread to Shanghai and other cities. Simmering unrest continued, encouraged by conflict at the top of the Party between hardliners and those more sympathetic to intellectuals. But the spark for the mass protests of April to June 1989 was the death of the former General Secretary Hu Yaobang, forced out of office by hardliners for alleged responsibility for the protests of December 1986. Students massed in Tiananmen Square in April to lay wreaths to Hu, and the protest rapidly developed through marches, occupation of the Square, boycott of classes and formation of autonomous student unions. The demonstrations won support from workers and other Beijing residents and spread to other parts of the country. Some Party leaders tried to conciliate the students, but in May the rise of a more radical student leadership and the launching of a hunger strike, coinciding with the visit of President Gorbachev, led most of the Politburo to endorse the imposition of martial law. This met widespread popular resistance. Numerous collections of documents and accounts of both protest and repression were compiled at the time. The sources selected here seek to give an overall perspective on events.

269.Cherrington, Ruth, China's Students: The Struggles for Democracy, London, Routledge, 1991, pp. 239.

270.Duke, Michael S., The Iron House: A Memoir of the Chinese Democracy Movement and the Tiananmen Massacre, Layton, Utah, Gibbs Smith, 1990, pp. 180.

Eyewitness account from May 19 by Chinese-speaking American professor.

271.Fang Lizhi, Bringing Down the Great Wall: Writings on Science, Culture and Democracy, translated and edited J.H. Williams, New York, Alfred A. Knopf, 1990, pp. 336.

Fang Lizhi, a prominent astrophysicist, became an increasingly vocal critic of the regime in the 1980s and was linked to the 1986 student protests. Introduction by Orville Schell.

272.Han, Minzhu (ed.), Cries for Democracy: Writings and Speeches from the 1989 Chinese Democracy Movement, Princeton NJ, Princeton University Press, 1990, pp. 401.

Collection of materials from the protest movement.

273.Mok, Chiu Yu and J. Frank Harrison (eds.), Voices from Tiananmen Square: Beijing Spring and the Democracy Movement, Montreal, Black Rose Books, 1990, pp. 203.

Collection of documents from participants in demonstrations.

274.A Moment of Truth: Workers Participation in China's 1989 Democracy Movement and the Emergence of Independent Unions, Hong Kong, Asia Monitor Resource Center, 1991, pp. 254.

275.Oksenberg, Michael, Lawrence R. Sullivan and Marc Lamberts (eds.), Beijing Spring 1989: Confrontation and Conflict, The Basic Documents, Armonk NY, M.E. Sharpe, 1990, pp. 403.

Collection of documents from official perspective.

276.Saich, Tony (ed.), The Chinese People's Movement: Perspectives on Spring 1989, Armonk NY, M.E. Sharpe, 1991, pp. 207.

Includes both an account of the protests and the authorities' response, and scholarly essays interpreting the context. Has extensive bibliography.

277.The Tiananmen Papers, compiled by Zhang Liang and edited by Andrew J. Nathan and Perry Link, London, Little Brown, 2001, Abacus. 2002, pp. 679.

Secret Party papers leaked to the west provide details of the meetings, negotiations and communications between the top leaders about how to deal with the protests, and the triumph of the hardliners over Zhao Ziyang, General Secretary of the Party, who wished to be conciliatory. Western scholars generally accepted the papers as authentic.

278.True, Michael, 'The 1989 democratic uprising in China from a nonviolent perspective' in M. Kumar and P. Low (eds.), Legacy and Future of Nonviolence, New Delhi, Gandhi Peace Foundation, 1996, pp. 141-57.

279.Unger, Jonathan (ed.), The Pro-Democracy Protests in China: Reports from the Provinces, Armonk NY, M.E. Sharpe, 1991, pp. 239.

See also: Schock, Unarmed Insurrections, pp. 98-119 on reasons for failure, and Thompson, Democratic Revolutions, pp. 65-83 for comparison with government responses in Eastern Europe (A.1.); and Simpson, Dispatches from the Barricades, which has two chapters on Tiananmen, Chapter 4 'The river of protest', pp. 64-88 and Chapter 5 'Death in the Square', pp. 89-113 (C.1.1.b.).

d. China Since 1990

There has been a gradual but unpredictable relaxation of controls over freedom of speech and publication and some evidence of a developing civil society. The abandonment of former socialist policies has increased the wealth of some but encouraged corruption, and left many workers, peasants and those dependent on state benefits economically insecure. As a result there has been a dramatic increase in worker unrest, public protests by pensioners, and some criticism of economic globalization. There has also been resistance to the Three Gorges Dam, which has thrown many peasants off their land. (Jaspar Becker, 'World's third largest river starts to rise by 400 ft to create the great wall of water', Independent on Sunday, 1 June 2003, pp. 12-13) There is in addition evidence of rising rural unrest over sale of land to developers, local corruption and destruction of the environment. Campaigners are both putting up candidates in local elections and demonstrating. The government admitted that there had been 74,000 'mass incidents' in 2004.

The incorporation of Hong Kong into China in 1995 created a zone with a special status and a lively democracy movement that had sprung up in the period leading to Britain's transfer of control to Beijing. Nationalist dissent has not prompted the kind of problems experienced in the USSR because, in the China created in 1949, over 90 per cent of the population were ethnic Chinese. But reports have emerged of significant dissent among the Muslim population of Xinjiang. (Tibet is treated in this bibliography as a separate country.)

280.'China: "Let us speak!"', New Internationalist, no. 371 (September 2004), pp. 9-28.

Overview of Chinese society today, role of the media, the conditions in the workplace, and the scope for and limits to debate and dissent. Yu Jianrong charts the growth of direct action among farmers resisting heavy taxes, protesting against irregularities in village elections or challenging corruption among local cadres (pp. 16-17).

281. Han Dongfang, 'Chinese labour struggles', New Left Review, no. 34 (July/August 2005), pp. 65-85.

Interview with a former railway worker involved in trade union activity at time of Tiananmen, who now directs the China Labour Bulletin and broadcasts from Hong Kong to promote independent union activity in China.

282. He Qinglian, 'China's listing social structure', New Left Review, no. 5 (Sep/Oct 2000), pp. 69-100.

A critical assessment of Chinese society by a Chinese social scientist, widely discussed within China, indicating the context for unrest. Inset is an article describing a pensioner campaign led by a former Party official (pp. 82-83).

283. Jiang Xueqin 'Fighting to organize', Far Eastern Economic Review, (6 September 2001), pp. 72-75.

Gives examples of strikes and sit-ins and role of unofficial trade unions.

284. Perry, Elizabeth J. and Mark Selden (eds.), Chinese Society: Change, Conflict and Resistance, London, Routledge, 2000, pp. 249.

Analysis of reactions to government reforms, including both covert and open resistance, distinguishing between intellectual dissidents and popular rebellion. See especially 'Rights and resistance: The changing context of the dissident movement' (pp. 20-38); 'Pathways of labour insurgency' (pp. 41-61); and 'Environmental protest in rural China' (pp. 143-59) which includes reference to direct action against a factory polluting water.

285. Wasserstrom, Jeffrey N., 'Student protests in fin-de-siecle China', New Left Review, no. 237 (September/October 1999), pp. 52-76.

Discusses 1999 student demonstrations against the NATO bombing of Chinese Embassy in Belgrade, comparing them with earlier May 4th 1919 and June 1989 protests. Argues that, despite official support and encouragement, the 1999 protests did reflect significant degree of student autonomy and included allusion to 1989.

2. Tibet

Tibet has a long history as an effectively independent Buddhist state, but was claimed as part of China by the Chinese Communists, who occupied Tibet in 1950. Under the 1951 Agreement, signed by the Dalai Lama, the Chinese promised to respect the role of Buddhism and the authority of the Dalai Lama. Since then Chinese policy has reflected its internal politics. For example during the Cultural Revolution monasteries were destroyed and practice of Buddhism forbidden, but under Deng Xiaoping religious toleration was restored. In general, however, China has sought to modernize Tibet, promoted Chinese immigration and suppressed dissent.

Since 1959, when the Dalai Lama fled to India, he has been the key figure in exile and engaged in negotiations with the Chinese government. The Dalai Lama himself is strongly committed to nonviolence, but some of the exile organizations advocate violent revolt. Resistance inside Tibet has at times been violent, as in the 1959 uprising, but has also included nonviolent protests by monks and nuns.

286.Barnett, Robert and Shirin Akiner (eds.), <u>Resistance and Reform in Tibet</u>, Bloomington IN, Indiana University Press, 1994, pp. 314. Barnett also contributes an essay to Lehman, Steve, Robbie Barnett and Robert Coles, <u>The Tibetans: A Struggle to Survive</u>, New York, Powerhouse Cultural Entertainment Books, 2004, pp. 125, a primarily photographic record.

287.Dalai Lama, <u>Freedom in Exile: The Autobiography of the Dalai Lama</u>, London, Hodder and Stoughton, 1990, pp. 308.

288.Dalai Lama, <u>My Land and My People</u>, London, Weidenfeld and Nicholson, 1962, pp. 253.

Autobiography of his earlier years.

289.Donnet, Pierre-Antoine, <u>Tibet: Survival in Question</u>, Delhi, Oxford University Press, and London, Zed Books, 1994, pp. 267.

Examines Tibet from 1950 to early 1990s, and includes account of the 1959 uprising, the role of the Dalai Lama and protests in the 1980s (see chapter 4, 'The revival of nationalism', pp. 93-107).

290.Grunfeld, A. Tom, <u>The Making of Modern Tibet</u>, revised edition, Armonk NY, M.E. Sharpe, 1996, pp. 352.

Discusses the role of the Tibetan diaspora, and intrigues by the Indian government, the Chiang Kai-shek government of Taiwan and the CIA, as well as internal developments from the 1950s to 1995.

291.Kelly, Petra K, Gert Bastian and Pat Aiello (eds.), <u>The Anguish of Tibet</u>, Berkeley CA, Parallax Press, 1991, pp. 382.

Selection of documents and personal accounts, including eyewitness reports on demonstrations in Lhasa in 1988 and 1989.

292.Schwarz, Ronald D., <u>Circle of Protest: Political Ritual in the Tibetan Uprising</u>, London, Hurst, 1994, pp. 263.

293.Smith, Warren W. Jr., <u>Tibetan Nation: A History of Tibetan Nationalism and Sino-Tibetan Relations</u>, Boulder CO, Westview Press, 1996, pp. 732.

The Chinese occupation of Tibet in 1950 and subsequent changing Chinese policies and Tibetan responses are covered chapters 9-15. Various protests in 1980s are noted in chapter 15.

See also web source: Kramer and Moser Puangsuwan, (eds), <u>Truth is our Only Weapon: The Tibetan Nonviolent Struggle</u>, SE Asia, Nonviolence International, 2000, and Ram, Senthil, 'The Tibetian Nonviolent Resistance: Empowerment in an Extraordinary Situation' in Ney, Chris (ed) <u>Nonviolence and Social Empowerment</u>, War Resisters' International web (H.b.).

D. Resisting Rigged Elections, Oppression, Dictatorship, or Military Rule

I. Africa

Most examples of mass popular resistance in Africa have been to colonial rule (see Section B above) or to apartheid. The long struggle in South Africa, which involved a very wide range of nonviolent tactics, as well as (from the 1960s) limited guerrilla warfare, is covered below. The example of popular protest against rigged elections spread to Madagascar in 2001–2; and demonstrators in both Ethiopia and Egypt were fired on by the police in mid-2005. But the only sustained nonviolent campaign against political authoritarianism so far has occurred in Zimbabwe since 2000. (Campaigns against multinational corporations and neoliberal economic policies are listed under G.7.)

1. South Africa, Resisting Apartheid to 1994

Nonviolent resistance has a long history in South Africa, where Gandhi developed his methods of 'satyagraha' to assert the civil rights of the Indian community, and where the multiracial African National Congress (ANC) was officially committed to nonviolence in its struggle against apartheid from 1910 until 1961. After 1945, as apartheid was strengthened, there were impressive strikes, for example the 1946 miners' strike, and acts of civil disobedience against apartheid measures, for example by Indians opposing discriminatory legislation in 1946. The 1952 'defiance campaign', demanding the repeal of unjust laws, aspired to nation-wide noncooperation, and there was resistance to the removal of squatters, and boycotts of the newly introduced Bantu education system in 1954-55. Nonviolent protest continued in the late 1950s, and mounted in 1960-61 with resistance to the pass laws, including demonstrations and a general strike.

But the increasingly brutal government repression, and the banning of opposition organizations, convinced the ANC leadership that it was necessary to create Umkhonto we Sizwe (the 'Spear of the Nation') to carry out guerrilla warfare – though the emphasis was on sabotage, and the ANC itself remained committed to 'mass struggle'. Mandela's speeches during the 1960 Treason Trial and his later 1962 trial, when he was condemned to life imprisonment, still stressed commitment to what he called a 'nonracial' future. The rival Pan African Congress (PAC), which differed from the ANC over association with the Communist Party and organized the fateful Sharpeville demonstration of 1961 (when the police fired repeatedly into a peaceful crowd), also created a military wing, which targeted both whites and African collaborators. So there was a clear turn from nonviolence.

Mass popular protest did not occur again until 1976, when about 15,000 Soweto school children demonstrated against being forced to learn in Afrikaans, a protest which extended to opposing the Bantu education system and the regime itself. The bloody police response triggered school boycotts and mass protests throughout the country. Although the basic tactics were nonviolent, demonstrators often fought the police with sticks and stones. Many of the children were killed and injured, and the protests ended after six months of resistance. Funerals of militants and demonstrators killed by the security services were, however, a continued focus for defiant mass public protest.

During the 1980s protest in the form of consumer and school boycotts and student activism revived, independent grass roots organizations and community activism developed and the United Democratic Front (UDF), which resisted the apartheid constitution of 1983, coordinated community, student, church and trade union bodies. The trade unions consolidated their organization and their ability to conduct disciplined strikes, as in the 1979 Ford strike against relocation, and in 1989 COSATU (the trade union federation) together with the UDF created the Mass Democratic Movement to organize nationwide defiance. During the protracted negotiations to end apartheid in the early 1990s, symbolized by Mandela's release in February 1990 and the ending of the bans on the ANC, PAC, Communist Party and other political organizations, the ANC leadership turned to 'people power' and organized mass strikes and demonstrations to back their negotiating strategy. This period saw bloody confrontations between the ANC and the supporters of the Zulu Inkatha movement led by Chief Buthelezi (the security services helped to promote some of the worst acts of violence), but nevertheless heralded the moves towards reconciliation and the remarkably peaceful and successful elections under universal franchise of 1994.

The injustice of apartheid was opposed throughout much of the world and was frequently denounced at the United Nations. Popular campaigns to promote economic sanctions – including a wave of sit-ins at US universities in the mid-1980s – encouraged some institutions to disinvest from banks and corporations engaged in South Africa; economic sanctions were also endorsed by some governments. Demonstrations against South African sports teams and moves towards sporting boycotts also had a significant impact. International pressure therefore combined with internal resistance.

The opposition to apartheid both within the country and outside continued for over three decades, and there is a large literature on various forms of resistance and the role of different sectors of South African society, organizations and individuals, as well as numerous individual memoirs, many by white opponents of apartheid. The list of books below is highly selective, but covers major aspects of the struggle and key individuals.

a. Internal Resistance

294.Benson, Mary, The African Patriots: The Story of the African National Congress of South Africa, London, Faber and Faber, 1963, pp. 310 (Reprinted in USA as South Africa: The Struggle for a Birthright, New York, Funk and Wagnalls, 1966).

This history covers the period 1910 to 1960.

295.Biko, Steve, The Testimony of Steve Biko, edited Millard Arnold, London, Maurice Temple Smith, 1978, pp. 298 (published in the USA by Random House as Black Consciousness in South Africa).

Biko, a key figure in the move towards radical black consciousness in the 1970s, was killed, whilst in custody, by the South African security services.

296.Callinicos, Alex and John Rogers, <u>Southern Africa after Soweto</u>, 2nd edition, London, Pluto Press, 1978, pp. 246.

Includes critical assessment of the 1960s campaigns and examination of industrial action in the 1970s.

297.Feit, Edward, <u>African Opposition in South Africa: The Failure of Passive Resistance</u>, Stanford CA, Hoover Institution on War, Revolution and Peace, 1967, pp. 223.

A critical study of the 1954-55 campaigns.

298.Hope, Marjorie and James Young, <u>The South African Churches in a Revolutionary Situation</u>, New York, Orbis Books, 1981, pp. 268.

Covers opposition of many churches to apartheid.

299.Kuper, Leo, <u>Passive Resistance in South Africa</u>, London, Jonathan Cape, 1956, pp. 256. Reprinted 1957 and 1960 by Yale University Press.

A sociological study of the 1952 'Defiance Campaign'.

300.Lodge, Tom, <u>Black Politics in South Africa since 1945</u>, London, Longman, 1983, pp. 389.

Covers key campaigns up to Sharpeville and also the Soweto student rebellion.

301.Luckhardt, Ken and Brenda Wall, <u>Organize or Starve! The History of the South African Congress of Trade Unions</u>, New York, International Publishers, 1980, pp. 485.

302.Luthuli, Albert, <u>Let My People Go</u>, London, Collins, 1962, pp. 256.

Autobiography of a leading opponent of apartheid, President of the ANC from 1952 to 1967, and Nobel Prize winner.

303.Mandela, Nelson, <u>Long Walk to Freedom: The Autobiography of Nelson Mandela</u>, London, Little Brown, 1994, pp. 768; reprinted five times as an Abacus paperback in 1995.

Provides Mandela's own perceptions of the evolving struggle and his own role within it, including his views on nonviolence and support for the turn to violent resistance.

304.Mandela, Nelson, <u>No Easy Walk to Freedom</u>, London, Heinemann, 1965, pp. 189. Reprinted 1986.

Mandela's articles, speeches and addresses at his trials.

305.Marx, Anthony, <u>Lessons of Struggle: South African Internal Opposition 1960-1990</u>, New York, Oxford University Press, 1992, pp. 347.

Comprehensive survey and analysis.

306.Meredith, Martin, <u>Nelson Mandela: A Biography</u>, London, Hamish Hamilton, 1997, pp. 596.

Meredith has written widely on southern Africa.

307.Michelson, Cherry, <u>The Black Sash of South Africa: A Case Study in Liberalism</u>, London, Oxford University Press, 1975, pp. 204.

Analysis of (predominantly) white women's organization publicly opposing apartheid since 1950s; known especially for its black sash vigils.

308.Mufson, Steven, <u>Fighting Years: The Black Resistance and the Struggle for a New South Africa</u>, Boston, Beacon Press, 1990, pp. 360. Includes bibliography pp. 349-52.

309.Reeves, Ambrose, <u>Shooting at Sharpeville: The Agony of South Africa</u>, London, Gollancz, 1960, pp. 159.

Account by Anglican Bishop of Johannesburg, prominent in resisting apartheid, of the opposition to carrying passes.

310.Scott, Michael, <u>A Time to Speak</u>, London, Faber, 1959, pp. 365.

Autobiography of well known supporter of human rights in South Africa, who spoke for the Herero people of South West Africa before the United Nations when they were opposing incorporation into the Union of South Africa. Chapter 8 describes the Indian resistance to discriminatory legislation in 1946.

311.Smuts, Dene and Shauna Westcott, <u>The Purple Shall Govern: A South Africa A to Z of Nonviolent Action</u>, Cape Town, Oxford University Press and Centre for Intergroup Studies, 1991, pp. 165.

Seeks to document examples from the history of nonviolent action from the 1950s to 1990s (Luthuli to Tutu) which amounts to 'probably the largest grassroots eruption of diverse nonviolent strategies in a single struggle in human history'. Brief extracts illustrating tactics such as boycotts, courting arrest, funerals, graffiti, ostracism, prayer, resisting removal, voluntary exile and 'wading in' (segregated beaches). Includes some distinctively South African expressions of protest.

312.Tutu, Desmond, <u>The Rainbow People of God</u>, ed. John Allen, London, Bantam, 1995, pp. 286.

Archbishop Tutu, a highly respected opponent of the regime who influenced world opinion in the 1980s and 1990s, played a key role in the Truth and Reconciliation Commission after the ANC came to power. This is a collection of his sermons on Christianity and apartheid, race relations and politics.

b. External Boycotts

313.Hain, Peter, <u>Don't Play with Apartheid: Background to the Stop the Seventy Tour</u>, London, Allen and Unwin, 1971, pp. 232.

See also: 'Direct action and the Springbok tours' in Benewick and Smith (eds.), <u>Direct Action and Democratic Politics</u>, pp. 192-202 (A.1.).

314.Lapchick, Richard, <u>The Politics of Race and International Sport: The Case of South Africa</u>, Westport CT, Greenwood Press, 1975, pp. 268.

Analysis of sports boycott and its impact on white South Africans.

315.Orkin, Mark (ed.), <u>Sanctions Against Apartheid</u>, New York, St. Martin's Press, 1989, pp. 328.

c. Resisting South African Military Policies

In order to shore up the apartheid regime, the South African government used its security service and military forces to prevent majority African rule in other southern African countries, such as Namibia. After Portugal agreed to decolonization in Mozambique and Angola, South Africa fomented civil war. This policy meant that South African conscripts were sent to fight in neighbouring countries. From the 1970s there was growing opposition to being conscripted either to suppress the black townships within South Africa, or to fight in neighbouring countries. South African draft resisters abroad also began to organize in the late 1970s.

316.Catholic Institute for International Relations, <u>Out of Step: War Resisters in South Africa</u>, London, CIIR, 1989, pp. 141.

Resistance to conscription in apartheid South Africa.

317.Clark, Howard, <u>When the Best Say No: Impressions from a Visit to South Africa in Support of War Resisters</u>, London, War Resisters' International, 1989, pp. 27.

Report from a War Resisters' International delegation, noting the widespread recognition of the potential for nonviolent action.

318.Cock, Jacklyn and Lawrence Nathan (eds.), <u>War and Society: The Militarisation of South Africa</u>, New York, St Martin's Press, 1989, pp. 361.

319.Cock, Jacklyn, <u>Women and War in South Africa</u>, London, Open Letters, 1992, pp. 254.

This is primarily an analysis of the nature and effects of violence in South Africa in the 1980s and how the politics of gender underpins the South African Defence Force. But it also looks at whites resisting conscription. Different responses – compliance, evasion and resistance – are examined pp. 75-90, including accounts of some individual objectors and the role of the End Conscription campaign.

320.Nathan, Lawrence, <u>Force of Arms, Force of Conscience: A Study of Militarisation, the Military and the Anti-Apartheid War Resistance Movement in South Africa, 1970-1988</u>, Bradford, M.Phil. Thesis, 1990.

Discusses the increasing incidence of conscientious objection to compulsory military service as the SADF was deployed to suppress resistance in the townships. Notes that the End Conscription Council, in which he was centrally involved, 'became a significant force' in the opposition to apartheid and was eventually outlawed by the authorities.

321.Seegers, Annette, 'South Africa: From laager to anti-apartheid', in Charles C. Moskos and John Whiteclay Chambers (eds.), <u>The New Conscientious Objection</u>, New York, Oxford University Press, 1993, pp. 127-34 (see G.3.b.ii).

Survey of development of conscientious objection from 1960.

See also on anti-apartheid struggle: Schock, <u>Unarmed Insurrections</u>, pp. 56-68 (A.1.).

2. Zimbabwe, Resisting Mugabe's Autocracy Since 2000

After a bitter civil war Zimbabwe achieved independence in 1980, and the Zimbabwe African National Union – Patriotic Front (ZANU-PF), one of the political movements engaged in the guerrilla struggle, won an overwhelming majority in the elections, with Robert Mugabe as President. Mugabe reached an accommodation with the white population and the prospects for stability and economic prosperity looked good.

The main problem in the early years of the new regime was the conflict between ZANU-PF and the rival Patriotic Front – Zimbabwe African People's Union (PF-ZAPU) party, led by Joshua Nkomo, with its base in Matabeleland. Small numbers of former ZAPU guerrillas challenged the government and Mugabe launched a four year war in Matabeland in which 10,000 civilians were killed. But in December 1987 PF-ZAPU was incorporated into ZANU-PF, with Nkomo becoming Vice President.

The country then enjoyed peace and reasonable prosperity, although the economy began to decline in the 1990s. However, the predominantly white ownership of the best farmland, whilst large numbers of Africans lacked land, was a continuing source of resentment. A land reform law in 1992, proposing white farmers would be compensated for transferring some of their land, petered out. Pressure from the War Veterans Association for land encouraged Mugabe to commit himself to seizing white farmers' land without compensation. These provisions were included in a new draft constitution, which also enhanced the President's powers, which was defeated in a referendum in February 2000. A new opposition party, the Movement for Democratic Change, was prominent in opposing the clause.

Mugabe then sanctioned violent invasions of white farms by 'veterans' of the independence struggle, with an eye to support from the Shona peasantry in the June 2000 parliamentary elections. Repression of the farmers and their black workers coincided with rising opposition to Mugabe's rule in the urban centres and in the trade unions. Since 2000 there has been increasing poverty and lack of food, and widespread resistance by many sectors of the African population, including sections of the press, judiciary and the churches. The MDC has continued to contest elections (despite severe harassment of candidates and supporters), claimed the elections have been rigged (claims supported by many but not all external observers) and called a number of general strikes. The regime has responded to opposition with legal bans, imprisonment, beatings and torture, and distributed food so as to reward supporters and penalize opponents.

There is a growing literature analysing developments in Zimbabwe, but much of it focuses on the developments since 1980 and the context of opposition since 2000. Information on campaigning groups active within Zimbabwe is mostly available on the web sites listed below.

322.Buckle, Catherine, <u>African Tears: The Zimbabwe Land Invasions</u>, London, Covos Day Books, 2001 and Johannesburg, Jonathan Ball, 2002, pp. 243. Foreword by Trevor Ncube.

Cathy Buckle, a supporter of the new inter-racial Zimbabwe, was forced off her farm. This book focuses on invasions of white farms by Mugabe's 'veterans' but also stresses suffering of black farm workers, and documents the developing resistance round the Movement for Democratic Change in the June elections. A postscript provides a chronology of events from October-December 2000, including repression of protests and the resistance by Supreme Court justices. See also: Buckle, Catherine, <u>Beyond Tears: Zimbabwe's Tragedy</u>, Johannesburg, Jonathan Ball, 2002, pp. 218; sequel to her earlier book, continuing her account of repression and resistance.

323.Chan, Stephen, 'Zimbabwe: The old fox eludes the hunt', <u>World Today</u>, vol. 61 no. 4 (April 2005), pp. 22-23.

Assesses the faction fights within Mugabe's party and the role of South Africa, and forecasts likely split in the MDC.

324.Cross, Eddie, 'Zimbabwe: Body blow', <u>World Today</u>, vol. 59, no. 12 (December 2003), pp. 20-21.

A member of the MDC looks back at rising opposition, especially in trade unions, to Mugabe and his party in 2000, particularly resistance to the new constitution, and support for the newly formed MDC in the June elections. Also notes the challenge to Mugabe in 2002 Presidential elections and outlines the government's subsequent sustained campaign to crush opposition.

325.MacLean, Sandra J. 'Mugabe at war: The political economy of conflict in Zimbabwe', <u>Third World Quarterly</u>, vol. 23 no. 3 (June 2002), pp. 513-28.

Examines deterioration of governance in Zimbabwe since independence and notes effectiveness of the opposition movement since 2001.

326.Meldrun, Andrew, <u>Where We Have Hope: A Memoir of Zimbabwe</u>, London, John Murray, 2004, pp. 272.

Personal account by <u>Guardian</u> journalist of Zimbabwe's politics and people since 1980. Chapters 12-19 (pp. 114-241) cover the rise of MDC, the debates about the new constitution, resistance and repression, and Chapter 20 describes his own expulsion from the country.

327.Ranger, Terence, 'Zimbabwe: Cultural Revolution', <u>World Today</u>, vol. 58, no. 2 (February 2002), pp. 23-25.

Analysis of Mugabe's rhetoric and strategy of launching a third revolution against imperialism, and his policy on violence.

328.Sithole, M., 'Fighting authoritarianism in Zimbabwe', <u>Journal of Democracy</u>, vol. 12 no. 1 (January 2001), pp. 160-69.

329.Windrich, Elaine, 'Then and now: Reflections on how Mugabe rules Zimbabwe', <u>Third World Quarterly</u>, vol. 23 no. 6 (December 2002), pp. 1181-88.

Feature review of several books on Zimbabwe, including Buckle, <u>African Tears</u>, with historical analysis.

330.'Zimbabwe Focus': 'When to call black white: Zimbabwe's electoral reports', <u>Third World Quarterly</u>, vol. 23 no. 6 (December 2002), pp. 1145-58.

Analysis of March 2002 Presidential election and conflicting assessments of its fairness from organizations within Zimbabwe and teams of electoral observers from the west and Africa.

For web sources on internal opposition see: Enough is Enough: www.sokwanele.com/ and Women of Zimbabwe Arise and Gays and Lesbians of Zimbabwe, both at: www.kubatana.net See also: Goddard, Keith, 'Inside Out', in Ney, Chris (ed.), Nonviolence and Social Empowerment, War Resisters International web (see H.b.)

II. Asia

It was in Asia that key theorists and leaders of two types of popular struggle emerged in the first half of the 20th century: Gandhi's satyagraha in India and Mao's guerrilla warfare in China. Guerrilla warfare has been widely used in various struggles for independence from colonialism and western intervention (notably in Vietnam). Armed violence has also been a resort for minorities opposing political oppression (as in Burma) or major social injustice (for example the Naxalites in India).

Nevertheless, there have been significant nonviolent struggles in many parts of Asia, both in India where the Gandhian legacy is still important, and in a number of other countries, notably the Philippines and Burma. There has also been a trend towards mass popular demonstrations to demand democracy in recent years, for example in South Korea and Thailand. In some cases nonviolent tactics have been linked to street fighting or riots (for example in Pakistan), but if the overall strategy has promoted noncooperation and unarmed opposition they are relevant to this bibliography.

A useful source for researching the development of particular campaigns in Asia is Far Eastern Economic Review, which carries frequent, but usually brief, reports on important developments.

Asian Survey is an academic journal which publishes broader political assessments. For a more radical perspective see: Critical Asian Studies, published by Routledge (formerly Bulletin of Concerned Asian Scholars).

Two interesting campaigns which have not been listed separately because of a dearth to date of accessible printed sources occurred in Nepal (1990) and Kyrgyzstan (2005).

The Movement for the Restoration of Democracy in Nepal, inspired by events in Eastern Europe, launched a campaign, 'the stir', to end the panchayat (council) system and restore multiparty democracy. After mass demonstrations and the calling of two general strikes between February and April 1990, the King lifted the ban on political parties in April and approved a new draft constitution in September. These events are covered by the Far Eastern Economic Review and the Economist (see issues of April 7 1990, p.83; April 14, pp. 67-68; April 21, p. 72 and May 5, p. 88 summarizing the protests, their causes, and the political responses). See also:

331.Koirala, Niranjan, 'Nepal in 1990: End of an era', and Michael Hutt, 'Drafting the Nepal Constitution', 1990', in Asian Survey, vol. 31 (1991): February, pp. 134-39; and November, pp. 1020-39. See also: Schock, Unarmed Insurrections, pp. 121-25 and 130-41 (A.1.).

The Kyrgyzstan protests in March 2005 (the 'tulip revolution') were, as in Georgia and the Ukraine, at least partly a response to rigged parliamentary elections. But the demonstrations which erupted in the southern city of Osh, before spreading to the capital Bishek, also appeared to be a protest against presidential nepotism and economic hardship. The protesters were more violent than in Georgia and the Ukraine, looting and rioting as they attacked the presidential and parliamentary buildings. Some observers queried how far the uprising was spontaneous or was organized by opposition leaders seeking to assume power. The immediate outcome was that President Akayev fled to Russia and an opposition leader, Kurmanbek Bakiyev, became interim president and prime minister, but agreed to work with the newly elected parliament. He won a landslide victory in the presidential election held in early July 2005, in an election approved by OSCE monitors. See:

332. International Crisis Group, 'Kyrgyzstan: After the Revolution', Asia Report no. 97, 4 May 2005, pp. 1-20 plus appendices (map of area, key members of interim government, and information about the International Crisis Group). There are also later ICG reports on Kyrgyzstan. Available on the web from: www.crisisgroup.org

1. Burma, Resisting Military Dictatorship 1988, and Ongoing Protest

Burma gained independence from the British immediately after the Second World War, and after a period of civilian government has been subjected to a series of military regimes. There has been continuing guerrilla resistance by national minorities in Burma since its independence. But in 1988 there was mass nonviolent resistance to military dictatorship, which met with brutal repression. Ever since the peaceful opposition has been led and symbolized by Aung San Suu Kyi (daughter of the leader of Burma's armed struggle for independence), who has adopted a Gandhian philosophy of nonviolence. Her party, the National League for Democracy, was elected by a clear majority in elections held in 1990, despite harassment by the military, but the military junta then refused to recognize the elections and placed Suu Kyi under house arrest, where she has remained, with occasional partial lifting of restrictions, ever since. She and her party have, however, continued to defy the regime.

Suu Kyi called for an economic and tourist boycott of Burma (Myanmar), and there has been a transnational campaign in support of democracy in Burma. North American students in the 1990s spearheaded a campaign for disinvestment, persuading a significant number of major corporations to withdraw by using consumer boycotts and other forms of protest. Continuing boycott campaigns in the west are still forcing companies (such as sportswear manufacturers), attracted to Burma by low wages, to pull out. Some individuals have also entered Burma to demonstrate and hand out leaflets – for example 18 who protested in Rangoon in August 1998. (On this transnational support see: Naomi Klein, No Logo, London, Flamingo, 2000, pp. 402-4, and pp. 410-16.).

333. Aung San Suu Kyi, Freedom from Fear and Other Writings, ed. Michael Aris, London, Viking, 1991, pp. 338.

See especially Suu Kyi's writings on the democracy struggle in 'Part II', pp. 167-237 and essays by Josef Silverstein, 'Aung San Suu Kyi: Is she Burma's woman of destiny?', pp. 267-83 and Philip Kreager, 'Aung San Suu Kyi and the peaceful struggle for human rights in Burma', pp. 284-325.

334.Aung San Suu Kyi, The Voice of Hope: Conversations with Alan Clements with Contributions by U Kyi Maung and U Tin Oo, London, Penguin, 1997. pp. 301.

335.Beer, Michael A., 'Violent and Nonviolent Struggle in Burma: Is a Unified Strategy Workable?', in Zunes et al (eds.), Nonviolent Social Movements, pp. 174-84 (A.1.).

336.Fink, Christina, Living Silence: Burma under Military Rule, London, Zed Books, 2001, pp. 286.

Provides brief historical background and surveys the regime in its internal and international context. Chapter 2 notes students', monks' and workers' protests against General Ne Win in 1970s (pp. 42-45). Chapter 3 describes national nonviolent resistance 1988-90 and subsequent opposition to military rule led by Aung San Su Kyi (pp. 50-72). Chapter 12 looks at campaigns by transnational civil society.

337.Littner, Bertil, Outrage: Burma's Struggle for Democracy, [1989] London and Bangkok, White Lotus, 1990, pp. 208.

Covers the 1988 mass nonviolent resistance and its suppression.

See also: Helvey, On Strategic Nonviolent Conflict, pp. 51-65; Schock, Unarmed Insurrections; pp. 92-98 and 102-119, and Sharp et al, Waging Nonviolent Struggle, pp. 245-52 (A.1.).

2. Korea (South), Demanding Democracy, 1979-80 and 1986-87

There was a history of nonviolent resistance by the Koreans to Japanese occupation during the first half of the 20th century. After the division of Korea in 1945, the death and destruction of the Korean War, 1950-53, and Korea's continuing role as a front line in the cold war, with American troops guarding the armistice line, South Korea was subject to the dictatorship of the western-backed Syngman Rhee until 1960. Then popular desire for democracy, demonstrated in mass protests in which students were prominent, brought down the dictatorship. But it was replaced by a new military regime under Park Chung Hee from 1961-1979. There were renewed student protests in 1979, and a 1980 student revolt in Kwangju was brutally repressed by the army, which killed up to 2000 people and arrested thousands more. General Chun Doo Hwan won the 1981 elections, and students continued to protest, often resorting to firebombing government buildings or fighting the police. But in 1986 students began to mobilize worker and rural support and a dozen students set fire to themselves (an act of traditional remonstrance to unjust rulers). Widespread popular opposition persuaded Chun not to stand for a second term in 1987, and led to gradual democratization of the previously authoritarian regime.

338.Clark, Donald N. (ed.), The Kwangju Uprising: Shadows over the Regime in South Korea, Boulder CO, Westview Press, 1987, pp. 101. Includes bibiography pp. 95-96.

339.Cotton, James (ed.), <u>Politics and Policy in the New Korean State</u>, New York, St Martin's Press, 1995, pp. 246.

Proceedings of conference in Melbourne 1992.

340.Kim Chong Lim (ed.), <u>Political Participation in Korea: Democracy, Mobilization and Stability</u>, Santa Barbara CA and Oxford, Clio Books, 1980, pp. 238.

Includes chapter on student activism in 1960 and 1971.

341.Kim Dae Jung 'Interview: Democracy and dissidence in South Korea', <u>Journal of International Affairs</u>, vol. 38 no. 2 (1984-1985), pp. 181-92.

Kim Dae Jung had been a leading figure in the Democratic Opposition of South Korea since 1971, when he ran for president against the dictator Park Chung Hee, was imprisoned and then exiled. He gave this interview in November 1984, setting out his policies and hopes, when planning to return to join in the struggle against dictatorship.

342.Kim Shinil 'South Korea' in Philip G. Altbach, <u>Student Political Activism: An International Reference Handbook</u>, Westport CT, Greenwood Press, 1989, pp. 173-8.

343.Kluver, Alan R., 'Student movements in Confucian society' in Gerard J. DeGroot, <u>Student Protest: The Sixties and After</u>, London, Addison Wesley, 1998, pp. 219-31.

Discusses role of self-immolation by Korean protesters.

344.Shorrock, Tim, 'The struggle for democracy in South Korea in the 1980s and the rise of anti-Americanism', <u>Third World Quarterly</u>, vol. 8 no 4 (October 1986), pp. 1195-1218.

Analyses the Park Chung Hee regime, looks back to the Kwangju massacre and the role of the US, and comments on the student and worker demonstrations in the spring of 1986 and US/Korean government attempts to channel unrest from the streets into electoral activity. Refers to his earlier article 'Korea: Stirrings of resistance', <u>The Progressive</u>, February 1986.

3. Pakistan, Resisting Military Rule, 1968 and 1980s

Pakistan was created out of the partition of the Indian sub-continent in 1947, which led to mass migrations and terrible massacres of both Muslims and Hindus. Pakistan suffered a further partition when East Pakistan broke away in 1971 and claimed independence. The secession met with harsh repression by the Pakistan army, thousands of refugees fled to India, and the Indian army invaded East Pakistan, ensuring recognition of an independent Bangladesh. Pakistani politics has also been marked by long periods of military rule.

There have, nevertheless, been campaigns of predominantly nonviolent resistance to the military using boycotts, strikes, demonstrations and hunger strikes, although protest often turned into riots and there was also fighting between factions, often in the universities. (Factional strife became more bloody in the 1980s when guns were widely available, as Pakistan became enmeshed in the guerrilla warfare in neighbouring Afghanistan).

The first campaign of popular resistance took place in 1968-69, when workers and students, supported by peasants, women and school children, brought an end to the government of General Ayub Khan in March 1969. Although he handed over power to the commander-in-chief General Yahya Khan, who immediately imposed martial law, this was a significant example of people power. The resistance, in which Zulfikar Bhutto, leader of the Pakistan Peoples Party, played a prominent role, involved remarkable solidarity between West and East Pakistan, and continued after the imposition of martial law.

Bhutto headed a civilian government from the end of 1971 to 1977, when he was ousted by General Zia, and executed after a sham trial in 1979. The second campaign of national resistance to military rule began in April 1980, the anniversary of Bhutto's execution, with pilgrimages to his grave. In 1981 opposition parties came together to form the Movement to Restore Democracy – the Bhutto family, held under arrest, were a focal point for much of the opposition. Students took the initiative in demonstrating, supported openly by academics, doctors and lawyers and less openly by many others. When the regime arrested leaders of the Movement to Restore Democracy, the Movement called for mass strikes and political noncooperation across Pakistan. In 1983 the Movement again launched a mass protest movement, courting arrest. Popular resistance in Sindh spread to other provinces, with the Bar Associations demanding genuine elections. This campaign was not quelled until October 1983, after hundreds had been killed by the army, villages destroyed and crops burned. When in December 1984 Zia held a referendum on his policy of imposing Islamic law, and in March 1985 held an 'election' to the National Assembly, in which political campaigning was banned, the Movement called on the people to boycott them. After martial law was ended at the end of 1985 political campaigning by opposition parties, in particular the Pakistan Peoples Party increased. But genuine elections were not granted until after the death of Zia in an air crash in August 1988. Benazir Bhutto, Zulfikar's daughter, was elected as prime minister in December 1988.

These campaigns against military rule have not received much attention in the west, books on Pakistan tend to focus entirely on government actions and on political leaders, but a few relevant books are listed below.

345.Ali, Tariq, <u>Pakistan: Military Rule or People's Power</u>, London, Jonathan Cape, 1970.

The first four chapters cover the period 1947 to 1968. Chapters 5-7 (pp. 156-216) discuss the mass revolt from November 1968 to March 1969, which the author compares to the May 1968 Events in France.

346.Bhutto, Benazir, <u>Daughter of the East: An Autobiography</u>, London, Mandarin, 1989, pp. 402.

A memoir by Bhutto's daughter, who was central figure in the campaign for democracy in the 1980s, which takes her story up to the period just before the November 1988 elections and her becoming prime minister of Pakistan in December 1988. Although the focus is personal, includes material on the wider political context and on the growing popular resistance.

347.Feldman, Herbert, <u>From Crisis to Crisis: Pakistan 1962-1969</u>, London, Oxford University Press, 1972, pp. 344.

The main emphasis of this book is on Ayub Khan's government, but chapter 9 'The last phase' (pp. 237-71) does cover the '132 days of uninterrupted disturbances'. Author stresses the rioting and factional violence, but does note the significant role of the urban working classes and the students.

348.Sobhan, Rehman, 'Pakistan's political crisis', <u>World Today</u>, vol. 24, no. 5 (May 1969), pp. 203-11.

Examines Zulfikar Bhutto's style of opposition and growth of popular opposition, especially role of students, in 1968-69.

349.Wolpert, Stanley, <u>Zulfi Bhutto of Pakistan: His Life and Times</u>, New York and Oxford, Oxford University Press, 1993, pp. 378.

The focus is on Bhutto's political role and leadership and there is only very brief mention of popular agitation in chapter 7 'Winters of his discontent' (1965-1969), pp. 100-34.

4. Philippines

The resistance in the Philippines popularized the now widely used term 'people power'. The authoritarian Marcos regime, established in 1972, faced popular challenge during the early 1980s. The fraudulent parliamentary elections of 1984 prompted mass demonstrations of protest. When Marcos called an election for the presidency in 1986, Cory Aquino, widow of the assassinated opposition leader Benigno Aquino, stood as a candidate. The regime's rigging of the election to deny her success led to a nonviolent uprising which overthrew Marcos. The role of the armed forces – the Defence Minister Juan Enrile appealed to the army and people to support Aquino – has been much debated. The role of the Catholic Church was also central. Catholic bishops backed Aquino, and when Marcos called on units of the army to attack Enrile's headquarters, priests and nuns led many thousands of people to prevent their advance.

The success of the 1986 protests prompted a renewed expression of people power in January 2001. When President Estrada was accused of major corruption and a Senate investigation failed to pursue the charges seriously, tens of thousands took to the streets. In the absence of military support, Estrada rapidly resigned to be replaced by Gloria Macapagel Arroyo.

a. Resisting Marcos, 1983-86

350.Arillo, Cecilio T., <u>Breakaway: The Inside Story of the Four-Day Revolution in the Philippines, February 22-25 1986</u>, Manila, CTA and Associates, 1986, pp. 288.

Account focusing primarily on role of military and using extensive military sources, but also discusses role of 'people power'.

351.Bello, Walden, 'From the ashes: The rebirth of the Philippine revolution – a review essay', Third World Quarterly, vol. 8 no. 1 (January 1986), pp. 258-76.

Left wing academic discusses sympathetically the role of the left and armed revolution in the countryside, but also explores the 'legal, semi-legal and clandestine mass struggles in the cities'. Notes the creation by 1975 of a militant workers' movement and the 1975 year-long wave of over 400 strikes, as well as networks among Catholics, professionals and students.

352.Bello, Walden, 'Aquino's elite populism: initial reflections', Third World Quarterly, vol. 8 no. 3 (July 1986), pp. 1020-30.

Observes that Cory Aquino's movement seen as a third force by the US, though author rebuts US claims to have supported her before the fall of Marcos. Comments that the movement 'is a genuine populist phenomenon', with base in urban middle class, and brought onto the streets the lower middle class, unemployed workers and shanty town residents. Aquino avoided ties to the left and did not need them to win the election, though – Bello claims – the left had paved the way for her ultimate success.

353.Cortright, David and Max Watts, Left Face: Soldier Unions and Resistance Movements in Modern Armies, Westport CT, Greenwood Press, 1991.

In the chapter 'The Philippines: Another Portugal?', pp. 220-28, the authors challenge the view that the Reformed Armed Forces Movement was ever a revolutionary movement, suggest that Enrile was seeking power, and conclude:'The primary thrust for the overthrow of Marcos and the installation of Cory Aquino came from the people themselves, notably the church and the middle classes'.

354.Elwood, Douglas J., Philippines Revolution 1986: Model of Nonviolent Change, Quezon City, Philippines, New Day Publishers, 1986, pp. 60.

Includes material on role of local peace movement, nonviolent training and a 1983 statement on 'creative nonviolence'.

355.Fenton, James, 'The snap revolution', Granta, 18 (1986), pp. 33-155.

Eyewitness account

356.Johnson, Bryan, The Four Days of Courage: The Untold Story of the People Who Brought Marcos Down, New York, Free Press, 1987, pp. 290.

Emphasis on role of military and Catholic Church.

357.Komisar, Lucy, Corazon Aquino: The Story of a Revolution, New York, George Brazillier, 1987, pp. 290.

Discusses role of Benigno Aquino and Corazon Aquino's involvement in politics; pp. 105-23 focus on mutiny and popular protests.

358.Mercado, Monina Allarey (ed.), People Power: An Eyewitness History: The Philippine Revolution of 1986, Manilla, J.B. Reuter, 1986 and New York, Writers and Readers Publishing, 1987. Preface and scenarios by Francisco S. Tatad. pp. 320.

359.Pascual, Dette, 'Organizing "People Power" in the Philippines', <u>Journal of Democracy</u>, vol. 1 no. 1 (Winter 1990), pp. 102-109.

Brief but illuminating account by the founder and chair of the National Women's Movement for the Nurturance of Democracy in the Philippines of the role played by her organization and two other civil society groups with which she was involved between 1983 and 1986.

360.Schwenk, Richard L., <u>Onward Christians! Protestants in the Philippines Revolution</u>, Quezon City, New Day Publishers, 1986, pp. 102.

Examines role of various Protestant groups and stresses Christian basis of nonviolence.

361.Thompson, Mark R, <u>The Anti-Marcos Struggle: Personalistic Rule and Democratic Transition in the Philippines</u>, New Haven CT, Yale University Press, 1995, pp. 225.

362.Zunes, Stephen Z, 'The origins of people power in the Philippines', in Zunes et al (eds), <u>Nonviolent Social Movements</u>, pp. 129-57 (A.1.).

See also: Ackerman and Duvall, <u>A Force More Powerful</u>, pp. 369-95; Diokno, Maria Serena I in Martin et al, <u>Nonviolent Struggle and Social Defence</u>, pp. 24-29; Schock, <u>Unarmed Insurrections</u>, pp. 68-90; Sharp et al, <u>Waging Nonviolent Struggle</u>, pp. 239-44, and Thompson, <u>Democratic Revolutions</u>, pp. 18-34, 'The Puzzle of the Philippine "People Power"', and pp. 35-50, comparing Aquino, Bhutto, Suu Kyi and other Asian women leaders of democractic revolutions. (A.1.).

b. Challenging Estrada, 2001

363.'Documents on democracy: Philippines', <u>Journal of Democracy</u>, vol. 12 no. 2 (April 2001), pp. 184-85.

Excerpts from inaugural address of Gloria Macapagel Arroyo.

364.Labrador, M.C., 'The Philippines in 2001: High drama, a new president and setting the stage for recovery', <u>Asian Survey</u>, vol. 42 no. 1 (Jan/Feb 2002), pp. 141-49.

365.Lande, Carl H., 'The return of "people power" to the Philippines', <u>Journal of Democracy</u>, vol. 12 (April 2001), pp. 88-102.

Discusses the continuing problems of Philippine democracy and the role of an elite above the law.

366. Macapagal, Maria Elizabeth and Jasmin Nario Galace, 'Social psychology of People Power II in the Philippines', <u>Peace and Conflict: Journal of Peace Psychology</u>, vol. 9 no. 3 (2003), pp. 219-33.

Includes assessment of nonviolence.

367.Mitchell, M. 'Shut out of people power', <u>Far Eastern Economic Review</u>, vol. 164 no. 5 (8 February 2001), pp. 22-23.

Comments on leftist groups seeking support from the poor majority.

368.Reid, Ben, 'The Philippine democratic uprising and the contradictions of neoliberalism: EDSA II'. Third World Quarterly, vol. 22, no. 5 (2001), pp. 777-93.

Analysis of Estrada regime and the protests that led to the overthrow of Estrada and his replacement by Gloria Aroyo – EDSA stands for Epifanco de los Santos, the location of both 1986 and 2001 uprisings. The article is also a critique of western commentators who deplore the popular uprising, and an attack on a neoliberal conception of democracy. The author concludes that the 2001 rebellion was ultimately an elite controlled process, transferring power to a different faction of the elite, but also a model of popular mobilization and empowerment.

5. Taiwan, 1970s and 1980s

As Chiang Kai-shek was driven out of mainland China by the Communists in the late 1940s, he consolidated Kuomintang rule over Taiwan (Formosa), whilst looking to the future reunification of China on KMT terms. From the end of 1949 until the mid-1980s Taiwan was effectively ruled by a one-party dictatorship with the help of martial law. It was also the rule of mainland Chinese over native Taiwanese. In 1987, after a year's discussion, martial law was lifted and the regime, under Chiang Kai-shek's son, Chiang Ching-kuo, began to take steps towards liberalization, such as easing restrictions on the press, freeing many imprisoned dissidents and allowing opposition parties. The ossified structure of the Leninist-style KMT and the legislature also underwent reform. Democratization could be seen in part as an adjustment to an increasingly prosperous capitalist economy, a response to US pressure and as enlightened reform from above. But it also reflected strong pressure from below, and the regime discussed reforms with leaders of the opposition.

In the early 1970s the changing international context and US recognition of Communist China sparked a major debate among intellectuals and students. After Chiang Kai-shek's death in 1975 there was renewed intellectual ferment, and dissent intensified after the KMT tried in 1977 to rig the election of a local magistrate against an independent candidate, prompting 10,000 people to attack the local police station. National opposition, centred on new dissident periodicals, included moderate and Marxist groups, but was spearheaded by the radical 'Formosa' group. This wave ended in 1979 when a mass rally in Kaohsiung on December 10, Human Rights Day, was bloodily suppressed, and leaders of 'Formosa' jailed.

During the 1980s, however, a moderate opposition regrouped and used the loophole of independent individual candidacies for elections to gain electoral support, won seats for the wives of jailed dissidents and other independents, and laid the basis for an opposition party. Growing liberalization after 1986 encouraged marches, demonstrations, strikes and boycotts on a range of political, economic and environmental issues, and between July 1987 and July 1988 there were over 1,400 reported protests, many by students, workers and farmers.

369.Cheng Tun-jen and Stephen Haggard, 'Taiwan in transition', Journal of Democracy, vol. 1 no. 2 (Spring 1990), pp. 62-74.

Discusses models of democratization, opting for an emphasis on processes rather than preconditions. Examines rather dismissively role of protest in 1970s but notes evolving opposition in the 1980s and concludes that although 1986 did not mark a Philippine-style people power transition it was a 'tacit negotiation' between the regime and the opposition. Tun-jen Cheng provides a similar analysis in 'Democratizing the quasi-Leninist regime in Taiwan', World Politics vol. 41 (July 1989), pp. 471-99.

370.Chou Yangsun and Andrew J. Nathan, 'Democratizing transition in Taiwan', Asian Survey, vol. 27 no. 3 (March 1987), pp. 277-99.

371.Kaplan, John, The Court Martial of the Kaohsiung Defendants, Berkeley CA, Berkeley University Press, 1981, pp. 79.

372.Long, Simon, Taiwan: China's Last Frontier, Basingstoke, Macmillan, 1991, pp. 264.

After sketching in Taiwan's earlier history and the evolution of the KMT, chapter 3 describes Taiwan's political development up to 1986 including a brief summary of the birth of opposition (pp. 66-72). Chapter 8 looks at political reform from 1986-89, the founding of the opposition Democratic Progressive Party and the rise in protest.

373.Roy, Denny, Taiwan: A Political History, Ithaca NY, Cornell University Press, 2003, pp. 255.

Chapter 6 examines the opposition's struggle and breakthrough.

6. Thailand, Demanding Democracy 1973 and 1992

Thailand has suffered frequent intervention by the military in politics: since the end of absolute monarchy in 1932 Thai history has been marked by a series of coups. Popular opposition began to contest this pattern: mass protests led by students in 1973 led to the fall of the existing military dictatorship. But military influence in politics was not at an end.

After a military-dominated government seized power in February 1991, a renewed popular campaign for democracy began in early 1992, which crystallized round the demand that General Suchinda resign as Prime Minister. Nonviolent resistance began in April with a hunger strike by a prominent politician and continued with weeks of popular demonstrations and public assemblies demanding democracy. When moves to resolve the crisis within parliament failed, hundreds of thousands gathered to protest on May 15. The government violently suppressed the demonstration, killing a minimum of 52 protesters, but General Suchinda was forced to resign and new elections were held in September 1992 leading to a coalition government headed by a civilian. Thailand has not had any coups since then.

374.Boonyarattanasoontorn, Jaturang and Gawin Chutima (eds.), Thai NGOs: The Continuing Struggle for Democracy, Bangkok, Thai NGO Support Project, 1995, pp. 188.

375.Callahan, William A., Imagining Democracy: Reading 'The Events of May' in Thailand, Singapore and London, Institute of Southeast Asian Studies, 1998, pp. 199.

376.Hewison, Kevin (ed.), <u>Political Change in Thailand: Democracy and Participation</u>, London, Routledge, 1997, pp. 301.

The book is an overview of society and politics in Thailand. The Introduction briefly discusses the background to May 1992. The chapter by Andrew Brown 'Locating working class power' (pp. 163-78) challenges the mainstream interpretation of May 1992 as an expression of the increased power of the middle class and civil society groups, which demonstrated the absence of working class power. He suggests commentators have an oversimplified model of united working class action.

377.Moncrieff, Anthony, 'Thailand: staggering back to democracy', <u>World Today</u>, vol. 48 no. 3 (March 1992), pp. 48-50; and 'Thailand's slow march to democracy', <u>World Today</u>, vol. 49 no. 3 (March 1993), pp. 56-59.

378.Paisal, Sridaradhanya (ed.), <u>Catalyst for Change: Uprising in May</u>, Bangkok, Post Publishing, 1992, pp. 116.

379.Paribatra, Sukhumbhand, 'State and society in Thailand: How fragile the democracy?', <u>Asian Survey</u>, vol. 33 (September 1993), pp. 879-93.

380.Samudavanija, Chai-Anan 'Thailand' in Philip G. Altbach, <u>Student Political Activism: An International Reference Handbook</u>, Westport CT, Greenwood Press, 1989, pp. 185-96.

Covers student activism in the 1960s and 1970s.

381.Sivaraska, Sulak, <u>Loyalty Demands Dissent: Autobiography of a Socially Engaged Buddhist</u>, Berkeley CA, Parallax Press, 1998, pp. 248.

Sivaraska (who is close to the Vietnamese Buddhist Thich Nhat Hanh) is a prominent social critic, who dared to compare the military to 'termites'. He edits the journal <u>Seeds of Peace</u>, which comments on problems in the region.

See also Sharp et al, <u>Waging Nonviolent Struggle</u>, pp. 299-314; Schock, <u>Unarmed Insurrections</u>, pp. 125-41, and Satha-Anand, Chaiwat, 'Imagery in the 1992 nonviolent uprising in Thailand' in Zunes et al (eds.), <u>Nonviolent Social Movements</u>, pp. 158-73 (A.1.).

III. Europe

After the end of the Second World War, Western Europe was generally seen as a bulwark of liberal democracy. There were however notable exceptions. Both Spain and Portugal (which had not taken part directly in the war) continued to be ruled until the 1970s by dictatorships dating from the 1930s. Spain moved peacefully towards parliamentary democracy after Franco's death in 1975, but there had been significant dissent and protest since the 1940s, mostly (with the exception of the Basque guerrilla movement ETA) nonviolent (see below). Portugal, on the other hand, moved towards parliamentary democracy (after a period of revolutionary turmoil) as a result of a widely popular military coup d'etat in 1974, when supporters placed carnations in the guns of the soldiers on guard in the streets. The military, disillusioned by having to fight brutal colonial wars in Africa, had, even before 1974, been at the forefront of opposing both dictatorship at home and continuing colonial rule abroad, although there was evidence of civilian resistance, especially in the form of worker strikes. Portugal is not included as a separate section in this bibliography, but is an interesting example of the military acting on behalf of the people, and of a coup d'etat igniting mass popular action. See:

382.de Figueiredo, Antonio, Fifty Years of Dictatorship, Harmondsworth, Penguin, 1975, pp. 261; and Insight on Portugal, by Sunday Times Insight Team, London, Andre Deutsch, 1975, pp. 273.

383.Harman, Chris, The Fire Last Time: 1968 and After, London, Bookmarks, 1988 (2nd edition 1998), pp. 410.

Chapter 13 'Portugal: the revolution that wilted', recounts from a revolutionary socialist perspective the extraordinary ferment of 1974-75, a period of 'dual power' between radical workers going on strike and occupying their workplaces and the provisional government and increasing polarization between left and right.

The third country which did not achieve a genuine and stable liberal democracy until the later 1970s was Greece, which moved from rightwing authoritarianism to temporary liberal government (1963-65), to harsh military rule from 1967-1974. The struggle against dictatorship was predominantly nonviolent.

France, racked by its colonial wars in Indo China and then in Algeria, was threatened by a military coup d'etat and invasion sponsored from Algeria in 1961. This coup attempt was thwarted by mass demonstrations and a token general strike, and by the authority of General de Gaulle, who eventually extricated France from Algeria. See: Adam Roberts, 'Civil resistance to military coups', Journal of Peace Research (A.1.).

But after the collapse of the Fourth Republic, de Gaulle imposed semi-authoritarian rule in 1958, creating a new constitution enshrining Presidential dominance over parliament. The student ferment of 1968 came closer in France than any other West European country to turning into a genuine revolution and almost toppled de Gaulle (see the New Left, G.2).

Since the collapse of the Berlin Wall in 1989 and the end of the Cold War, Eastern Europe and states formerly within the Soviet Union have achieved the transition to liberal democracy with very varying degrees of success. Serb oppression of the Albanian majority in the Kosovo region prompted prolonged nonviolent resistance before a minority resorted to guerrilla warfare. Recent examples of people power against authoritarian rule come from Serbia (2000), Georgia (2003) and the Ukraine (2004), although there are doubts whether all, or any, of these should be celebrated uncritically as expressions of popular democracy. For a comparative analysis of these three cases and the conditions for success see:

384.McFaul, Michael, 'Transitions from Postcommunism', Journal of Democracy, vol. 16, no. 3 (July 2005), pp. 5-19.

One authoritarian regime in a European ex-Soviet republic which has not (yet) experienced a people power revolution is Belarus. But there is a significant dissident movement among intellectuals and young people grouped round Charter 97, Zubr (Bison) committed to nonviolence, and other organizations. Commemoration of

Chernobyl in April 2005 resulted in large scale arrests. Although Amnesty International regularly reports on arrests and beatings of dissidents and silencing of human rights protesters, Belarus is not well covered in the west. But see:

385. Stoppard, Tom, 'Accidental tyranny', Guardian (Review), (October 5 2005), pp. 4-6.

1. Former Yugoslavia After 1990

From 1990, a combination of a changing international context at the end of the Cold War, economic crisis inside Yugoslavia and nationalist tensions promoted by politicians in the individual republics within Yugoslavia, led to the dissolution of the Federation. The breakdown started with the relatively painless secession of Slovenia, followed by bloody wars over the secession of Croatia and the future of Bosnia Hercegovina. The map of Yugoslavia was redrawn by the Dayton Accords of 1995, which left Kosovo as a province of Serbia, until increasing repression by the Serbian government and growing Albanian popular resistance led to crisis and NATO military intervention in late 1999. Despite the widespread use of military power and atrocities against civilians, this period also saw examples of impressive nonviolent popular resistance in Kosovo and in Serbia. How far western powers were pursuing their own interests in the Balkans, and gave active support to popular resistance is an important political question, but certainly does not nullify the significance of civilian resistance.

To understand the context of campaigns in different parts of the former Yugoslavia, a number of titles on the disintegration of Yugoslavia as a whole are included.

386.Glenny, Misha, The Fall of Yugoslavia: The Third Balkan War, Harmondsworth, Penguin Books, 1992, pp. 194.

Account by BBC Central Europe correspondent.

387.Magas, Branka, The Destruction of Yugoslavia: Tracking the break-up 1980-1992, London, Verso, 1993, pp. 336.

A compendium of essays and interviews commenting on events in the 1980s and 1990s, drawing on close contacts with social activists.

388.Ramet, Sabrina P., Balkan Babel: The Disintegration of Yugoslavia from the Death of Tito to the Fall of Milosevic, 4th edition, Boulder CO, Westview Press, 2002, pp. 426.

Frequently cited analysis.

389.Silber, Laura and Allan Little, The Death of Yugoslavia, London, Penguin Books/ BBC Books, 1995, pp. 400.

390.Thompson, Mark, A Paper House: The Ending of Yugoslavia, London, Hutchinson Radius/Vintage, 1992, pp. 288.

The author, associated in 1980s with European Nuclear Disarmament movement, is closer to the perspective of groups committed to nonviolence than other writers on this topic.

a. Serbia, Resisting Milosevic 1996-2000

After the end of the war in Bosnia in 1995, a range of groups inside Serbia (including students and intellectuals and extreme nationalists) began to rally against the increasingly authoritarian and corrupt regime of Milosevic. There were daily mass demonstrations in the winter 1996-97 over rigging of town hall elections. The student group OTPOR played an important role in planning resistance in 2000, but the miners and mass involvement were decisive in the final days leading to the fall of Milosevic. The most detailed account of the fall (hard to obtain outside Belgrade) is: October 5 – A 24-hour Coup, Media Center Belgrade (Press Documents), 2000, pp. 315, which is based on interviews with 60 people and includes photos and map of Belgrade.

391.Cohen, Lenard J., Serpent in the Bosom: The Rise and Fall of Slobodan Milosevic, Boulder CO, Westview, 2001, pp. 438.

Assesses Milosevic's role in Yugoslav and Serbian politics from 1980 to his overthrow.

392.Hudson, Kate, Breaking the South Slav Dream: The Rise and Fall of Yugoslavia, London, Pluto Press, 2003, pp. 192.

Account of fall of Milosevic, pp. 138-51, stresses US aid to the opponents of Milosevic such as OTPOR, not role of popular protest.

393.Krnjevic-Miskovic, Damjan de, 'Serbia's prudent revolution', Journal of Democracy, vol. 12 (July 2001), pp. 96-110.

394.Lebor, Adam, Milosevic: A Biography, London, Bloomsbury, 2002, pp. 386.

Chapter 24 'Toppling Milosevic from Budapest', pp. 298-312 covers role of OTPOR demonstrations in 2000, but focuses on role of outside powers in toppling Milosevic and of ensuring TV coverage.

395.Thomas, Robert, Serbia Under Milosevic: Politics in the 1990s, London, Hurst, 1999, pp. 443.

See especially pp. 263-318 on formation of united opposition and mass protests from March 1996 to Feburary 1997. Account goes up to 1998.

396.Thomspon, Mark R. and Philipp Kuntz, 'Stolen elections: The case of the Serbian October', Journal of Democracy, vol. 15, no. 4 (October 2003), pp. 159-72.

Analysis of the Milosevic regime and the reasons for the October 2000 uprising, plus brief reflections on links between stolen elections and democratic revolutions in the the Philippines 1986, Madagascar 2002 and Georgia 2003. Useful references to other literature.

397.US Institute of Peace, Whither the Bulldozer? Nonviolent Revolution and the Transition to Democracy in Serbia, Washington DC, USIP Special Report 72, 2001, pp. 12 (downloadable from http://www.usip.org/pubs/specialreports/sr72.html).

Based in part on a conference held in Belgrade with the USIP and the Belgrade Helsinki Committee for Human Rights.

398.Women in Black, <u>Women for Peace</u>, Belgrade, Yearbook, published in English, Spanish and Serbian since 1994.

Resistance to Serbia's wars and support for Serb militias in Bosnia.

See also Sharp et al, <u>Waging Nonviolent Struggle</u>, pp. 315-39; and Thompson, <u>Democratic Revolutions</u>, pp. 84-98, (A.1.).

b. Kosovo, Resisting Serbian Oppression 1988-98

Kosovo, with a large and growing Albanian population suspected of separatist leanings, suffered serious repression in Tito's Yugoslavia until 1966, when the powers of the Yugoslav political police were significantly curbed. The province of Kosovo within Serbia then enjoyed greater political autonomy, and Albanians had greater cultural rights until the 1980s, when there were signs of increasing tension between the (minority) Serbs and Albanians within Kosovo, and between the Serbian regime and the province. This Serbian nationalism was translated into a policy of oppressing the Albanians and suppressing their institutions from 1988. There was an impressive predominantly nonviolent mass struggle by the Albanian population from 1988 to 1998. But a group committed to guerrilla warfare (the Kosovo Liberation Army) began attacks in 1996 which led to a Serbian military offensive involving brutal retaliation in 1998, international condemnation of Serb actions and NATO bombing of Serb forces and Serbia in 1999.

For an insightful series of essays, which may not, however, be easily available, see: Maliqi, Shkelzen, <u>Kosova: Separate Worlds: Reflections and Analyses</u>, Peja/Pec, Dukagjini, 1998, pp. 261.

399.Clark, Howard, <u>Civil Resistance in Kosovo</u>, London, Pluto, 2000, pp. 266.

This study, whilst explaining the historical and political context of the civil resistance, focuses primarily on the strategy, institutions and weaknesses of the nonviolent struggle.

400.Kostovicova, D. <u>Parallel Worlds: Response of Kosovo Albanians to Loss of Autonomy in Serbia</u>, Keele European Research Centre, 1997, pp. 109.

Kostovicova's commentaries also appeared frequently in the on-line journal <u>Transitions</u>: http://www.tol.cz

401.Maliqi, Shkelzen, 'The Albanian movement in Kosova' in David A. Dyker and Ivan Vejoda, <u>Yugoslavia and After: A Study in Fragmentation, Despair and Rebirth</u>, London, Longman, 1996, pp. 138-54.

402.Mertus, Julie, <u>Kosovo: How Truths and Myths Started a War</u>, Berkeley CA, University of California Press, 1999, pp. 378.

Interviews with both Serbs and Albanians about key events in the escalation from 1981 to an alleged 'poisoning' in 1990 are juxtaposed with a written history. See also: Mertus, Julie, 'Women in Kosovo: Contested terrains – the role of national identity in shaping and challenging gender identity' in Sabrina P. Ramet (ed.), <u>Gender Politics in the Western Balkans</u>, University Park PA, Pennsylvania State University Press, 1999, pp. 171-86.

403.Waller, Michael, Kyril Drezov and Bulent Gokay (eds.), <u>Kosovo the Politics of Delusion</u>, London, Frank Cass, 2001, pp. 190.

Main focus on developments after 1996, the role of the Kosovo Liberation Army and the NATO war on Serbia (including documents such as the Rambouillet Text and UN Security Council Resolution of June 1999). But chapter 2 (pp. 11-19) discusses Albanian schooling in Kosovo 1992-1998, and chapter 18 'The limitation of violent intervention' raises questions about nonviolent alternatives.

2. Georgia, Challenging 'Rigged' Elections 2003

After the break-up of the Soviet Union many of the former republics faced multiple problems. Georgia inherited a legacy of widespread corruption from the Soviet era, and immediately after independence suffered two bitter ethnic conflicts when in 1990 the Ossetian region tried to break away and in 1993 Abkhazian separatists claimed the strategically vital area on the Black Sea. The first elected President of independent Georgia, Zviad Gamsakhurdia, was overthrown by the military in 1992 and Gorbachev's former Foreign Minister, Edvard Shevardnadze took over. He won an election in October 1992, but faced continuing civil war with the supporters of Gamsakhurdia based in western Georgia.

Georgia has strong economic and political links to Russia, but the US took an increasing interest in the region after 2001, both because of its commitment to extend its strategic reach and because of the planned gas and oil pipelines from Baku to run through Georgia and Turkey to the Mediterranean. When parliamentary elections were held in November 2003 opposition parties and foreign observers claimed that they were rigged, and thousands blocked the streets of the capital, halted traffic and then occupied the parliament building. Some army units offered support. After intensive negotiations Shevardnadze agreed to resign from the presidency, and in the elections of January 2004 the main leader of the protests, Mikhail Saakashvili, who had connections in the USA, won a landslide victory. Kmara (Enough), one of the activist groups in the 'rose revolution', had had close contacts with their Serbian counterparts in OTPOR (which has some official US backing). Western observers debated how far it was an inspiring example of people power (Saakashvili stressed the need for nonviolence), how far it undermined parliamentary constitutionalism, and how far it was a victory for the Bush Administration.

404.Broers, Laurence, '"After the Revolution": Civil society and the challenges of consolidating democracy in Georgia', <u>Central Asian Survey</u>, vol. 24 no. 3 (2005), pp. 333-50.

Analysis of the revolution including some mention of nonviolence.

405.Cohen, Jonathan, 'Georgia: Changing the Guard', <u>World Today</u>, vol. 60 no. 1 (January 2004), pp. 16-17.

Summarizes political background of the 'semi-constitutional coup that accompanied an orchestrated mass demonstration of people power'.

406.Fairbanks, Charles H., 'Georgia's Rose Revolution', Journal of Democracy, vol. 15 (April 2004), pp. 110-24.

Explains background to the demonstrations, and elaborates on the role of the US government in relation to the elections, and of the George Soros' Open Society Foundation in funding opposition and promoting nonviolent protest. Comments also on the role of TV stations owned by private entrepreneurs.

407.Karumidze, Zurab and James V. Wertsch (eds.), Enough! The Rose Revolution in the Republic of Georgia, New York, Nova Science Publishers, 2005, pp. 143.

This book features interviews with a number of Georgian political figures. Most of its contents are reproduced from the Spring 2004 issue of Caucasus Context, also published by Nova Science Publishers. The editors of the journal edited this book.

408.Khidasheli, Tinatin, 'Georgia: The Rose Revolution has wilted', International Herald Tribune, 8 December, 2004.

The chair of the Georgian Young Lawyers' Association assesses Saakashvili's record in office, noting his consolidation of presidential powers and attacks on press freedom.

409.Nodia, Ghia 'The meaning of Georgia's latest revolution', Caucasus Context, vol.1 no. 1 (Spring 2004), pp. 67-76.

410.'Special report: The Caucasus', Economist, 29 November 2003, pp. 23-25.

Assesses why opposition successful in Georgia, but not in Armenia and Aberzaijan, and discusses geopolitical and economic context of Georgian politics.

For sources on the web: The International Crisis Group, 'Georgia: What Now?', Europe Report No. 151 (December 3 2003) gives background to crisis and makes recommendations. The ICG has also published later reports on: www.crisisgroup.org

3. Greece, Resisting the Colonels, 1967-74

At the end of the Second World War Greece was plunged into a civil war between the Communists and the right. Britain and the USA intervened to ensure the Communists were defeated, and supported the creation of a political system in which, though there was a facade of parliamentary democracy, the monarchy, the security services and the military had significant influence, suppressed dissent and upheld right wing values. The Communist Party was banned. But by 1963 liberal and left wing groupings began to gain ground both through popular protest and parliamentary elections. In April 1963 a nonaligned peace group, the Bertrand Russell Committee, organized a march from Marathon to Athens. The Karamanlis government feared that, in the wider context of worker unrest, it would become a focus of opposition to the regime, banned the march and arrested the organizers. Police beat up over a thousand of those who tried nevertheless to demonstrate. Grigoris Lambrakis, a United Democratic Left Party deputy, who had parliamentary immunity, completed the march alone. A month later he was assassinated by right wing thugs. His funeral turned into a peaceful mass demonstration, and when it was eventually revealed that the Salonika police had assisted the assassination, the Palace forced Karamanlis out of office. New elections in

November 1963 brought George Papandreou's Centre Left government to power. This created a context for legal demonstrations – 500,000 people gathered at Marathon in April 1964 to commemorate Lambrakis. The Greek left and peace movement also received transnational support, for example from the British Committee of 100 which, together with the Campaign for Nuclear Disarmament, demonstrated against the Greek King's visit to London in 1963.

But in July 1965 the King dismissed Papandreou, responding to rightwing fears about the neutralist tendencies of the government – especially the influence of George's son Andreas, and appointed a more right wing prime minister. Popular protest then grew, including strikes for higher wages and anti-monarchist agitation. To forestall new elections and the possibility of the re-election of George Papandreou, sections of the military organized a coup in April 1967. The Colonels, led by George Papadopoulos, dissolved all political parties and imposed censorship. The King, after an abortive counter coup attempt, fled abroad in December 1967.

The Colonels' dictatorship, which lasted from April 1967 to July 1974, brought intense pressure on people to conform, for example by displaying portraits of Papadopoulos, and savagely repressed dissent. Suspected opponents were routinely tortured, and even distributing leaflets carried a prison sentence of several years. Some opponents responded by trying to assassinate the leaders of the military coup and planting bombs. But most of the resistance was either hidden, for example 'go slows' by civil servants, or at the level of writing up slogans and distributing leaflets. Underground political organization, including an underground press, rapidly developed. The coup united intellectuals from the left and the right for the first time since the Civil War. But the first major public demonstration occurred at the funeral for George Papandreou in November 1968, when up to 500,000 people defied martial law and shouted slogans. A smaller protest of about 100,000 took place at the funeral of Nobel Prize winning poet George Seferis in September 1971.

International pressure resulted in some relaxation of censorship from 1970, but harassment of suspected opponents continued. Students were particularly active in resisting the regime throughout, and undertook sustained agitation in 1973 in Athens and the provinces, culminating in the student occupation of the Athens Polytechnic in November 1973. They broadcast appeals for public support and thousands, including workers, demonstrated in response. The Colonels then turned tanks and guns on the students, killing scores, wounding hundreds and arresting about 7000. This confrontation was followed by an internal coup ousting Papadopoulos. Soon afterwards the new regime brought Greece to the verge of war with Turkey over Cyprus, and sections of the military stepped in to oust the junta. They recalled Karamanlis to become Prime Minister and set in train the revival of parliamentary democracy.

The literature on the opposition to the Colonels includes both analysis by academic experts on Greek politics and accounts by key individuals involved. Much was published before the events of 1973, but later accounts do cover the student resistance.

411.'Athenian', Inside the Colonels' Greece, London, Chatto and Windus, 1972, pp. 215. Translated and introduced by Richard Clogg.

The author, writing from inside Greece, outlines the background to the coup, going back to the 1930s, and analyses the nature of the regime. See especially chapter 8. 'The great fear', pp. 123-31, and chapter 9, 'The resistance', pp. 132-44.

412.Clogg, Richard and George Yannopoulos (eds.), <u>Greece under Military Rule</u>, London, Secker and Warburg, 1972.

See especially chapter 3, 'The ideology of the revolution of 21 April 1967', pp. 36-58; chapter 4, 'The Colonels and the press', pp. 59-74; chapter 8, 'Culture and the military', pp. 148-62, which includes materials on censorship and repression and on forms of intellectual resistance, such as circulating 'samizdat', and liberal protests and manifestos; and chapter 9, 'The state of the opposition forces since the military coup', pp. 163-90.

413.Papandreou, Andreas, <u>Democracy At Gunpoint: The Greek Front</u>, London, Andre Deutsch, 1971, revised edition (published New York, Doubleday 1970), pp. 338.

Part one covers the coup and Papandreou's arrest and subsequent exile, part 2 explains political developments from the Civil War to the Coup, and part 3 focuses on 'The struggle for freedom', including international pressures on the regime.

414.Theodorakis, Mikis, <u>Journals of Resistance</u>, London, Hart-Davis MacGibbon, 1973. Translated from the French.

Theordorakis, widely known for his music (banned by the Colonels), was a prominent member of the broad-based Patriotic Front Movement created in May 1967 to oppose the junta. Like hundreds of other members he was arrested. This book recounts his successive arrests, internment and imprisonment, until external intervention secured his release from a prison hospital in 1970.

415.Vlachos, Helen (ed.), <u>Free Greek Voice</u>, London, Doric Publications, 1971, pp. 168.

Helen Vlachos, who refused to publish her right wing paper <u>Kathimerini</u> after the coup, was arrested for publishing an article critical of the regime abroad. She also wrote an account of her experience in <u>House Arrest</u>, London, Andre Deutsch, 1970, pp. 158.

416. Woodhouse, C.M., <u>The Rise and Fall of the Greek Colonels</u>, London, Granada, 1985, pp. 192.

Political overview, including relations with the USA. Chapter 3 'Resistance and reaction: April-December 1967', pp. 33-48, covers early opposition to the regime. Chapter 10 gives detail on 'The students' revolt: November 1973', pp. 126-41.

See also Harman, <u>The Fire Last Time</u>, pp. 305-10, which gives some weight to the 1973 Polytechnic rebellion (cited in Introduction to D.III).

4. Spain, Resisting Franco up to 1975

After the bitter and bloody civil war of 1936-39, Franco's regime subjected the defeated republicans to severe repression and many thousands fled into exile (especially into

France). Renewed resistance in the form of guerrilla fighting and major strikes organized by clandestine groups flared up in 1946-47, but was decisively crushed. In the longer term, however, the Francoist regime began to change, moving after 1957 from economic autarky and a Fascist Falangist ideal of an agricultural society towards incorporation into western capitalist development. In 1962 Spain applied to join the EEC, giving opposition intellectuals an opportunity to set out in the 'Munich Manifesto' the political reforms required to make Spain an acceptable member of the European Community.

From the 1960s there was both some reduction in poverty, as sectors of society benefited from economic growth and tourism, and a degree of liberalization. Many political prisoners had been released in a series of amnesties, and some discreet dissent was tolerated. Although the regime still harshly repressed any active forms of dissent, worker and student resistance grew. There was a wave of strikes and student demonstrations in 1956, and 1962 saw the biggest strike since the Civil War, led by the miners of Asturias; students joined the protests. Throughout the 1960s, and with added momentum in the early 1970s, workers engaged in wild cat strikes (all strikes were officially illegal and workers were controlled by the fascist-style syndicates). Alongside underground trade unions, workers' committees bridging old ideological divides sprang up to organize the strikes and infiltrate the official syndicates. Student protest increased and intellectuals also engaged more openly in dissent. Apart from the Basque country, where ETA developed its long running campaign of guerrilla warfare, opposition groups relied primarily on nonviolent tactics (although demonstrations quite often erupted into street battles, sometimes with the right wing Falangists). After Franco's death in November 1975 Spain began its transition to democracy, holding free elections in 1977, which the previously underground opposition parties contested legally.

Most of the literature on the Franco regime and opposition to it is of course in Spanish, including the most comprehensive book on the opposition: Harmut Heine, La oposicion al franquismo, Critica, 1983. But there are a number of English language studies of Francoism which give some weight to the growing opposition from the 1950s to 1975.

417.Balfour, Sebastian, Dictatorship, Workers and the City: Labour in Greater Barcelona Since 1939, Oxford, Clarendon, 1989, pp. 290.

Analysis of labour resistance to Franco up to 1975, examining Barcelona in context of Spanish politics and labour movement.

418.Blaye, Edouard de, Franco and the Politics of Spain, Harmondsworth, Penguin, 1976, pp. 576.

Comprehensive and well informed, see especially chapter 18 'The Oppositions', pp. 490-513.

419.Carr, Raymond and Juan Pablo Fusi, Spain: Dictatorship to Democracy, London, Allen and Unwin, 2nd edition 1981, pp. 288.

See especially chapter 7, 'From "Conformism" to Confrontation', pp. 134-67, which covers not only regional, worker and student resistance, but also changes within the Catholic Church; and chapter 9 'The regime in crisis: Carrero Blanco and Arias Navarro 1969-1975', pp. 189-206.

420.Preston, Paul, The Triumph of Democracy in Spain, London, Routledge, 1986, pp. 274.

See chapter 1, 'Internal contradictions of Francoism 1939-69' which covers some of the major strikes and mass demonstrations, and chapters 2 & 3 on the Carrero Blanco years 1969-73 and the Arias Navarro government of 1974-76. Preston is a leading British expert on Spanish politics. For political developments from 1939 to 1975 see also: Paul Preston (ed.), Spain in Crisis: Evolution and Decline of the Franco Regime, Hassocks, Harvester Press, 1976, pp. 341.

421.Welles, Benjamin, Spain: The Gentle Anarchy, London, Pall Mall Press, 1965, pp. 386.

Welles was an American journalist in Spain. Chapter 7, 'The Opposition' pp. 185-228 includes some useful information.

5. Ukraine, People Power and Elections, 2004-2005

Ukrainian politics since independence in 1991 have been influenced by the division of the country between Ukrainian-speaking western Ukraine, which had been a base for nationalist dissent under the Soviet regime, and eastern Ukraine, where Ukrainians have been absorbed more closely into Russian culture and often speak Russian (there are also quite a few ethnic Russians in this area). This split is closely linked to ideological divisions between those in the east who wish to pursue pro-Moscow policies and resist western-style economic reforms, and those in the west who look to Europe and the USA.

Ukraine was after 1991 governed by former Communist leaders who espoused nationalism. Under pressure from opposition parties parliamentary elections were held in 1994, but the government continued to be dominated by a coalition between Communists and financial oligarchs in a corrupt semi-authoritarian regime.

Initial protests in the Ukraine focused on corruption and lack of freedom. In 2000 journalists launched the 'Wave of Freedom' protests, starting in the western city of Lvov and developing in Kiev. One of its key organizers, investigative journalist Gyorgy Gongadze, was later found murdered, and secret tape recordings suggested that President Leonid Kuchma had been complicit. An opposition member of parliament, who released the tapes, demanded the President's impeachment. Demonstrators representing both right wing and leftist parties marched in Kiev in early February 2001 to demand Kuchma's resignation and set up a protest camp in the centre of the city. The government tore down the camp on March 1 and was able to suppress the relatively small protests. In April 2001 the prime minister, Viktor Yushchenko, who had been trying to end corruption and introduce controversial economic reforms, was forced from office, whilst thousands of supporters outside demanded the impeachment of Kuchma.

These issues came to the fore again in November 2004, when Yushchenko, despite an attempt to poison him, stood in the presidential elections to replace Kuchma who was retiring. In the second round of the elections Yushchenko opposed the then prime minister, Viktor Yanukovitch, who was the candidate backed by Kuchma and the government, and who was declared the winner. Yushchenko's supporters and OSCE observers claimed that the poll was marked by intimidation and ballot rigging and, emulating Georgia a year earlier, thousands of people poured into the streets of Kiev and set up a protest camp, which they maintained for days despite freezing temperatures. Three western Ukrainian cities, where thousands also took to the streets, declared Yushchenko the winner despite the official results. After prolonged protests, parliamentary debates and top-level negotiations (in which President Putin of Russia, who openly backed Yanukovitch, was involved) and a referral to the Supreme Court, a re-run ballot was organized, which Yushchenko won. But Yanukovitch refused to concede defeat, claiming evidence of fraud and he took his case to the central election committee and Supreme Court, which both ruled against him. Despite threats of civil war, serious violence was averted.

But the protests did demonstrate the deep divisions in the country – pro-Yanukovitch supporters also came to demonstrate in the streets of Kiev and the voting was very close in the re-run ballot. The events also illustrated strong involvement by both Russia and the USA. Although the mainstream western media generally celebrated the 'orange revolution' as a victory for democracy, sceptical journalists raised questions about the constitutionality of the protests, western support for Yushchenko, and the integrity of some of his own supporters. After Yushchenko came to power concern was soon expressed that his government was, despite the arrest of two policemen, failing to investigate fully top level complicity in the murder of journalist Gongadze.

For the historical and political background to Ukraine politics see:

422.Reid, Anna, <u>Borderland: A Journey Through the Ukraine</u>, London, Weidenfeld and Nicolson, 1997 (Phoenix paperback 1998), pp. 258.

Includes several chapters on Ukraine during the Soviet era, including collectivization and the great hunger of the 1930s, and the Chernobyl nuclear disaster in the 1980s. Chapter 10 examines post-1991 politics and the nature of the Kuchma regime.

Since there has been little time for academic articles or books on the 'orange revolution' to appear, some sources listed here are from newspapers, which also illustrate a variety of interpretations.

423.Ackerman, Peter and Jack DuVall, 'Peaceful protest brings justice to Ukraine', <u>Chicago Sun-Times</u> (14 December 2004); '"People power" wins in Ukraine', <u>Boston Globe</u>, (26 December 2004); 'The secret to success in Ukraine', <u>International Herald Tribune</u> (29 December 2004).

424.Ash, Timothy Garton, '"The country called me" – Ukraine's newly sovereign society is throwing off the governing mob', <u>Guardian</u> (9 December, 2004). See also 'The $65m question: When, how – and where – should we promote democracy? First we need the facts', <u>Guardian Weekly</u>, 24 December 2004, p. 13, which suggests six principles that should govern funding for opposition 'people power' movements.

425.Elliot, Iain, 'Ukraine: Different country, different people', <u>World Today</u>, vol. 61, no. 1 (January 2005), pp. 15-17.

426.Kuzio, Taras, 'The Opposition's road to success', <u>Journal of Democracy</u>, vol. 16 (April 2005), pp. 117-30.

Looks at background of 'Kuchmagate' in 2000, and the failure of opposition parties to unite in 2002, whereas they coalesced in 2004. Argues that the revolution revealed the existence of civil society in the Ukraine and that it was mostly funded from within the country. But Kuzio stresses the role of external civil society groups (especially in training the youth group 'Pora') and of international election monitors. The neutrality of the security forces and partial defections from their ranks were also crucial.

427.Steele, Jonathan, 'Ukraine's postmodern coup d'etat', <u>Guardian</u> (26 November 2004).

Steele's critical analysis prompted a host of letters representing conflicting viewpoints, some printed in the <u>Guardian</u> on 27 November, and a follow-up article by Steele himself replying to critics on 31 December.

428.Way, Lucan A, 'Kuchma's failed authoritarianism', <u>Journal of Democracy</u>, vol. 16 (April 2005), pp. 131-45.

Looks at nature and weaknesses of Kuchma's regime, the failure of police to prevent demonstrators pouring into Kiev and defections of sections of police, military and intelligence services to opposition after 'stolen second round'. Way also notes that businesses flocked to Yushchenko in the repeat of the second round on December 26th.

429.Wilson, Andrew, 'Ukraine: Wild dances', <u>World Today</u>, vol. 61, no 4. (April 2005), pp. 19-21.

On background to December 2004 elections and the nature of the opposition, including the role of Yushchenko in parliamentary elections of March 2002 and government manipulation.

IV. Latin America

Central and South America have in general an unhappy history of wars, coups d'etat, assassination squads and military dictatorships, and the best known mode of resistance to oppression – at least up the 1970s – has been guerrilla warfare: Castro's overthrow of Batista in Cuba and the struggle by the Sandanistas against Somoza in Nicaragua are two key examples. Nevertheless, there is also a long tradition of peasant and worker militancy which is predominantly nonviolent. National nonviolent insurrection has also overthrown a number of dictatorships, two impressive examples occurred in El Salvador in April-May 1944 and in Guatemala in June 1944. See:

430.Parkman, Patricia, <u>Insurrectionary Civic Strikes in Latin America 1931-1961</u>, Cambridge MA, Albert Einstein Institution, 1990, pp. 55; see also her <u>Nonviolent Insurrection in El Salvador</u>, Tucson, University of Arizona Press, 1988, pp. 168.

Catholic activists committed to nonviolence have gained influence since the 1960s, especially through the organization Service for Peace and Justice (SERPAJ) created in 1974, and played a part in promoting the increasing use of nonviolent methods in the last 30 years. (There are numerous SERPAJ websites in Spanish, some also in English translations). However, broad social and political trends, including the growing impact of transnational opinion and solidarity mobilized by the internet, also underlie a turn towards nonviolence since the 1970s. These factors are particularly notable in relation to some of the movements for social justice (see Sections F and G), although economic demands and campaigns for political freedom and democracy sometimes overlap. The literature focused specifically on nonviolence in Latin America is still limited, but many effectively nonviolent campaigns are covered in the broader literature on social movements and resistance.

For historical background see: Galeano, Eduardo H., Open Veins of Latin America: Five Centuries of the Pillage of a Continent, New York, Monthly Review Press, 1973, pp. 313.

For a survey of growing challenge to military rule by the 1980s see: Cammack, Paul and Philip O'Brien (eds.), Generals in Retreat: The Crisis of Military Rule in Latin America, Manchester, Manchester University Press, 1985, pp. 208. Papers from International Congress of Americanists held in Manchester in 1982.

Relevant journals include, The Bulletin of Latin American Research (quarterly) and Revista. Harvard Review of Latin America (three times a year), which brings out issues on specific themes such as 'Social Justice' (Spring 1998), 'Women in Latin America' (Winter 1998), putting together different voices and giving prominence to Harvard-related research.

For a wide range of case studies and some individual testimonies, focusing on nonviolence, see:

431. McManus, Philip and Gerald Schlabach (eds.), Relentless Persistence: Nonviolent Action in Latin America, Philadelphia PA, New Society Publishers, 1991, pp. 312. (Individual essays are also cited in sections below).

For role of radical Catholics see:

432. Lernoux, Penny, Cry of the People. The Struggle for Human Rights in Latin America: The Catholic Church in Conflict with US Policy, Garden City NY, Doubleday, 1980; reprinted Harmondsworth, Middlesex, Penguin Books, 1982, pp. 535 (with new preface).

433. Pagnucco, Ronald and John D. McCarthy, 'Advocating nonviolent direct action in Latin America: The antecedents and emergence of SERPAJ' in Zunes et al (eds.), Nonviolent Social Movements, pp. 235-58 (see A.1.); see also, Perez Esquivel, Adolfo, Christ in a Poncho: Testimonies of the Nonviolent Struggle in Latin America, edited by Charles Antoine, Maryknoll NY, Orbis 1983, pp. 139. Perez Esquivel, winner of the Nobel Peace Prize in 1980, has been a leading SERPAJ activist in Argentina, and in Latin America generally.

For the role of women in Latin American protest see:

434. Radcliffe, Sarah and Sallie Westwood, Viva: Women and Popular Protest in Latin America, London, Routledge, 1995, pp. 270.

In addition to the countries listed in sections below, nonviolent action under very repressive circumstances has occurred in Colombia and Guatemala. For reports on oppression see America's Watch (now incorporated into Human Rights Watch) and Amnesty International. The latter has provided some extensive reports on the 'peace communities' in Colombia.

Colombia: There have been heroic attempts by displaced people forming 'communities of peace', indigenous and women's groups to create autonomous spaces and to bring an end to four decades of warfare between guerrillas and successive governments; and there have also been environmental and social justice campaigns.

An important work available only in Spanish is: Cante, F and I. Ortiz (eds.), Accion Politica No-Violenta: Una opcion para Colombia, Centro de Estudios Politicos e Internacionales, Facultades de Ciencia Politica y Gobierno y de Relaciones Internacionales, Bogota, Centro Editoral Universdad del Rosario, 2005. This includes articles by Gene Sharp, Roger Peterson and Jenny Pearce arguing that nonviolence is not only possible, but the best option. Also includes chapters on indigenous movements in south west Colombia.

English sources are more limited. But see:

435. American Friends Service Committee and US Fellowship of Reconciliation, Building from the Inside, Philadelphia PA, AFSC, 2005, pp. 36. (available at: http://www.afsc.org/colombia/learn-about/default.htm)

Account of several nonviolent initiatives involving peace communities of displaced people, indigenous, women's and youth groups. See also: Peace News, no. 2449 (Dec. 2002 – Feb. 2003), Special section on Colombia covering peace communities, indigenous and women's campaigns and work of the Peace Brigades International.

436.Laan, E. 'Citizens take the initiative in Uraba, Colombia: Zone of peace in the heart of a bitter war', in People Building Peace: 35 Inspiring Stories from around the World, Utrecht, European Centre for Conflict Prevention, 1999, pp. 180-97; and Sanford, Victoria, 'Peacebuilding in a war zone: The case of Colombia peace communities', International Peace Keeping, vol. 10, no. 2 (Summer 2003), pp. 107-18. See also: Accord, the Journal of Conciliation Resources, 'Alternatives to War: Colombia's Peace Processes', edited by Mauricio Garcia-Duran, no. 14 (2004).

See also Bradford University theses on nonviolence in Colombia (H.c.) and Revista 'Colombia: Beyond armed actors: A look at civil society',(Spring, 2003); net address: (http://drelas.fas.harvard.edu.publications/revista/colombia)

Guatemala: The people enjoyed 10 years of democratic rule from the civil resistance of 1944 to the CIA-backed overthrow of President Arbenz in 1954, but since then human rights and popular protest have come under savage attack. In recent years this repression has been highlighted by the 1992 award of the Nobel Peace Prize to Rigoberta Menchu, the indigenous woman involved in the struggles of the Peasant Union. See:

437.Menchu, Rigoberta, I Rigoberta Menchu: An Indian Woman in Guatemala, edited and introduced by Elisabeth Burgos-Debray, London, Verso, 1984, pp. 252.

438.Ecumenical Program on Central America (EPICA) and Center for Human Rights Legal Action (CHRLA), Out of the Shadows: The Communities of Population in Resistance in Guatemala, Washington DC, EPICA and CHRLA, 1993.

See also Stanfield, Pablo 'When spring turned to winter' in McManus and Schlabach (eds.), Relentless Persistence, pp. 14-32 on earlier post-war period. See also Griffin-Nolan (ed.), Witness for Peace and Mahoney and Eguren, Unarmed Bodyguards, especially on accompaniment of returning refugees in 1989 (A.4.).

A third country not listed separately below, but important to note here is Venezuela. Mass popular resistance by the poor and the left blocked a right-wing military coup in 2002. But President Chavez, who pursues a militant anti-American economic and foreign policy and promotes the interests of the poor, has also been faced by mass demonstrations by the right. Chavez himself is a controversial figure, viewed critically by some on the left as well as by the right. For the broader politics see: Ellner, Steve and Daniel Hellinger (eds.), Venezuelan Politics in the Chavez Era: Class, Polarization and Conflict, Boulder CO, Lynne Rienner, 2003, pp. 257.

For an analysis of the thwarted two-day coup-attempt see:

439. McCaughan, Michael, The Battle of Venezuela, London, Latin American Bureau, 2004, pp. 116. See also: Gott, Richard, Hugo Chavez and his Bolivarian Revolution, London, Verso, 2005, pp. 315, which includes a section on the popular uprising following 2002 coup, by an analyst sympathetic to Chavez.

This section focuses primarily on resisting official and unofficial military repression. For popular land reform movements in Latin America, see section F.1. For the growing number of rebellions against neoliberal capitalism and privatization (sometimes intertwined with others issues) see G.7.b.ii for Argentina, Bolivia and Ecuador; and G.7.e. for the Zapatistas and other Mexican movements.

1. Argentina, Resisting the Military Dictatorship, 1977-81

Argentine politics has (until recently) been marked by frequent military coups d'etats. But from 1946-1955 an elected government led by General Peron and his flamboyant wife, Evita, established a distinctive style of populism and a Peronist party. Peron returned to power in 1974, and after his death his new wife Isabella governed until 1976, when a combination of economic chaos and political violence by both the extreme left and extreme right prompted another military coup. This new military government set out to impose order through a ferocious 'Dirty War', detaining, torturing and in many cases murdering thousands of supposed leftists, including many students. Up to 30,000 people 'disappeared'. In this atmosphere of terror some of the mothers of the disappeared began to demonstrate publicly in 1977, and continued to do so until the junta collapsed after losing the 1981 Falklands War. Then the mothers campaigned to bring guilty members of the military regime to justice, and to find their grandchildren born in prison, who had been given to military families. 'Las Madres de Plaza de Mayo' inspired the creation of other human rights groups in Argentina, and mothers of the disappeared in other repressive regimes, like Chile, to follow their example.

This experience of military rule has created determination among many Argentinians never to suffer such oppression again: in 1986 over a million people took to the streets when groups in the military seized barracks in an attempted coup, which failed.

For background on Argentina's politics: Nouzeilles, Gabriele and Graciela Montaldo, The Argentine Reader, Durham NC, Duke University Press, 2002, pp. 600.

440.Bouvard, Marguerite Guzman, Revolutionizing Motherhood: The Mothers of the Plaza de Mayo, Wilmington, Delaware, Scholarly Resources, Inc., 1994. pp. 278.

441.Cox, Robert, 'At least 10,000', Index on Censorship vol. 9 no 3 (1980), pp. 43-52.

The exiled co-editor of the Buenos Aires Herald describes the effect of abduction on families and lists writers and journalists 'disappeared' since March 1974. See also: Coad, Malcolm, 'The "disappeared" in Argentina 1976-1980', Index on Censorship, vol. 9 no. 3 (1980), pp. 41-43.

442.Fisher, Jo, Mothers of the Disappeared, London, Zed Books, 1989, pp. 168.

443.Graham-Yool, Andrew, A State of Fear: Memories of Argentina's Nightmare, London, Eland, 1986, pp. 180.

As a journalist in Argentina the author tried to compile a day-to-day chronicle of violence and repression. His life was often threatened and he was forced into exile in 1976. A later expanded version of his book was published as Portrait of an Exile, which describes his return in 1984 to give evidence at trial of commander of the Montoneros guerrillas.

444.Simpson, John and Jana Bennett, The Disappeared and the Mothers of the Plaza, New York, St Martin's Press, 1985, pp. 416.

See also Ackerman and Duvall, A Force More Powerful, pp. 270-78 (A.1.) McManus, Philip, 'Argentina's mothers of courage' in McManus and Schlabach (eds.), Relentless Persistence: Nonviolent Action in Latin America, pp. 79-99 (D.IV introduction).

2. Bolivia, Resisting Repression, 1964-82

After a revolution in 1952, the Nationalist Revolutionary Movement introduced nationalization of the tin mines, agrarian reform and universal franchise. A military coup in 1964 led to the regime of General Barrientos, which after a confrontation with the miners dismantled worker power, whilst cultivating the peasantry. Guerrilla resistance (which Che Guevara tried to foster) developed during the 1960s. Manifestations of mass discontent in 1971 led to planned destabilization by the right, the overthrow of the leftist government of General Torres (1970-71) and the imposition of the right wing Banzer dictatorship from 1971 to 1978. Banzer consolidated support by granting extensive rights to large landholders.

Popular resistance to the government, led by the tin miners, emerged in the later 1970s. Four women initiated a 23-day hunger strike from December 1977 to January 1978, which had church support and eventually involved 1,200. This led to the release of most political prisoners and recognition of trade unions. It was also the signal for renewed political organization. Responding to pressure from below and from the Carter Administration in the US, Banzer held elections. Political polarization between left and right resulted, however, in frequent elections and turnover of presidents, and a series of coups, including a ruthless two-year military dictatorship deploying death squads. But the military were overthrown by successful nonviolent resistance, which led to the election of a civilian president in 1982.

Since the mid-1980s the imposition of IMF austerity programmes has led to frequent peasant and worker unrest, strikes and hunger strikes. (For recent popular uprisings against economic policies see G.7.b.ii.)

445.Boots, Wilson T, 'Miracle in Bolivia: Four women confront a nation' in McManus and Schlabach (eds.), Relentless Persistence, pp. 48-62 (D.IV. Introduction).

On 1977-78 hunger strike. In the 1980s, some groups used the term 'firmeza permanente' (in English widely rendered as 'relentless persistence') to indicate nonviolence.

446.Crabtree, John and Lawrence Whitehead (eds.), Towards Democratic Viability: The Bolivian Experience, Basingstoke, Palgrave, 2001, pp. 256.

447.Dunkerley, James, Rebellion in the Veins: Political Struggle in Bolivia, 1952-82, London, Verso, 1984, pp. 385.

Notes that the revolution of 1952 not well covered in literature (even in Spanish). Charts changing political and economic context, giving weight to role of militant working class in mines, but also notes role of Catholic church on human rights (pp. 128-31).

448.Guillermo, Lora, A History of the Bolivian Labour Movement, 1848-1971, Cambridge, Cambridge University Press, 1977, pp. 380.

449.Malloy, James M. and Eduardo Gamarra, Revolution and Reaction: Bolivia 1964-1985, Oxford, Transaction Books, 1988, pp. 244.

450.Nash, June, We Eat the Mines and the Mines Eat Us: Dependency and Exploitation in Bolivian Tin Mines, New York, Columbia University Press, 1979, pp. 363.

The tin miners were at the forefront of political agitation against authoritarian rule in the 1970s. Includes material on strikes, demonstrations, hunger strikes and road blocks.

3. Brazil, Resisting Military Rule, 1964-85

The military, which had been exerting increasing pressure over the government of Brazil, demanded in 1954 the resignation of the popular President Getulo Vargas, who committed suicide. By the early 1960s there was growing popular unrest, which President Joao Goulart tried to mobilize against the military. The military responded with a coup in 1964, and military rule continued until 1985. Despite often brutal repression, including torture, there was a good deal of resistance to military rule, in which students, workers and Catholic Church groups all played a significant role.

The workers' struggle for basic economic rights has often become intertwined with the struggle against dictatorship (since the military backed the employers by targeting labour leaders), and the strength of Brazil's labour unions has been an important factor in politics.

For Brazil's impressive movement of land occupations, Movimento Sem Terra, see F.1.

451.Alves, Maria Helena Moreira, State and Opposition in Military Brazil, Austin TX, University of Texas Press, 1985, pp. 352.

452.Antoine, Charles, Church and Power in Brazil, London, Sheed and Ward, 1973, pp. 275.

453.Carvalho de Jesus, Mario, 'Firmeza Permanente: Labor holds the line in Brazil', in McManus and Schlabach (eds.), Relentless Persistence, pp. 33-47 (D.IV. Introduction).

Account by Brazilian labour activist of protracted struggle from 1962 in PETRUS cement factory in Sao Paolo against strikebreaking, police repression and an alternative union created by the employer.

454.Camara, Helder, Spiral of Violence, London, Sheed and Ward, 1971, pp. 83.

Statement of case for nonviolent, not violent resistance, by Archbishop known for his support for the poor and his opposition to racism and militarism.

455.Erickson, Kenneth P., The Brazilian Corporate State and Working-Class Politics, Berkeley CA, University of California Press, 1977, pp. 225.

456.Stepan, Alfred (ed.), Democratizing Brazil, New York, Oxford University Press, 1989, pp. 404.

Includes chapters on local social movements, and on the role of strikes in promoting popular unrest and encouraging move to elections.

457.Zirker, Daniel, 'The Brazilian Church-State crisis in 1980: Effective nonviolent action in a military dictatorship', in Zunes et al (eds.), Nonviolent Social Movements, pp. 259-78 (A.1.).

4. Chile

Chile had, unlike many of its neighbours, an enviable record of civilian government. But the popular election of the Marxist President Salvador Allende in 1970 polarized the country. Whilst some left wing groups agitated for more rapid moves towards socialism, right wing parties, much of the middle class and small business mobilized to oppose moves towards nationalization. Although unrest was promoted by the military and rich elite, and many on the left argue the US used economic pressure to destabilize the regime, the lorry drivers' strikes of 1972 and 1973, supported by significant sections of the population, did reflect genuine popular opposition. But the military then intervened by overthrowing Allende in a coup.

a. The Right Mobilizes Against Salvador Allende, 1972-73

458.Alexander, Robert J., The Tragedy of Chile, Westport CT, Greenwood Press, 1978, pp. 509.

459.Bitar, Sergio, <u>Chile: Experiment in Democracy</u>, Philadelphia, Institute for the Study of Human Issues, 1986, pp. 243.

By former member of Allende's cabinet.

460.David, Nathaniel, <u>The Last Two Years of Salvador Allende</u>, London, I.B. Tauris, 1985, pp. 480.

Account of evolving crisis by former US Ambassador to Chile.

461.Petras, James and Morris A. Morley, <u>How Allende Fell: A Study in U.S.-Chilean Relations</u>, Nottingham, Spokesman Books, 1974, pp. 125.

462.Valenzuela, Arturo, <u>The Breakdown of Democratic Regimes: Chile</u>, Baltimore MD, John Hopkins University Press, 1978, pp. 140.

b. Resisting the Pinochet Dictatorship, 1973-90

After Salvador Allende was overthrown, General Pinochet headed a ruthless military regime which began with the murder of many leftists and drove thousands of others into exile. Suspected dissenters were tortured and jailed and for the first ten years opposition was limited. But protest, in which women were prominent, erupted in 1983-1984, and in 1988 the opposition mobilized to campaign successfully for a 'no' vote in the government's plebiscite designed to re-elect Pinochet.

463.Arriagada, Gennaro, <u>Pinochet: The Politics of Power</u>, Boston, Unwin Hyman, 1988, pp. 196.

Chapter 7 discusses the protests between 1983 and 1986.

464.Brown, Cynthia, <u>Chile Since the Coup: Ten Years of Repression</u>, New York, America's Watch, 1983, pp. 137.

465.Bunster, Ximena, 'The mobilization and demobilization of women in militarized Chile', in Eva Isaksson (ed.), <u>Women and the Military System</u>, Brighton, Harvester-Wheatsheaf, 1988, pp. 210-22.

Discusses how Pinochet regime mobilized women to support it, but also examines role of women in spearheading resistance in 1979 and their role in 1986.

466.Chavkin, Samuel, <u>Storm Over Chile: The Junta Under Siege</u>, Westport CT, Lawrence Hill, 1985, pp. 303.

Chapter 9 focuses on protest 1983-84.

467.Drake, Paul and Ivan Jaksic (ed.), <u>The Struggle for Democracy in Chile, 1982-1990</u>, Lincoln, University of Nebraska Press, 1991, pp. 321.

468.Spooner, Mary Helen, <u>Soldiers in a Narrow Land: The Pinochet Regime in Chile</u>, Berkeley CA, University of California Press, 1994, pp. 305.

469.Valenzuela, J. Samuel and Arturo Valenzuela, <u>Military Rule in Chile: Dictatorship and Opposition</u>, Baltimore, John Hopkins University Press, 1986, pp. 331.

470.Yanez Berrios, Blanca and Omar Williams Lopez, 'Cultural action for liberation in Chile', in McManus and Schlabach (eds.), <u>Relentless Persistence</u>, pp. 117-35 (D.IV. Introduction).

Discusses role of SERPAJ in struggle for survival by poor (including forms of community cooperation) and social mobilization in shanty towns, noting ingenious forms of protest against hunger and unemployment, such as blocking supermarket checkouts with trolleys. Mentions 'lightning action' (10 minute protest) by women demanding Pinochet should go in 1987.

See also Ackerman and Duval, <u>A Force More Powerful</u>, pp. 279-302, and Aliaga Rojas, Fernando, 'How we won democracy in Chile' in Martin et al, <u>Nonviolent Struggle and Social Defence</u>, pp. 51-54 (A.1.).

5. Panama, Resisting Noriega 1987-89

Panama has long been of key interest to the USA because of the Panama Canal, but in the 1970s the US agreed to transfer its direct control over the Canal to the Panama government – the handover occurred in October 1979. At the time Panama was effectively ruled by General Torrija, though politics became slightly more open after the Canal treaty was agreed, and a Constitutional Assembly was elected. When Torrija died in a plane crash in July 1981, de facto power passed to Noriega, who had run the security service for Torrija and achieved control of the National Guard. Noriega was able to force the official President to resign in both 1982 and 1985. Popular disillusion with repressive rule, and revelations about the murder of opposition activist Hugo Spadafora in 1985, sparked public protests from 1987. The opposition groups had begun in 1984 to cooperate more closely and broaden their base of support.

The US government initially backed Noriega, who was a long-term ally of the CIA and provided significant support for the Contra war against the Sandinista regime in Nicaragua. But Noriega's involvement in drug smuggling into the USA and Panama's reputation for money laundering were factors cited in a reversal of policy in 1987, and the US began to look to opposition leaders, perhaps encouraged by mass protests in July-August 1987. The US, followed by the World Bank, also imposed sanctions in 1987.

There were mass strikes and demonstrations in Panama in February/March 1988, partly prompted by the economic conditions created by sanctions. The opposition parties (supported by US President George Bush) chose candidates to oppose Noriega in the May 1989 elections, and won a large majority; but Noriega refused to go. Troops fired on mass demonstrations in support of the opposition candidates and a general strike called on May 17 fizzled out. The US gave up hope of internal change and invaded in December 1989.

471.Buckley, Kevin, <u>Panama: The Whole Story</u>, New York, Simon and Schuster, 1991, pp. 304.

Rather sensationalist account by journalist focusing on events from the 1985 coup to the US invasion, but stresses role of Noriega and the Panama Defence Force, and includes descriptions of popular resistance as well as elite manoeuvres.

472.Calderon, Ricardo Arias, 'Panama: Disaster or democracy?', Foreign Affairs, vol. 66 (Winter 1987/88), pp. 328-47.

The President of the Christian Democratic Party discusses the 1987 National Civic Crusade to coordinate the protest movement and formulate its key demands for justice, the removal of Noriega, and the democratization of government. Explains background to protest, notes the 1,500 arrests and numerous shootings of protesters, and comments on changing attitudes inside the US.

473.Eisenmann, Roberto, 'The struggle against Noriega', Journal of Democracy, vol. 1 no. 1 (Winter 1990), pp. 41-46.

Editor of La Prensa, Panama's leading daily, looks at the role of Panama's people and organized opposition in article written before the December 1989 US invasion.

474.Furlong, William L., 'The 1977 Panama Canal Treaties: The non-issue issue', World Today, vol. 44 no. 1 (January 1988), pp. 10-15.

Focuses particularly on the US handing over control of the Canal but also discusses internal Panamanian politics from 1978-1987 and the mass protests of 1987.

475.Scranton, Margaret E., The Noriega Years: US-Panamanian Relations 1981-1990, Boulder CO, Lynne Rienner, 1991, pp. 245.

Charts the sharp changes in US policy from collaboration with Noriega 1981-87, decision to oust him 1987-89, and decision to invade October-December 1989. Author also describes evolving internal politics, including elections and popular strikes and demonstrations.

476.Weeks, John and Andrew Zimbalist, 'The failure of intervention in Panama: Humiliation in the backyard', Third World Quarterly, vol. 11, no. 1 (January 1989), pp. 1-27.

Explores from leftist perspective failure of Reagan Administration to overthrow Noriega in Spring 1988 and the reasons why US turned against Noriega. Argues also that the internal opposition was led by an isolated upper class elite and 1988 protests indicated the limits of its effectiveness. The authors accept that the July-August 1987 strikes and demonstrations did mobilize workers and peasants, but suggest they were responding to the arrest of a popular politician and expressing mass resentment of World-Bank directed economic policies, rather than specifically opposing Noriega.

6. Uruguay, Resisting Military Rule 1973-84

Uruguay had, after its 1904 civil war, a reputation for stability for much of the 20th century. With a predominantly urban and educated population of about 3 million, and a system of 'co-participation' between parties in government, it was dubbed the 'Switzerland' of Latin America. But the poor were effectively marginalized from the 1950s, and during the 1960s rampant inflation and wage freezes, combined with increasing repression of labour and students, fuelled unrest. The Tupamaros guerrilla movement was also founded in the early 1960s. Against this background, the military seized power in 1973, suppressed all political activity, imposed sweeping controls over the media and imprisoned 7000 suspected political opponents.

However in 1980, when the government held a referendum on a new constitution to enshrine a single-candidate presidential election, despite the arrest of those campaigning for a 'no' vote, and propaganda linking a 'no' vote to terrorism, 57% (out of the 87 per cent of the electorate who voted) voted 'no'.

In 1981 a SERPAJ group was founded to agitate for human rights, and during 1983 public denunciations, fasts and marches (sparked by outrage about the torture and rape of a group of young people) culminated in general strikes in January and June 1984. Elections were held in November that year.

For a clear account of the political background see:

477.Weinstein, Martin, Uruguay: The Politics of Failure, Westport CT, Greenwood Press, 1975, pp. 190.

478.Finch, Henry, 'Democratization in Uruguay', Third World Quarterly, vol. 7 no. 3 (1985), pp. 594-609.

Analysis of evolution of opposition 1983-1985: from saucepan banging, one day general strikes and 250,000 strong rally on the last Sunday of November 1983 (the traditional day for elections); the electoral politics of 1984 and public sector strike of January-February 1985.

479.Kaufman. Edy, 'The role of the political parties in the redemocratization of Uruguay' in Saul Sosnowski and Louise B. Popkin (eds.), Repression, Exile and Democracy: Uruguayan Culture, Durham NC, Duke University Press, 1993, pp. 17-58.

Essay includes some references to role of 'truly peaceful resistance' in 1983.

480.Roberts, Katherine, 'Uruguay: Nonviolent resistance and the pedagogy of human rights', in McManus and Schlabach (eds.), Relentless Persistence, pp. 100-17 (D.IV. Introduction).

481.Weinstein, Martin, Uruguay: Democracy at the Cross Road, Boulder CO, Westview Press, 1988, pp. 160.

V. Middle East

The Middle East since 1945 is associated primarily with conventional wars (between Israel and Arab states and wars by and against Iraq) and with new forms of guerrilla warfare. Nevertheless, there have been some attempts to develop nonviolent theory and to practise an essentially nonviolent struggle. For a general overview see:

482.Crow, Ralph E, Philip Grant and Saad E. Ibrahim, Arab Nonviolent Political Struggle in the Middle East, Boulder CO, Lynne Rienner, 1990, pp. 129.

Two major examples of predominantly nonviolent resistance, the overthrow of the Shah of Iran in 1979 and the First Palestinian Intifada against Israeli occupation from 1987, are discussed below. For a separate, specific case study see:

483.Kennedy, R. Scott, 'The Druze of the Golan: A case study of nonviolent resistance', Holmes (ed.), Nonviolence in Theory and Practice, pp. 193-203 (A.1.), originally 'The

Golani Druze: A case of non-violent resistance', <u>Journal of Palestine Studies</u>, vol. 13, no. 2 (Winter 1984), pp. 48-64.

There are also signs that people power may become more frequent. In the Lebanon the assassination of a former premier prompted large numbers of people in March 2005 to take to the streets and to go on strike to protest against the dominance of Syria over internal politics. This 'cedar revolution' did succeed in securing the resignation of the pro-Syrian prime minister, and with the help of US pressure resulted in Syrian agreement to withdraw their troops. But the anti-Syrian demonstrators were mostly Sunni Muslims, Christians and Druze, and Hizbullah had mobilized a counter-demonstration of poor Shias in favour of Syria, raising concern about reviving the conflicts of the 15 year civil war from 1975-1991. Indeed, since March 2005 there have been a number of car bombs and assassination attempts, although in July large numbers of people celebrated a 'National Unity Week' to demonstrate their determination not to be intimidated or to return to civil war. See:

484. 'Something Stirs', <u>Economist,</u> March 5, 2005, pp. 24-26, on the rise of people power; and the <u>New Internationalist</u> which runs a monthly letter from Lebanon by journalist Reem Haddad. See 'Dear departed', no. 378 (May 2005), p. 3 and 'A test of wills', no. 380 (July 2005), p. 3.

485.Shehadi, Nazim, 'Lebanon: Battle resumes', <u>World Today,</u> vol. 61. no. 4 (April 2005), pp. 7-9 on the background to the assassination of prime minister Hariri, the role of Syria and of Hizbollah. For wider historical context, see: Ramsey, Allan, 'The Lebanon: Old Bottle, New Vintage?', <u>Contemporary Review</u>, no. 1676 (September 2005), pp. 135-41.

1. Iran, Overthrowing the Shah 1979-1980

After the Second World War Iranian moves towards electoral democracy were thwarted when the US and British intelligence services collaborated in 1953 to overthrow the elected prime minister Mohammed Mossadegh, who had nationalized the Anglo-Iranian oil company in 1951. The Shah had tried unsuccessfully to oust Mossadegh and had to flee the country, and the CIA was able to mobilize his supporters. The Shah returned to assert the dominance of the dynasty (founded in 1921 when his father had seized the throne). His regime was subsequently criticized for human rights violations.

The Shah's authoritarian regime was overthrown in 1979-80 by impressive, predominantly nonviolent mass protest which showed that people power can prevail over regime brutality. Millions went on strike and filled the streets, and resistance continued despite the shooting of many unarmed protesters. This led to a split in the armed forces, with the army deciding to stay in its barracks. A very wide range of groups with differing ideological perspectives took part in the mass strikes and demonstrations. But an important role was played by the exiled Ayatollah Khomeini, whose supporters were able to seize power. The subsequent rule by the Ayatollahs introduced a more draconian regime based on religious extremism, which has in recent years seen attempts at internal reform and the emergence of cautious opposition, but (so far) no major popular protest.

486.Abrahimian, Ervand, <u>Iran between Two Revolutions</u>, Princeton NJ, Princeton University Press, 1982.

For the protests leading to the overthrow of the Shah see pp. 496-537.

487.Albert, David H. (ed.), <u>Tell the American People: Perspectives on the Iranian Revolution</u>, Philadelphia PA, Movement for a New Society, 1980, pp. 212.

The editor is a practitioner and theorist of nonviolence. He comments briefly on the Iranian Revolution to illustrate the dynamics of power relationships (pp. 29-36) in his booklet: <u>People Power: Applying Nonviolence Theory</u>, New Society Publishers, 1985, pp. 64.

488.Bashirey, Hossein, <u>The State and Revolution in Iran 1962-1982</u>, London, Croom Helm, 1984, pp. 203. Chapters 5-7 focus on the demonstrations.

489.Stempel, John D., <u>Inside the Iranian Revolution</u>, Bloomington, Indiana University Press, 1981, pp. 324.

Book by US diplomat describing and assessing the evolution of protest.

2. Palestine

The creation of Israel in 1948 (and the expulsion of many Palestinians from their land) left Palestinians without political representation and subordinated to the conflicting goals of the Arab states and Israel. Organized independent Palestinian guerrilla resistance began to emerge by 1965, but Palestinian political consciousness grew after the 1967 Arab-Israeli war, which ended with the Israeli occupation of the remaining Palestinian areas of previously Arab Palestine – Gaza, the West Bank of the Jordan river (previously controlled by Jordan) and Jerusalem.

Palestinian resistance is often associated with the well-publicized guerrilla tactics of groups such as Al Fatah, headed by Yasser Arafat, which drew recruits from the refugee camps and put the Palestinian cause on the world's map from the late 1960s. But Palestinians inside the occupied territories did begin to resist in various ways the imposition of Israeli control and the taking of their land for Israeli settlements. The most effective internal opposition began in 1987 and continued into the early 1990s, though it had begun to flag by 1990. In combination with other developments in Arab and international politics, this campaign led to Israel entering negotiations for the creation of an independent Palestinian state. This (first) 'Intifada' – literally 'shaking off' – was a mass movement of active civil resistance involving old and young, men and women, and using a range of nonviolent methods, including mass boycotts. Although it did include a good deal of low level violence, such as stone-throwing – often by children, it avoided use of firearms. This movement also demonstrated not only Palestinian solidarity and determination, but the existence of an autonomous Palestinian people asserting their rights, drew international criticism of Israel's attempts to suppress the rising, and enabled the Palestinian Liberation Organization, then based in Tunisia, to become a genuinely national representative organization empowered to enter into negotiations with Israel.

In 1993 the PLO and the Israeli government signed a historic Declaration of Principles after secret talks, and negotiations openly sponsored by the US. Israel withdrew its troops from Gaza, and after further protracted negotiations also withdrew from parts of the West Bank in 1995. As a result a formal if largely powerless Palestinian state, threatened by increasing Israeli settlements, and de facto Israeli economic and military control, was created. The peace process was always opposed by sections of the Israeli population, in particular the new settlers, and by some Palestinians, including the armed group Hamas, which maintained the right to respond to Israeli provocation and exploded some bombs inside Israel. The peace process broke down at the Camp David summit in 2000, after President Arafat refused to endorse an ambitious plan by Prime Minister Barak (unacceptable to Palestinians on crucial issues) for a final settlement. The breakdown at Camp David, and Ariel Sharon's provocative visit soon afterwards to the Temple Mount/Haram Sharif, holy to both Muslims and Jews, ignited a new uprising, the second Intifada; and there was a turn to the right in Israeli internal politics.

The second Palestinian Intifada against Israeli military action, was much more violent than the first. The Israelis had responded immediately to renewed protests with shooting and systematic repression. Individuals and groups within the Palestinian territories argued early in 2001 for mass involvement and nonviolent methods, but the armed militias were at the forefront of the struggle, and sponsored the new tactic of suicide bombings in Israel. Israeli retaliation and major military incursions into Palestinian territory fuelled bitter resentment.

Despite increasing polarization, some Israelis and Palestinians continued to work together to promote peaceful alternatives, or to defend Palestinian land. The main recent examples of nonviolent resistance come from the Israeli side, for example soldiers refusing to serve in the occupied territories (see the next section). Transnational support for Palestinians has come from the International Solidarity Movement, and other groups committed to nonviolence, who have engaged in acts of nonviolent resistance, for example to the bulldozing of Palestinian homes, and by their presence tried to protect Palestinians and focus international attention on the area (see A.4.).

a. Palestinian Resistance after 1967 and the First Intifida, 1987-1992

490.Aronson, Geoffrey, <u>Creating Facts: Israel, Palestinians and the West Bank</u>, Washington DC, Institute of Palestine Studies, 1987, pp. 334.

Covers the growing resistance from 1967 inside the Occupied territories.

491.Awad, Mubarak E, 'Non-violent resistance: A strategy for the occupied territories', <u>Journal of Palestine Studies</u> (Washington DC), vol. 13, no. 4 (Summer 1984), pp. 22-36. Also available in Holmes, <u>Nonviolence in Theory and Practice</u>, pp. 155-63 (A.1.).

492.Bregman, Ahron and Jihan El-Tahri, <u>The Fifty Years War: Israel and the Arabs</u>, Harmondsworth, Penguin Books, 1998, pp. 301, Published in conjunction with a BBC 2 television series.

Accessible book on the overall conflict between Israel and the Arab states and the Palestinians. Chapters 27 and 28 (pp. 187-199) cover the first Intifada, the impact on Israel and the initiatives taken by the PLO.

493.Dajani, Souad, 1994, 'Between national and social liberation: The Palestinian Women's Movement in the Israeli Occupied West Bank and Gaza Strip', in Tamar Meyer (ed.), Women and the Israeli Occupation, London, Routledge, 1994. pp. 33-61.

Discusses women's initial major role in Intifada and why it declined by the second year.

494.Dajani, Souad R., Eyes Without Country: Searching for a Palestinian Strategy of Liberation, Philadephia PA, Temple University Press, 1995, pp. 238. See also: Dajani, Souad, 'Resistance in the occupied territories' in Zunes et al (eds.), Nonviolent Social Movements, pp. 52-74. (A.1.).

495.Finkelstein, Norman, Image and Reality of the Israel-Palestine Conflict, 2nd edition, London, Verso, 2003, pp. 287.

496.Galtung, Johan, Nonviolence and Israel/Palestine, Honolulu, University of Hawaii, Institute for Peace, 1989, pp. 79.

497.Hudson, Michael C., The Palestinians: New Directions, Washington DC, Center for Contemporary Arab Studies, Georgetown University, 1990, pp. 268.

Includes chapters on the role in the Intifada of the labour movement (chapter 3), of traders (chapter 2) and of women.

498.Hunter, F. Robert, The Palestinian Uprising: A War By Other Means, Berkeley, University of California Press, 1993 (2nd edition), pp. 356.

499.Khalidi, Rashid, 'The uprising and the Palestine question', World Policy Journal, vol. 5, no. 3 (Summer 1988), pp. 497-517.

500.Lustick, Ian S., 'Writing the Intifada: Collective action in the Occupied Territories', World Politics, no. 4 (July 1993), pp. 560-94.

Review article covering nine recent books providing overview of movement and noting impact on Arab world (Algeria and Jordan) and wider world.

501.O'Ballance, Edgar, The Palestinian Intifada, Basingstoke, Macmillan, 1998, pp. 252.

502.Peretz, Don, Intifada: The Palestinian Uprising, Boulder CO, Westview Press, 1990, pp. 246.

503.Rigby, Andrew, Living the Intifada, London, Zed Books, 1991, pp. 233.

Account of the 'unarmed resistance' of the first Intifada then analysed in the context of theories of non-violent action. Addresses issue of leverage when the regime has no direct dependence on a population but would rather expel them. See also Rigby Andrew, The Legacy of the Past: The Problem of Collaborators and the Palestinian Case, Jerusalem, PASSIA – Palestinian Academic Society for the Study of International Affairs, 1997, pp. 94, where the writer considers the issue of 'collaboration' in more detail.

504.Schiff, Ze-ev and Edud Ya'ari, The Intifada: The Palestinian Uprising, Israel's Third Front, New York, Simon and Schuster, 1989, pp. 352.

505.Sharp, Gene, 'The Intifadah and nonviolent struggle', Journal of Palestine Studies, vol. 19 no. 1 (1989), pp. 3-13. See also: 'Gene Sharp: Nonviolent struggle', interview with Afih Safieh, vol. 17 no. 1 (Autumn 1987), pp. 37-55.

506.Vogele, William, 'Learning and nonviolent struggle in the Intifadah', Peace and Change, vol. 17 no. 3 (July 1992), pp. 312-40.

Argues the need for nonviolent resisters to re-evaluate strategies and tactics in the light of their opponents' reactions; and (more exceptionally) to redefine their interests and goals.

See also: Ackerman and Duvall, A Force More Powerful, pp. 397-420 (A.1.).

b. Israeli Opposition to Israel's Occupation

Because Israel was created out of a war with the surrounding Arab states and faced the continuing threat of attack, military service was a citizen duty and the conditions were initially hostile to an Israeli peace movement (although there were some committed pacifists). However, after moves by Egypt to recognize Israel in the later 1970s, desire for a peaceful settlement with Israel's neighbours and a negotiated return of 'occupied territories' to the Palestinians (required by UN Resolutions) grew. Peace activism and opposition to the draft increased as a result of Israel's controversial 1982 invasion of Lebanon. After the first Intifada challenged Israeli occupation of the post-1967 territories, sections of public opinion in Israel became uneasy. The PLO's decision in 1988 to recognize the existence of Israel encouraged Israeli opposition to the occupation. Two organizations, Yesh Gvul (There is a Limit) created in 1982 in opposition to the invasion of Lebanon, and the 1988 Council for Peace and Security supported by high ranking officers, publicized their objections to Israel's military tactics, and some reservists refused to serve in the occupied territories. Peace groups committed to working with Palestinians met for joint discussions, and took part in acts of solidarity such as planting olive trees along the frontier between Israel and the West Bank to replaced those uprooted by the Israeli government. Cooperation was assisted by the Palestinian Centre for Nonviolence based in East Jerusalem. A joint demonstration between Israelis and Palestinians, supported by a transnational presence, occurred in December 1989.

The political context for Israeli opposition during the second Intifada has been much more hostile, but civil society groups have continued to cooperate with Palestinians, and groups like Physicians for Human Rights and the Israeli Committee Against House Demolitions challenge checkpoints and bulldozers. Some serving soldiers have publicly condemned Israeli military action or refused to serve in the occupied territories.

507.Bar-On, Mordechai, In Pursuit of Peace: The History of the Israeli Peace Movement, Washington D.C, US Institute of Peace, 1996, pp. 470. Includes bibliography pp. 419-29.

508.Chazan, Naomi, 'Israeli women and peace activism' in Barbara Swirski and Marylin Safir (eds.), <u>Calling the Equality Bluff in Israel</u>, New York, Pergamon Press, 1991, pp. 152-62.

509.Davis, Uri, <u>Crossing the Border: An Autobiography of an Anti-Zionist Palestinian Jew</u>, London, Books and Books, 1995, pp. 398.

510.Hall-Cathala, David, <u>The Peace Movement in Israel, 1967-87</u>, Basingstoke, Macmillan in association with St Antony's College Oxford, 1990, pp. 228.

511.Deutsch, Yvonne, 'Israeli women against the Occupation: Political growth and the persistence of ideology' in Tamara Mayer (ed.), <u>Women and the Israeli Occupation</u>, London, Routledge, 1994, pp. 88-105.

Describes the growing number of organizations engaged in demonstrating solidarity with the Palestinians (e.g. Women in Black), meeting with Palestinian women in Occupied Territories, helping Palestinian women political prisoners or proposing peace plans.

512.Hurwitz, Deena (ed.), <u>Walking the Red Line: Israelis in Search of Justice for Palestine</u>, Philadelphia PA, New Society Publishers, 1992, pp. 208.

513.Kaminer, Reuven, <u>The Politics of Protest: The Israeli Peace Movement and the Palestinian Intifada</u>, Brighton, Sussex Academic, 1996, pp. 174.

514.Keller, Adam, <u>Terrible Days: Social Divisions and Political Paradoxes in Israel</u>, Amstelveen, Cypres, 1987, pp. 200.

The final chapter is an authoritative account of the peace movement.

515.Kidron, Peretz (ed.), <u>Refusenik!: Israel's Soldiers of Conscience</u>, London, Zed Books, 2004, pp. 160.

Documents from the soldiers' resistance from the Lebanon War, the first Intifada and the second Intifada.

516.Linn, Ruth, <u>Conscience at War: The Israeli Solider as a Moral Critic</u>, Albany NY, State University of New York Press, 1996, pp. 245.

517.Sharoni, Simona, <u>Gender and the Israeli-Palestine Conflict: The Politics of Women's Resistance</u>, Syracuse NY, Syracuse University Press, 1994, pp. 199.

See also Rigby, <u>Living the Intifada</u> (D.V.2.) and further references on conscientious objection/draft refusal in Israel (G.3.b.ii).

E. Campaigns for Cultural, Civil and Political Rights

I. National Rights or Self Determination

Since the 1970s there has been an upsurge of campaigns by nationalist minorities, not only in newly created states, but also in the west. They usually demand full cultural rights, degrees of political autonomy and in some cases independence. These campaigns often draw on a much longer history of opposition to incorporation into a larger state, and have typically pursued a strategy of either cultural renewal, or party politics and fighting elections, or both.

In some cases radical nationalists have engaged in spectacular exploits – for example four Scottish students removed the symbolic Stone of Scone from Westminster Abbey on Christmas Day 1951 – or adopted guerrilla tactics to dramatize their struggle. But usually bombing or dynamiting of symbolic targets, such as letter boxes with the Queen's name in Scotland, has been a minority and temporary part of a predominantly constitutional campaign. In the Basque country, however, prolonged armed struggle has been maintained by a significant wing of the nationalist movement (ETA), despite electoral success by more moderate nationalists.

Nonviolent methods of protest, such as hunger strikes, have sometimes been adopted by nationalist movements. But Welsh nationalists have most consistently incorporated nonviolent direct action into their campaigns.

1. Welsh Nationalism and Nonviolent Action

The long campaign for the public use of the Welsh language – including Welsh language radio and TV stations, and for Welsh political autonomy or independence – has used a mix of constitutional tactics and more dramatic protest. Plaid Cymru has contested local, British and European elections in Wales, but Welsh language campaigners have also refused to pay BBC radio licences and prominent activist Gwynfor Evans engaged in public fasts. The movement has included some acts of sabotage, such as burning down English second homes in Wales, and a guerrilla style attack on a reservoir built in a Welsh valley to provide water for Liverpool, but the Welsh campaign has made varied use of nonviolent direct action tactics.

518.Evans, Gwynfor, <u>For the Sake of Wales: The Memoirs of Gwynfor Evans</u>, Caernarfon, Welsh Academic Press, [1986] 1996, pp. 257.

Memoirs of this key figure in the nationalist movement and committed advocate of nonviolence.

519.Evans, Gwynfor, <u>The Fight for Welsh Freedom</u>, Talybont, Y Lolfa, 2000, pp. 176.

Covers Plaid Cymru, history and Welsh politics and government. An earlier book by Evans from the same publisher is: Fighting for Wales, 1992, pp. 221.

520.Howys, Sian, 'Breaking the law to make change', in John Brierley et al (eds.) Gathering Visions, Gathering Strength, co-published by GVGS organising group and London, Peace News, 1998, pp. 13-15.

521.Madgwick, P.J., 'Linguistic conflict in Wales: A problem in the design of government', in Glyn Williams (ed,), Social and Cultural Change in Contemporary Wales, London, Routledge and Kegan Paul, 1978, pp. 227-41.

522.Morgan, Gerald, The Dragon's Tongue, Cardiff, The Triskel Press, 1966, pp. 144.

523.Osmond, John, Creative Conflict: The Politics of Welsh Devolution, Llandysul, Gomer Press, London, Routledge and Kegan Paul, 1978, pp. 305.

States the case for devolution, criticizes British regional policy, and traces the emergence and development of a distinctive Welsh politics.

524.Thomas, Ned, The Welsh Extremist, Gollancz, 1971, pp. 126.

Chronicles the Welsh cultural and national revival in the 20th century, including the nonviolent direct action campaign of the 1970s. Chapters on several of the leading figures in the movement, Critical assessment of the response of English socialists to movement.

II. Campaigns for Civil Rights

1. The Civil Rights Movement and Black Power in the USA, 1955-68

The Civil Rights Movement against 'Jim Crow', the racism and segregation practised in the southern states of the USA, became a key example of principled and effective nonviolent resistance, and its leading figure, Martin Luther King, was inspired by and sometimes compared to Gandhi.

There had been a long history of African American resistance to the systematic discrimination which was legally entrenched from the late 19th century until the 1960s. Often it took the form of promoting black education up to university level, and legal challenges to southern laws. The legal path, pursued primarily by the National Association for the Advancement of Colored People (NAACP), began to have major results from 1954, the year in which the Supreme Court ruled that segregated schools were unconstitutional. In addition to the NAACP, other key organisations were:

CORE – the Congress of Racial Equality – which pioneered nonviolent direct action such as the first freedom rides; later excluded whites;

SCLC – the Southern Christian Leadership Conference, the organization closely associated with Martin Luther King;

SNCC – Student Nonviolent Coordinating Committee – which organized lunch counter sit-ins and the Mississippi Freedom Summer School, but which later turned away from nonviolence and excluded whites.

By the later 1950s and early 1960s federal government began to exert its powers more effectively, culminating in the 1964 Civil Rights Act and the 1965 Voting Rights Act, which outlawed devices designed to prevent African Americans voting. This federal legislation was in large measure a response to the growth of nonviolent direct action in the South.

The year-long 1955 bus boycott in Alabama, which brought Luther King to prominence, began the more militant movement of mass nonviolent direct action. There had been earlier small scale direct action challenges to southern segregation, but in 1960 large numbers of African American students engaged in sit-ins and occupations of segregated facilities and many other forms of intervention and civil disobedience. These tactics spread throughout the south, taken up by all sections of the black population, including school children, and were supported by white sympathizers. From 1964 to 1965 there was also a concerted attempt, despite white southern violence and intimidation, to register black voters.

The March on Washington in 1963, where Martin Luther King made his 'I have a dream' speech, perhaps represented a peak in mobilization for civil rights. Subsequently, especially after 1965, the movement became more radical. Two key issues were black separatism (linked to an assertion of black pride and autonomy) and a move to carrying guns (initially for self-defence). The turn to 'black power' was also prompted by the fact that the methods of civil disobedience, so effective in the south, could not easily be transplanted to the northern cities, where African Americans suffered de facto discrimination, unemployment and poverty. The extent of anger in the ghettoes was demonstrated by widespread urban riots in the mid-1960s. Urban protest and a philosophy of black power became associated particularly with Malcolm X.

The growing American involvement in the Vietnam War, and the disproportionate numbers of poor blacks drafted and killed in the war, also became a key issue, dividing the Civil Rights Movement.

The Civil Rights Movement is not only an iconic example of nonviolent methods and of disputes between advocates of nonviolence and violence, it also inspired a range of later social movements. The New Left, and various pioneers of the women's liberation movement, were deeply involved with Civil Rights; Native Americans, too, began to assert and campaign for their rights (see G.6). Overseas, Aboriginal rights campaigners in Australia looked to the example of the freedom rides and the ideas of black power.

Civil Rights and black power have been exceptionally well documented by journalists, contemporary historians and by many activists themselves. The books listed below try to cover key political and theoretical issues, represent a range of important organizations, campaigns and personalities in the movement for African American equality, give a voice to prominent women activists, and reflect differing ideological perspectives.

The realities of life for African Americans have been captured in novels by Richard Wright and James Baldwin, and more recently Alice Walker and Toni Morrison. James Baldwin entered the political fray with his passionate polemic <u>The Fire Next Time</u> (Penguin, 1964; reissued London, Joseph, 1972, pp. 112).

For background of Southern segregation see:

525.Woodward, C. Vann, <u>The Strange Career of Jim Crow</u>, 2nd revised edition, London, Oxford University Press, 1966, pp. 205.

Classic 1955 account of the complex emergence and later consolidation of systematic segregation in the South after the Civil War and abolition of slavery. Updated to cover succinctly major moves towards desegregation from 1955 to 1965.

526.Abernathy, Ralph D., <u>And the Walls Came Tumbling Down</u>, New York, Harper, 1989, pp. 638.

Reverend Abernathy was one of King's chief associates in the SCLC. After King's assassination in 1968, Abernathy led the Poor People's Campaign in Washington DC.

527.Albert, Peter J, Ronald Hoffman (eds.), <u>We Shall Overcome: Martin Luther King and the Black Freedom Struggle</u>, New York, Da Capo Press, 1993, pp. 294.

528.Anderson, Jervis, <u>A Philip Randolph: A Biographical Portrait</u>, Berkeley CA, University of California, 1986, pp. 398.

Study of the leader of the black trade union, The Brotherhood of Sleeping Car Porters, whose threat to organize a mass march on Washington in 1941 led to President Roosevelt's issuing an Executive Order banning discrimination in Federal and defence employment. Some twenty-two years later was one of the principal initiators of the 1963 March on Washington.

529.Branch, Taylor, <u>Parting the Waters: America in the King Years, 1954-1963</u>, New York, Simon and Schuster, 1988, pp. 1064.

Detailed account and insightful analysis of the US Civil Rights movement during this period.

530.Branch, Taylor, <u>Pillar of Fire: America in the King Years 1963-1968</u>, New York, Simon and Schuster, 1998, pp. 746.

531.Brinkley, Douglas, <u>Mine Eyes Have Seen the Glory: The Life of Rosa Parks</u>, London, Weidenfeld and Nicholson, 2000, pp. 248 (published in USA as <u>Rosa Parks</u>, New York Viking, 2000).

Parks is famous for her role in starting the 1955 Montgomery bus boycott, but had been engaged in demanding civil rights earlier.

532.Carbado, Devon W. and Donald Weise (eds.), <u>Time on Two Crosses: The Collected Writings of Bayard Rustin</u>, San Francisco, Cleis Press, 2003, pp. 354.

Bayard Rustin was an influential adviser to King and the coordinator of the 1963 March on Washington. These writings on civil rights and gay politics from 1942 to 1986 include his classic 1964 essay 'From Protest to Politics' which argues that the Civil Rights movement should shift its emphasis towards mainstream politics through voter registration campaigns and involvement with trade unions.

533.Carmichael, Stokeley and Charles V. Hamilton, <u>Black Power: The Politics of Liberation in America</u>, London, Jonathan Cape, 1968, pp. 198.

Makes case for black separatism in the struggle for equality, to enable black people to lead their own organizations and establish their own power bases. It also describes the attempt to achieve these aims through the Mississippi Freedom Democrats in 1964 and the role of SNCC in voter registration 1965-66. There is also a chapter on problems facing blacks in the northern ghettoes.

534.Carson, Clayborne et al (eds.), The Eyes on the Prize Reader, 1954-1990, New York and London, Penguin Books, 1991, pp. 764.

Comprises documents, speeches and first hand accounts from the black freedom struggle during this period. Published to accompany a TV documentary series.

535.Carson, Clayborne, In Struggle, Cambridge MA, Harvard University Press, 1981, pp. 359.

Admired study of the Student Nonviolent Coordinating Committee (SNCC) by an activist in the Civil Rights Movement. An early book on this topic is Howard Zinn, SNCC: The New Abolitionists, Boston, Beacon Press, 1964.

536.Cone, James H., Martin and Malcolm and America: A Dream or a Nightmare, London, Fount/HarperCollins 1993, pp. 358.

Compares two key and contrasting figures in the movement for black liberation, who began wholly opposed to each other as ministers of, respectively the Baptist Church and the separatist Black Muslims. But they moved closer together in the later 1960s as King came out against the Vietnam War and Malcolm X moved away from black messianic separatism to increasing political engagement. They also worked with different constituencies: the black communities of the South, and the alienated residents of the northern ghettoes. This book is a useful source for criticisms of King and his strategy by Malcolm X and many other black militants; and also of the March on Washington (see pp. 117-18).

537.Crawford, Vicki L, Jacqueline Rouse and Barbara Woods (eds.), Women in the Civil Rights Movement: Trailblazers and Torchbearers – 1941-1965, Bloomington, Indiana University Press, 1993, pp. 290.

Articles originally presented at conference in 1988.

538.D'Emilio, John, Lost Prophet: The Life and Times of Bayard Rustin, New York, Free Press, 2003, pp. 568.

The most comprehensive account to date of the work and ideas of this leading civil rights activist. Shows also how Rustin's gay lifestyle was continually brought up by political enemies intent on undermining the movement and by political rivals wanting to marginalize his role within it.

539.Farmer, James, Lay Bare the Heart: An Autobiography of the Civil Rights Movement, New York, Arbor House and Plume, 1985, pp. 370.

Central figure in CORE outlines its origins and later campaigns (chapters 9, 10 and 19) and recounts involvement in the 1960s movement.

540.Forman, James, The Making of Black Revolutionaries, New York, Macmillan and Washington DC, Open Hand, 1972, pp. 568.

Autobiography of one of the key activists in SNCC. Touches on issue of SNCC volunteers in the South carrying guns to deter assassination attempts.

541.Garrow, David J, Bearing the Cross: Martin Luther King Jr and the Southern Christian Leadership Conference, New York, Morrow, 1986, pp. 800.

542.Giddings, Paula, When and Where I Enter: The Impact of Black Women on Race and Sex in America, Toronto, Bantam Books, 1984, pp. 408.

543.Harding, Vincent, The Other American Revolution, Los Angleles, Center for Afro-American Studies, University of California; Atlanta, Institute of the Black World, 1988, pp. 261.

544.Holt, Len, The Summer That Didn't End, London, Heinemann, 1966, pp. 351. Reissued New York, Da Capo Press, 1992, with new introduction by Julian Bond.

On the 1964 Mississippi Freedom Summer.

545.King, Martin Luther, Letter from Birmingham City Jail, Philadelphia PA, American Friends Service Committee, 1963, pp. 15.

Answer to critics during the major campaign to desegregate Birmingham, Alabama. President Kennedy intervened to get King released from prison.

546.King, Martin Luther, Loving Your Enemies, New York, A.J. Muste Institute, pp. 50.

547.King, Martin Luther, Stride Towards Freedom: The Montgomery Story, London, Victor Gollancz, 1958, pp. 216.

Account of year-long 1955 bus boycott which heralded new era of nonviolent direct action against segregation and made King the most central figure of Civil Rights Movement.

548.King, Martin Luther, Why We Can't Wait, New York, Harper and Row, 1963, pp. 159.

Answer to white political and religious leaders urging less militant confrontation and greater patience.

549.King, Mary, Freedom Song: A Personal Story of the 1960s Civil Rights Movement, New York, William Morrow, 1987, pp. 592.

Insider account by white woman working in SNCC office. Meticulously detailed, with extensive quotes from key documents.

550.Klarman, Michael J., From Jim Crow to Civil Rights: The Supreme Court and the Struggle for Racial Equality, Oxford, Oxford University Press, 2004, pp. 655.

551.Levine, Daniel, Bayard Rustin and the Civil Rights Movement, Rutgers NJ, Rutgers University Press, 2000, pp. 307.

552.Lewis, John (with Michael D'Orsa), <u>Walking with the Wind: A Memoir of the Movement</u>, New York, Simon and Schuster, 1998, pp. 496.

By one of the early leaders of SNCC who came from the South.

553.Malcolm X (with assistance of Alex Haley), <u>The Autobiography of Malcolm X</u>, New York, Grove Press, 1965 pp. 455; republished several times, most recently by Penguin, 2001, with new introduction by Paul Gilroy, pp. 512.

See also <u>Malcolm X Speaks: Selected Speeches and Statements</u>, ed. George Breitman, New York, Grove Press, 1966, pp. 226.

554.Meier, August and Elliott Rudwick, <u>CORE: A Study in the Civil Right Movement 1942-1968</u>, Oxford, Oxford University Press, 1973 and Urbana IL, Illini Books, 1975, pp. 563.

Extensive analysis of rise and fall of CORE drawing on interviews with key members and CORE archives. Covers the 1960 sit-ins, 1961 Freedom Ride, mass campaigns in 1963 to desegregate Southern cities and the impact of black power ideology.

555.Morris, Aldon, <u>The Origins of the Civil Rights Movement: Black Communities Organising for Change</u>, London, Collier Macmillan, 1984, pp. 354.

556.Oates, Stephen B, <u>Let the Trumpet Sound: A Life of Martin Luther King Jr.</u>, Edinburgh, Playback, 1998 (first published New York, Harper and Row 1982), pp. 560.

557.Peck, James, <u>Freedom Ride</u>, New York, Simon and Schuster, 1962, pp. 160. Foreword by James Baldwin.

First hand account by activist who participated in both the 1947 'Journey of Reconciliation' (jointly organized by the Fellowship of Reconciliation and CORE) and the 1961 Freedom Rides organized by CORE at the height of the Civil Rights campaign.

558.Ransby, Barbara, <u>Ella Baker and the Black Freedom Movement: A Radical Democratic Vision</u>, Chapel Hill NC, University of North Carolina Press, 2003, pp. 470.

Recounts life and work of black woman activist who played key role in three major civil rights organizations – the NAACP, SCLC and SNCC.

559.Waldman, Louis, 'Civil Rights – Yes – Civil Disobedience – No' (a reply to Dr Martin Luther King)' in Bedau (ed.), <u>Civil Disobedience</u> (see A.1.).

See also, Dalton, <u>Mahatma Gandhi</u>, chapter 6 'Mohandas, Malcolm and Martin', pp. 168-87 (A.2.); Hentoff (ed.) <u>Essays of A.J. Muste</u>, 'Rifle squads or the beloved community' (pp. 426-37) on the debate about African-American activists carrying guns, and 'The Civil Rights Movement and the American Establishment' (pp. 451-61) (G.3.b.i).

2. Northern Ireland

The 1920 Government of Ireland Act created a Northern Ireland state within the UK with its own devolved parliament and government in the six North East counties of Ireland, which had constituted part of the nine counties of the province of Ulster. This constitutional arrangement was strengthened by the 1921 Anglo-Irish Treaty which created the Irish Free State, and also provided for Northern Ireland to choose to remain separate. The Treaty split the nationalist movement in the South and led to a bitter civil war between those for and against the Treaty.

Since Catholics/Nationalists formed a majority in two of the six counties of Northern Ireland and in the city of Derry/Londonderry, and since Irish republicans had fought for a united independent Ireland, the settlement created continuing sources of conflict. The demography of the new state and the political divide on Protestant/Unionist and Catholic/Nationalist lines ensured permanent Unionist control of the Provincial government at Stormont and the exclusion and political alienation of the Catholic minority. Unionist governments, fearful of this minority which mainly looked to the south and cherished the hope of a united Ireland, enshrined Protestant dominance through restricting voting rights of Catholics in local elections, altering local electoral boundaries and controlling most aspects of government and society, including law and order. Thus judges and magistrates were almost all Protestants, many members of the Unionists Party. The police force, the Royal Ulster Constabulary (RUC) was 90 per cent Protestant and the Ulster Special Constabulary – the 'B-Specials' – entirely so. Discrimination in jobs and housing, which pre-dated the creation of the new state, also continued.

This was the background to intermittent unrest, bombings and other military attacks by the Irish Republican Army (IRA) from the inception of the new state, and to the rise of the Civil Rights movement in the 1960s. For an overview of the history, governmental politics and moves towards change in the 1970s see:

560. Buckland, Patrick, <u>A History of Northern Ireland</u>, Dublin, Gill and Macmillan, 1981, pp. 195.

561. Murphy, John, <u>Ireland in the Twentieth Century</u>, Vol. 2 in The Gill History of Ireland, Dublin, Gill and Macmillan, 1975, pp. 180.

Chapter 1 'The independence struggle' and chapter 2 'Treaty and Civil War' set the historical context in which the Free State and Northern Ireland came into existence. Chapter 8, 'Northern Ireland' deals specifically with the Province from its inception until the collapse of the Power Sharing Executive in 1974.

562. O'Dowd, Liam, Bill Rolston and Mike Tomlinson, <u>Northern Ireland: Between Civil Rights and Civil War</u>, London CSE Books, 1980, pp. 224.

Examination of key issues by three Northern Ireland academics from a socialist perspective – includes a chapter on reform of the RUC in the 1970s.

563. Rose, Richard, <u>Northern Ireland: A Time of Choice</u>, London, Macmillan, 1976, pp. 175.

Clear analysis by British-based political scientist, which does not assume prior knowledge, tracing developments up to 1975.

a. The Civil Rights Movement 1967-72

The Civil Rights movement had its origins in various community initiatives in the early 1960s, but was launched on a countrywide basis in January 1967 when the Northern Ireland Civil Rights Association (NICRA) was created with support from trade unions, community and campaigning groups, republican bodies and all the Northern Ireland political parties. (Although the Unionist Party delegate walked out of the initial meeting, the Executive Committee subsequently co-opted two young Unionists.) The Unionist government, however, saw the movement from the start as a republican ploy to undermine the state and achieve a united Ireland.

Initially NICRA focused on defence of individual rights, but it then switched to demanding an end to collective discrimination against Catholics on voting, housing and employment, the repeal of the Special Powers Act (which gave police sweeping powers of search and arrest and the right to ban meetings or publications), the disbandment of the B Specials and the disarming of the RUC.

In August 1968 NICRA organized the first civil rights march to support a local campaign against continuing Council discrimination in allocating housing in Dungannon. Though prevented by police from entering the city centre, and facing provocation from a loyalist crowd led by Ian Paisley, the majority of the march remained nonviolent. Violence against demonstrators escalated on subsequent marches: in October 1968 a police baton charge injured 77 protesters at the end of a march organized jointly by NICRA and the Derry Citizens Action Committee, and in January 1969 a march from Belfast to Derry organized by Peoples Democracy (PD) – a radical socialist-oriented, campaigning body which began life at Queens University Belfast – was attacked by Protestant loyalists at Burntollet Bridge. A subsequent People's Democracy march in Newry, Co. Down, was followed by rioting and damage to property.

The turning point came in Derry on 12 August 1969 following clashes between the Protestant Apprentice Boys March and residents of the Catholic Bogside area of the city. The Bogside came under siege from loyalists, largely backed by the RUC and B-Specials. The rioting escalated and spread to Belfast on 14 August, where 150 Catholic homes were burned, eight people killed and hundreds injured. The British government sent troops into the province, who were initially welcomed by Catholics. But the troops were increasingly seen as serving the interests of the Unionist government.

In August 1971, amid a renewal of armed attacks and terrorist bombings by the Provisional IRA and loyalist paramilitaries, the British government introduced internment. Over 2,400 people were arrested in the first six months, though most were soon released. Internment further antagonized the Catholic community and the (mainly Catholic) Social Democratic and Labour Party announced a campaign of civil disobedience, including a rent and rates strike. Many Catholics also withdrew from public bodies. The last civil rights march took place in Derry in January 1972, when the British army opened fire on unarmed demonstrators, killing 14 people. Thereafter military resistance predominated.

Despite the descent of Northern Ireland into violence, the Civil Rights movement did draw world attention to the injustices suffered by the minority community and forced the Northern Ireland and British governments to introduce reforms which met its principal demands. Reforms included one-person-one-vote in local council elections (1969), proportional representation in local and European elections (1972), the replacement of the B-Specials with the Ulster Defence Regiment (1970) and the creation of Parliamentary and local commissioners for complaints in 1969. A new housing executive (1971), local government reorganization (1972) and the 1976 Fair Employment Act were designed to end discrimination. The movement also brought forward a new generation of political leaders.

564.Arthur, Paul, The People's Democracy 1968-1973, Belfast, Blackstaff Press, 1974, pp. 159.

565.Devlin, Bernadette, The Price of My Soul, London, Pan, 1969, pp. 205.

Devlin, a student in 1968, came to the fore as a fiery speaker and increasingly militant opponent of the Protestant supremacy and the British government role in Northern Ireland.

566.Farrell, Michael, Twenty Years On, Dingle, Brandon, 1988, pp. 160.

Contributions by nine activists who had been involved in the Civil Rights movement in 1968 and were still trying to secure social and political change in Northern Ireland, Contributors include Gerry Adams (of Provisional Sinn Fein) and Bernadette (Devlin) McAliskey.

567.McCann, Eamonn, War and an Irish Town, London, Pluto, 1980, pp. 176. (first edition published by Penguin 1974).

Account by one of leaders of Civil Rights movement of events in Derry from October 1968 to August 1969, and the aftermath, from a radical socialist and anti-capitalist perspective.

568.McCluskey, Conn, Up Off Their Knees: A Commentary on the Civil Rights Movement in Northern Ireland, Republic of Ireland, ConnMcCkuskey & Associates, 1989, pp. 245.

Account of origins and development of the movement by an activist who played a key role in its foundation.

569.McKittrick, David and David McVea, Making Sense of The Troubles, Belfast, The Blackstaff Press, 2000, pp. 353.

Provides excellent coverage of major events and includes a useful chronology covering period from the Government of Ireland Act 1920 to October 2000.

570.O'Brien, Conor Cruise, States of Ireland, London, Hutchinson, 1972, pp. 327.

Mixture of history, personal memoir and analysis by a noted author and Labour parliamentarian in Ireland. Chapter 8 'Civil Rights: the Crossroads' (pp. 147-77) is a detailed study of the movement and discussion of why the broader Irish context meant civil disobedience had limitations as a lever for change.

571.O'Connor, Fionnuala, <u>In Search of a State: Catholics in Northern Ireland</u>, Belfast, The Blackstaff Press, 1993, pp. 393.

Incisive analysis of underlying factors in Catholic/Nationalist and Protestant/Unionist tensions.

572.O'Dochartaigh, Niall, <u>From Civil Rights to Armalites: Derry and the Birth of the Irish Troubles</u>, Cork, Cork University Press, 1997, pp. 364.

Traces the slide from nonviolent protest to riots and military violence in the city of Derry. A central thesis of the book is that 'occasions of violent confrontation play a crucial role in promoting the escalation and continuation of conflict'.

573.Purdie, Bob, <u>Politics in the Streets: The Origins of the Civil Rights Movement in Northern Ireland</u>, Belfast, Blackstaff, 1990, pp. 286.

Argues in conclusion that the movement made a strategic error in taking to the streets because of the connection between street demonstrations and sectarian conflict in Northern Ireland. Although activists drew inspiration from the US Civil Rights Movement they did not take sufficient account of the different circumstances in the two countries.

574.Sunday Times Insight Team, <u>Ulster</u>, Harmondsworth, Penguin, 1972, pp. 311.

Detailed account of the evolution of events from 1967 to 1971.

b. The Protestant Workers' Strike 1974

The power-sharing executive, created as a result of the Sunningdale Agreement in December 1973, took office in January 1974 with ministers drawn from the Ulster Unionist Party, the SDLP and the Alliance Party. However it was opposed by many Unionist politicians, as well as by the IRA on the nationalist side, and prompted widespread grassroots Protestant resistance. Anti-Sunningdale Unionist candidates won 11 out of 12 Westminster seats with 51 per cent of the votes in the UK February 1974 general election. The Executive was finally brought down by a mass strike in May 1974 organized by the Ulster Workers' Council, in which gas and electricity workers played a critical role. In one sense it was an impressive demonstration of 'people power', but it was far from being nonviolent as there was widespread intimidation by Protestant para-military groups to enforce the strike. It also coincided with bomb explosions in Dublin and Monaghan in which 30 people were killed. Power sharing was deferred until the election of an assembly in 1998 following the Good Friday Agreement.

575.Fisk, Robert, <u>The Point of No Return: The Strike which Broke the British in Ulster</u>, London, Deutsch, 1975, pp. 264.

See also: McKittrick and McVea, <u>Making Sense of the Troubles</u> Chapter 5, 'Sunningdale, strike and stalemate' which notes the intimidation accompanying the strike (E.II.2.a.).

c. The Peace People, Nonviolent Intervention to Halt Violence 1976-1979

The growing tension between the Protestant and Catholic communities in the 1970s and the rising violence by both Catholic and Protestant paramilitary groups led to a number of attempts to prevent violence and promote reconciliation, for example Witness for Peace created by a Protestant clergyman in 1972, and Women Together founded in 1970 to stop stone throwing and gang fights. But the best publicized and most controversial protest against violence was the Peace People, founded in 1976 after three young children were killed by a runaway IRA car whose driver had been shot by the army. Two women initiated the movement, Protestant Betty Williams, who saw the tragedy, and Catholic Mairead Corrigan, the children's aunt. The Peace People brought 10,000 and then 20,000 out onto the streets in Belfast in August and 25,000 in Derry in September to demand an end to paramilitary violence. By November 1976 the Peace People had over 80 local groups, offices in both Belfast and Derry and its own paper. The movement was criticized, especially by Sinn Fein, for its initial failure to condemn violence by the British Army and the Protestant-dominated RUC; and attacked by the militant Protestant leader Ian Paisley for being a Catholic front. Over time, under the influence of the third key figure in the movement, former journalist Ciaran McKeown, the Peace People turned to long term community organization.

Two periodicals which ran articles on the Peace People from a nonviolent perspective are Peace News (London) and the monthly Dawn (published by a collective from Belfast, Derry and Dublin). In the latter, see especially issues no. 25 (November 1976), editorial on Peace People leadership in no. 26 (Christmas 1976), and analyses of Peace People strategy in nos. 27 and 28 (January and February 1977). Dawn also published a combined issue, 'Nonviolence in Irish History', no. 38-39, (April-May 1978), which traced nonviolence in Ireland back to the arrival of the Quakers in the 17th century, through the campaign of Daniel O'Connell for Catholic Emancipation, the Land League agitation in the 19th century and nonviolent elements in the national and labour movements (late 19th and early 20th centuries) to the Peace People.

576.Deutsch, Richard, Mairead Corrigan, Betty Williams, Woodbury NY, Barrons, 1977, pp. 204. Foreword by Joan Baez.

Account of the genesis, development and programme of the Peace People by French journalist resident in Belfast at the time.

577.Fannin, Anne, The Peace People Experience 1976-1979, Anne Fannin, 1986, pp. 114.

578.McKeown, Ciaran, The Passion of Peace, Belfast, Blackstaff Press, 1984, pp. 319.

579.O.Connor, Fionnuala, 'Community politics in Northern Ireland', in Michael Randle (ed.), Challenge to Nonviolence, Bradford, University of Bradford, 2002, pp. 207-22.

580.O.Donnell, Dalry, The Peace People of Northern Ireland, Camberwell VIC, Widescope, 1977, pp. 122.

Description of the movement which covers marches and rallies against sectarian violence (chapter 4-6) and participants' own perspectives (chapter 7).

581.Overy, Bob, How Effective Are Peace Movements?, Bradford School of Peace Studies and London, Housmans, 1982.

There is a sympathetic analysis of the Peace People pp. 30-38.

582.Overy, Bob, The Price of Peace, Belfast, 1976, pp. 34.

See also McKittrick and McVea, Making Sense of the Troubles, for very brief assessment pp. 117 (E.II.2.a.).

F. Campaigns for Social and Economic Justice

A significant part of the repertoire of nonviolent direct action derives from movements for economic justice in the past. Strikes and boycotts of all kinds arose out of the evolving trade union movement. Peasant farmers have frequently attempted to occupy and cultivate land which is unused or owned by wealthy landowners. Refusal to pay exorbitant rents has been a tactic of both the rural and urban poor.

Since the 1990s there have been numerous nonviolent campaigns against forms of economic injustice, the dominant role of multinational corporations, and against global neoliberal policies such as privatization – promoted by international bodies such as the IMF, World Bank, World Trade Organization and regional groupings like the North American Free Trade Agreement (NAFTA). These are listed under G.7.a and G.7.b.

So this section focuses primarily on the period 1945-1990, though it includes land occupations which have occurred more recently.

1. Demands for Land Reform and Land Occupations

In Europe peasant seizure of land has often been part of a wider revolutionary upsurge, as in France in 1787 and Russia in 1905 and 1917 and Italy 1919. But there is a long history in Latin America of peasants seizing land (with varying degrees of nonviolence or violence) from absentee or large landowners and planting crops on the land. Sometimes land seizures were retrospectively legalized by government laws or by sale of the land, or even encouraged by leftist politicians. Peasant leagues in Colombia in the 1930s created an independent communist republic in the mountains based on land seized. In the 1950s and 1960s peasants seized land in Colombia, Bolivia, Brazil, Peru and Venezuela.

A major movement of the landless in Brazil, Movimento Sem Terra, formally created in 1984, arose out of the industrial and rural militancy of the late 1970s, when there were many land seizures. Sem Terra has continued to organize the landless and unemployed in seizing land from large landowners and multinationals, and in setting up cooperative farms. Their work has also extended to organizing slum dwellers on the outskirts Rio de Janeiro and other large cities in the southeast, providing them with allotments.

583.Branford, Sue and Oriel Glock, <u>The Last Frontier: Fighting Over Land in the Amazon</u>, London, Zed Press, 1985, pp. 336.

584.Branford, Sue and Jan Rocha, <u>Cutting the Wire</u>, London, Latin American Bureau, 2002, pp. 305.

Well researched account of Movimento Sem Terra.

585.Hammond, J.L. 'Law and disorder: The Brazilian Landless Farmworkers' movement', <u>Bulletin of Latin American Research</u>, vol. 18 no. 4 (1991), pp. 269-89. See also Hammond, John L, 'The MST and the media: competing images of the Brazilian Landless Farmworkers' Movement', <u>Latin American Politics and Society</u>, vol. 46, no.4. (Winter, 2004), pp. 61-90.

586.Hurley, Judith, 'Brazil: A troubled journey to the promised land' in McManus and Schlabach (eds.), <u>Relentless Persistence</u>, pp. 174-96 (D.IV. Introduction).

The author, who founded a US support group for the landless, provides excerpts from her journal of visiting sites of the land struggle in 1987. She notes intensified confrontations in 1980s between the landed elite and the landless, resorting to lawsuits, demonstrations, fasts, vigils, marches, funerals and above all land occupation.

587.Kingsnorth, Paul, <u>One No, Many Yeses</u>, London, Faber, 2003, pp. 355.

Chapter 7 'Land and freedom', pp. 241-71, is lively account of visit to Sem Terra projects in Brazil and provides some wider analysis.

588.Schlabach, Gerald, 'The nonviolence of desperation: Peasant land action in Honduras' in McManus and Schlabach (eds.), <u>Relentless Persistence</u>, pp. 48-62 (D.IV. Introduction).

Examines 200 peasant occupations in 1972 (assertion of a tradition of 'les recuperaciones') in context of developing forms of protest since the 'great strike' against United Fruit Company in 1954.

589.Stedile, Joao Pedro, 'Landless battalions', <u>New Left Review</u>, no 15 (May/June 2002), pp. 77-104.

An account by a participant in the evolution of land seizures and how Sem Terra in Brazil eventually achieved legal possession.

590.'Uncapping the bottle: Father Andres Giron and the clamor for land in Guatelama: Interview', in McManus and Schlabach (eds.), <u>Relentless Persistence</u>, pp. 225-36 (D.IV. Introduction).

Examines role of this radical Catholic priest in a campaign for land reform. Describes his 100-mile 'hunger march' in 1986 to demand land, and his 1987 fast and occupation of the square in front of the National Palace; but queries his emphasis on buying land as a solution.

591.Urrutia Montoya, Miguel, <u>The Development of the Colombian Labor Movement</u>, New Haven, Yale University Press, 1969, pp. 297.

Includes material on land seizures, though uses the term 'violent' ambiguously to include forms of direct action.

592.Warriner, Doreen, <u>Land Reform in Principle and Practice</u>, Oxford, Clarendon Press, 1969, pp. 457.

An overview of land reform assessing political, economic and ideological factors and looking at land reform in practice in particular countries. Much of the emphasis is on government reforms and economic outcomes. But chapter 7 'The Latin American background' examines the role of revolutions in Mexico and Cuba, and action by farm worker syndicates, including land invasions, in Bolivia, Brazil, Peru and Venezuela. Chapter 10 looks at the central role of the trade union movement in Venezuela in land reform, and the history and politics of the movement.

2. Protests by the Unemployed

Protests by the unemployed have considerable resonance in Britain, where demonstrators and commentators still refer back to the 'hunger marches' of the 1930s. In the USA during the great depression the unemployed created a tent city in Washington to dramatize their desperate situation. Other protesters around the world have attempted to find more direct answers to their plight. Movements by both the rural and urban unemployed have included seizing land to live on and grow food; workers thrown out of their jobs have occupied and begun to run their factories; and since the unemployed are quite often homeless they also join campaigns to occupy empty buildings.

a. Dolci and the Reverse Strike

One unusual tactic, associated with the prominent nonviolent activist Danilo Dolci, were the 'reverse strikes' organized in Sicily in December 1955-February 1956 as part of a series of campaigns between 1952 and 1965 to relieve the extreme poverty. When unemployed men started to repair a road outside Partinico, appealing to their constitutional right and duty to work, the police sent them home, and banned a second attempt to repair the road, arresting Dolci and six others.

593. Dolci, Danilo, The Outlaws of Partinico, London, Macgibbon and Kee, 1960, pp. 316.

Describes context of his campaigns – not much detail on the campaigns themselves.

594. McNeish, James, Fire Under the Ashes: The Life of Danilo Dolci, London, Hodder and Stoughton, 1965, pp. 256.

3. Factory Occupations

Various forms of worker control or worker ownership have at times been introduced by governments or philanthropic industrialists, negotiated between unions and management if a business is failing, or created as experiments in cooperation and worker democracy. This section looks only at some examples of laid-off workers taking direct action leading to worker control, though government intervention and negotiations with former management may arise out of the workers' actions. Recent factory occupations in Argentina, as part of the popular response to the collapse of the Argentinian economy in November 2001, come under G.7.b.ii.

a. Britain and Europe

595.Coates, Ken, <u>Work-ins, Sit-ins and Industrial Democracy</u>, Nottingham, Spokesman Books, 1981, pp. 175.

An account of sit-ins or work-ins to prevent factory closure in Britain in early 1970s and an examination of subsequent developments.

596.Greenwood, J., <u>Worker Sit-ins and Job Protection: Case Studies of Union Intervention</u>, Farnborough, Gower Press, 1977, pp. 121.

Discusses sit-down strikes in Britain, the occupation of the Lip factory in France in 1973 and West European sit-ins and work-ins protesting against redundancy.

597. <u>Lip and the Self-Managed Counter-Revolution</u>, Negation no. 3, Detroit, Black and Red, 1975, pp. 91.

The takeover of the Lip watch making factory in 1973 by workers who had been laid off became a noted example of worker struggle.

598.McGill, Jack, <u>Crisis on the Clyde: The Story of the Upper Clyde Shipbuilders</u>, London, Davis-Poynter, 1973, pp. 143.

See also: 'Forging links in Ozarow' in Notes from Nowhere (ed.), <u>We Are Everywhere</u>, pp. 450-55, on Polish worker occupation to prevent closure of factory in 2000, supported by local community and anarchist groups (see G.7.a.).

4. Significant Strikes

The labour movement has evolved a wide range of tactics associated with strikes to meet specific circumstances – for a detailed breakdown see Gene Sharp, <u>The Politics of Nonviolent Action</u>, Part Two (A.1.). In countries where trade unions are well established strikes have continued to be a useful tactic, but often as an adjunct of bargaining. Many economic strikes since 1945 have not therefore been particularly notable.

This bibliography selectively covers one strike by the poor and underprivileged seeking union organization and minimum economic justice: the California grape pickers. It also deals with one strike with major political implications: the 1984-5 miners' strike in Britain. (Strikes by women opposing discrimination and demanding equal pay are covered under 'Feminism', Section G.4. below)

Since the 1980s the decline in union power, in parallel with the triumph of a neoliberal global economy, and the evolution of new forms of unionism, has meant that labour protest even in the west is often becoming part of a fundamental struggle for basic social justice, and strikes against sweatshop conditions have become widespread (see section G.7.).

a. California Grape Pickers' Strike, 1965-1970

This important struggle for fair pay and the right to union organization was led by Cesar Chavez, who adhered to a philosophy of nonviolence. It was supported by a wider boycott of Californian grapes.

599.Day, Mark, Forty Acres: Cesar Chavez and the Farm Workers, New York, Praeger, 1971, pp. 222

600.Dunne, John Gregory, Delano: The Story of the California Grape Strike, New York, Farrar, Strauss and Giroux, 1967, pp. 202

601.Jenkins, J. Craig, The Politics of Insurgency: The Farm Worker Movement in the 1960s, New York, Columbia University Press, 1985, pp. 131-74.

602.Levy, Jacques, Cesar Chavez: Autobiography of La Causa, New York, W.W. Norton, 1975, pp. 546.

603.Matthiesen, Peter, Sal Si Puedes: Cesar Chavez and the New American Revolution, New York, Random House, 1969, pp. 372

604.Taylor, Ronald B., Chavez and the Farm Workers, Boston, Beacon Press, 1975, pp. 342.

Includes assessment of impact of grape pickers' strike on immigrant labour in other industries.

See also Sharp et al, Waging Nonviolent Struggle, pp. 173-87 (A.1.).

b. The British Miners' Strike, 1984-85

The miners' strike to defend their industry against extensive pit closures was also a highly politicized conflict between the National Union of Mineworkers (under the leadership of Arthur Scargill) and the Conservative government under Margaret Thatcher. Scargill hoped to repeat the success of the NUM in the early 1970s in undermining the then Conservative government, and Mrs Thatcher was determined to force the miners into surrender. The strike, which the miners eventually lost, saw a government assault on civil liberties and high levels of tension between the police and strikers, and was a turning point in industrial relations in Britain. Its significance is suggested by the large number of books and pamphlets it generated, some of which are listed below.

One unexpected, and more positive, by-product was that the strike mobilized many women in the mining communities (not previously active in industrial disputes) to organize support for the strikers (see section G.4).

605.Beynon, Huw (ed.), Digging Deeper: Issues in the Miners' Strike, London, Verso, 1985, pp. 280.

606.Callinicos, Alex and Mike Simons, The Great Strike: The Miners' Strike of 1984-5 and its Lessons, London, Socialist Worker, 1985, pp. 256.

607.Goodman, Geoffrey, The Miners' Strike, London, Pluto, 1985, pp. 224.

608. McCabe, Sarah et al, The Police, Public Order and Civil Liberties: Legacies of the Miners' Strike, London, Routledge, 1988, pp. 209.

609. Milne, Seumas, The Enemy Within: The Secret War Against the Miners, London, Verso, 1994, and Pan, 1995, pp. 511

610. Samuel, Raphael (ed.), The Enemy Within: Pit Villages and the Miners' Strike of 1984-5, London, Routledge and Kegan Paul, 1986, pp. 260.

611. Saunders, Jonathan, Across Frontiers: International Support for the Miners' Strike, London, Canary, 1989, pp. 288.

612. Wilsher, Peter, Donald MacIntyre and Michael Jones with the Sunday Times Insight Team, Strike: Thatcher, Scargill and the Miners, Sevenoaks, Coronet, 1985, pp. 304.

613. Winterton, Jonathan and Ruth Winterton, Coal, Crisis and Conflict: The 1984-85 Miners' Strike in Yorkshire, Manchester, Manchester University Press, 1989, pp. 360.

5. Campaigns by Homeless (Squatting)

There have been two types of movement to occupy empty buildings, action by the homeless to find somewhere to live; and counter-cultural movements to create new social spaces and new kinds of society in miniature in parts of modern cities, as for example the Kabouters (successors to the Dutch Provos) did in the 1970s, and groups in Italy are doing today.

614. Anarchy, no. 102 (vol. 9 no. 8), (August 1969).

Issue on 'Squatters', on London Campaign starting in 1968, including extract from Kropotkin on 'The expropriation of dwellings'.

615. Bailey, Ron, The Squatters, Harmondsworth, Penguin, 1973, pp. 206.

Covers the London Squatters Campaign 1968-1971, but notes background of the mass movement by homeless people in Britain to occupy military bases, and later luxury flats, in 1945-46.

616. Klein, Naomi, 'Italy's Social Centres' in Fences and Windows, London, Flamingo, 2002, pp. 224-27.

617. Ward, Colin, Housing: An Anarchist Approach, London, Freedom Press, 1976, pp. 182.

Ward, a leading anarchist theorist and expert on housing, examines the post-1945 British squatters movement (pp. 13-27) and assesses the revival of squatting between 1968 and early 1970s.

6. Protests Against Unjust Taxes and Rent Strikes

a. Taxes

Opposition to taxes deemed unjust or illegitimate has long been part of popular resistance, as in the preludes to the English Civil War and the American Revolution.

Taxes may also be withheld to demonstrate opposition to particular policies, such as war (see section G.3). Sometimes withholding taxes is part of a wider revolt against state policies, as in the Poujadist movement among small farmers in France in the 1950s. At other times the imposition of a tax may be the spark for a movement of resistance, as in the case of Mrs Thatcher's introduction of a 'poll tax' – a new flat rate local government tax on all individuals regardless of their income.

i. Poll tax protests, Britain, 1989-90

618.Bagguley, Paul, <u>The Mobilization of Anti-Poll Tax Protest in Leeds</u>, University of Leeds, School of Sociology and Social Policy, 1995.

619.Bagguley, P., 'Protest, poverty and power: A case study of the anti-poll tax movement', <u>Sociological Review</u>, vol. 43 (1995), pp. 693-719.

620.Haringey Solidarity Group, <u>The Poll Tax Rebellion in Haringey</u>, London, Haringey Solidarity Group, 1999, pp. 30.

621.Ramsey Kanaan interviewed by David Solnit, 'How one small anarchist group toppled the Thatcher Government', in David Solnit (ed.), <u>Globalize Liberation:</u> San Francisco, City Lights, 2004, pp. 397-410. (See G.7.a).

Discusses how the anti-poll tax campaign spread beyond its origins in Edinburgh to the rest of Britain, and describes its main tactics.

ii. Fuel tax protests, 2000

The campaign of direct action in autumn 2000 against fuel price rises, which spread from France and other European countries, was in Britain focused partly on government taxes on fuel. Whilst poor farmers were active in these protests, direct action seemed to represent the interests of trucking businesses and even the oil companies themselves, and the blockading of fuel depots with lorries was an aggressive form of direct action which threatened the British economy.

622.Lyons, Glenn and Kiron Chatterjee (eds.), <u>Transport Lessons from the Fuel Tax Protests of 2000</u>, Aldershot, Ashgate, 2002, pp. 338.

Includes material on the direct action protests as well as broader issues.

b. Rent Strikes

623.Brill, Harry, <u>Why Organizers Fail: The Story of a Rent Strike</u>, Berkeley CA, University of California Press, 1971, pp. 192.

Examines community action by the poor in Californian studies of urbanization and the environment series.

624.Lipsky, M. <u>Protest in City Politics</u>, Chicago, Rand McNally, 1970, pp. 214.

625. Moorhouse, Bert, Mary Wilson and Chris Chamberlain, 'Rent strikes – direct action and the working class', in Ralph Miliband and John Saville (eds.), <u>The Socialist Register, 1972</u>, London, Merlin Press, 1972.

Starts with an account of the major rent strikes on the Clyde in 1915 and 1921-26, but includes materials on rent strikes in London, 1959-61 and 1968-70 and their implications.

G. Nonviolent Action in Social Movements

This section covers a wide range of movements resorting to nonviolent action as part of their strategy. Most of the protests date from the 1960s or later and many (especially the campaigns against nuclear weapons, the green movement and feminism) have been categorized as 'new social movements'. There is a burgeoning literature on social movements, much of it with a strong theoretical slant, but which, as Kurt Schock (A.I) has cogently argued, tends to ignore scholarship on nonviolence. This bibliography does not attempt to cover the theoretical debates, but lists a few of the well known texts where they bear on particular campaigns and examples of nonviolent action. For a discussion of methods see:

626.Rucht, Dietrich, 'The strategies and action repertoires of New Movements' in Dalton, Russell J and Manfred Kuechler, Challenging the Political Order: New Social and Political Movements in Western Democracies, Cambridge, Polity, 1990, pp. 156-75.

a. National/Area Studies

627.Brierley, John et al (eds.), Gathering Visions, Gathering Strength, Bradford and London, GVGS Publishing Group and Peace News, 1998, pp. 39.

Report of conference of that title bringing together nonviolent activists from different campaigns and different generations.

628.Burgmann, Verity, Power and Protest: Movements for Change in Australian Society, St Leonards, New South Wales, Allen and Unwin, 1993, pp. 302. See also: Burgmann, Verity, Power, Profit amd Protest: Australian Social Movements and Globalisation, Crows Nest NSW, Allen and Unwin, 2003, pp. 393.

629.Escobar, Arturo and Sinia E. Alvarez (eds.), The Making of Social Movements in Latin America: Identity, Strategy and Democracy, Boulder CO, Westview Press, 1992, pp. 383.

Essays on conceptualizing and understanding social movements in Latin American context, as well as indigenous, peasant and urban protests, and on feminist and ecology movements. See also: Oxhorn, P. 'From human rights to citizenship rights: Recent trends in the study of Latin American social movements', Latin American Research Review, vol. 36 no. 3 (2001), pp. 163-82.

630.Routledge, Paul, Terrains of Resistance: Nonviolent Social Movements and the Contestation of Place in India, Westport CT, Praeger, 1993, pp. 170.

The theoretical emphasis of this book is on the spatial components to sites of resistance. Chapter one looks at the developing resistance to aspects of economic development (industrialization, dams, deforestation) and the numerous movements since independence among tribal people, peasants, women and squatters. Chapters 3 and 4 analyse the Baliapal Movement against a missile testing range and the Chipko Movement against logging.

631.Tracy, James, <u>Direct Action: Radical Pacifism from the Union Eight to the Chicago Seven</u>, Chicago, University of Chicago Press, 1996, pp. 196.

Examines how a small group of radical pacifists (such as David Dellinger, A.J. Muste and Bayard Rustin) played a major role in the rebirth of US radicalism and social protest in the 1950s and 1960s, applying nonviolence to social issues and developing an experimental protest style.

b. Transnational Issues and Campaigns

There are several edited collections (in addition to those already listed under A.1.) which include relevant essays:

632.Cohen, Robin and Shirin M. Rai, <u>Global Social Movements</u>, London, Athlone Press, 2000, pp. 231.

Essays examining aspects of indigenous peoples', women's, labour, religious and Islamic movements, as well as human rights, environmental and peace movements.

633.Della Porta, Donatella and Sidney Tarrow (eds.), <u>Transnational Protest and Global Activism</u>, Lanham MD, Rowman and Littlefield, 2005, pp. 287.

Collection of essays exploring globalization and its varying impact on social movements, comparing today's movements with earlier movements and examining specific examples.

634.Edwards, Michael and John Gaventa, <u>Global Citizen Action</u>, London, Earthscan Publications, 2001, pp. 327.

Discusses transnational civil society, its impact on international financial institutions and a range of specific campaigns, e.g. to ban landmines, Jubilee 2000, campaigns against corporations.

1. The New Left and Student Movements, 1960s

The ideas of the New Left and the wave of student protests in the western world in the 1960s are closely linked, although student protests often had specific national characteristics. In general, however, students protested against the intrusion of military and corporate interests into the academic world and heavy-handed university bureaucracy, as well as about wider human rights and anti-militarist issues – West German student protests began with opposition to the repressive regime of the Shah of Iran. In the USA student protest was closely linked to the Civil Rights movement, in Britain (in the later 1950s and early 1960s) to the campaign against nuclear weapons, and in France to resisting the authoritarianism of the Gaullist regime. Students in many parts of the world, especially the USA, Japan and Australia, became in the later 1960s key participants in the resistance to the Vietnam War.

The impetus behind the New Left was an attempt to chart an alternative both to western corporate and consumerist capitalism and the oppressive bureaucratic regimes of the Soviet bloc. Early US experiments, associated with Students for a Democratic Society, stressed community, participatory democracy and social justice. The New Left looked for inspiration to non-authoritarian strands in earlier socialism, and was also influenced by the development of the 1960s counter culture and the hippies. By the end of the 1960s the polarization encouraged by the escalation of the Vietnam War and the influence of various far-left groups created divisions, pushing some New Leftists towards more extreme and sectarian leftist positions and/or support for North Vietnam. A very small minority, in the USA, West Germany and Italy, decided to go underground and adopt guerrilla tactics.

The New Left was primarily a western phenomenon, but New Left ideas and student activism had repercussions in both Czechoslovakia, where students were prominent in the protests leading to the Prague Spring, and in Yugoslavia in 1968. (For these protests see relevant country subsections under C.) There was also a significant New Left student movement in Japan which engaged in university occupations 1965-70, opposed the US-Japan 1960 Security Treaty, and had a guerrilla wing, the Red Army. See:

635.McCormack, Gavan, 'The student left in Japan', New Left Review, no. 65 (January/ February 1971), pp. 37-53.

a. General and Comparative

636.Caute, David, Sixty Eight: The Year of the Barricades, London, Hamilton, 1988, pp. 464. (Published in USA as The Year of the Barricades: A Journey Through 1968, New York, Harper and Row.)

637.Cockburn, Alexander and Robin Blackburn (eds.), Student Power: Problems, Diagnosis, Action, Harmondsworth, Penguin, 1969, pp. 378.

A survey reflecting the standpoint of New Left Review, which includes general political analysis and particular examples of confrontation. Fred Halliday's chapter 'Students of the world unite' briefly covers a range of international campaigns.

638.Fraser, Ronald, 68 – A Generation in Revolt, London, Chatto and Windus, 1988, pp. 370.

An oral history focusing on the student protests.

639.Young, Nigel, An Infantile Disorder? The Crisis and Decline of the New Left, London, Routledge, 1977, pp. 490.

A history and analysis focusing primarily on the American New Left, critical of many of the developments in 1968 and afterwards, from a pacifist and nonaligned perspective.

See also: Harman, The Fire Last Time, Part 1 covers transnational student protests of 1968 and New Left, and Part II later developments, by an activist in the Socialist Workers' Party (D.III.Introduction).

b. Britain

640.Oxford University Socialist Discussion Group, <u>Out of Apathy: Voices of the New Left 30 years On</u>, London, Verso, 1989.

See Stuart Hall, 'The "First" New Left, Life and times', pp. 11-38; Michael Rustin, 'The New Left as a social movement', pp. 115-28.

641.Widgery, David, <u>The Left in Britain</u>, Harmondsworth, Penguin, 1976, pp. 549.

c. France, May Events of 1968

642.Posner, Charles (ed.), <u>Reflection on the Revolution in France: 1968</u>, Harmondsworth, Penguin, 1970, pp. 318.

Essays by French participants and left wing intellectuals on the key protests, organizations and strategy of the movement, its social context and lessons to be drawn.

643.Seale, Patrick and Maureen McConville, <u>French Revolution 1968</u>, Harmondsworth, Penguin, 1968, pp. 238.

Account and analysis by two Observer correspondents who witnessed the May Events.

d. Germany (West)

644.Becker, Jill, <u>Hitler's Children: The Story of the Baader-Meinhof Gang</u>, London, Michael Joseph, 1977 (and Granada, revised edition 1978).

This is primarily an account of leftwing urban guerrilla warfare in West Germany, but Part 1, pp. 25-75, covers the evolution of the German New Left from 1965-68, from which the small Baader-Meinhof group sprang.

645.Hunnius, F.C., <u>Student Revolts: The New Left in West Germany</u>, London, War Resisters' International, 1968, pp. 40.

e. USA

646.Jacobs, Paul and Saul Landau, <u>The New Radicals: A Report with Documents</u>, Harmondsworth, Penguin, 1966, pp. 331.

Sympathetic account of early New Left. Most of the book is composed of a wide range of documents indicating ideas and organizations involved, in particular Students for a Democratic Society, black voter registration, the Berkeley Free Speech Movement and anti-Vietnam War campaigns. Also includes chronology of key events.

647.Lipset, Seymour Martin and Sheldon S. Wolin (eds.), <u>The Berkeley Student Revolt: Facts and Interpretation</u>, New York, Doubleday, 1965, pp. 585.

Documents on and analyses of a key campaign in the evolution of the New Left, which lasted from September 1964 to January 1965, compiled by academics at Berkeley.

648.Newfield, Jack, <u>A Prophetic Minority: The American New Left</u>, London, Anthony Blond, 1967.

Survey of evolution of New Left up to 1965 by a participant.

649.Sale, Kirkpatrick, <u>SDS</u>, New York, Random House, 1973, pp. 752.

Traces history of Students for a Democratic Society from its emergence out of the Student League for Industrial Democracy in 1960 to its demise in 1970. Major focus on SDS campaigns against the Vietnam War, including the 1965 March on Washington.

650.Slate, W.M. (ed.), <u>Power to the People: New Left Writings</u>, New York, Tower Publications, 1970.

Selection of writings by activists and theorists of the New Left. The chapter by Carl Oglesby, 'Notes on a decade ready for the dustbin', pp. 99-130, charts the evolution of the New Left throughout the 1960s and the turn towards more violent protest.

2. Resistance to the Vietnam War, 1961-73

The evolution of the US-led war in Vietnam was complex. To understand events in Indo-China it is necessary to go back to 1945, when Japanese occupation of the area ended. The Communist-led guerrillas under Ho Chi Minh then established an independent state, whilst the French attempted to restore their former colonial empire and took control of South Vietnam. The French were decisively defeated by the Communist Vietminh forces in 1954 at the battle of Dien Bien Phu, and withdrew. But the US took over support for a South Vietnamese anti-communist state, and the international agreement about the future of Vietnam, reached at the Geneva Conference of 1954, was ignored. As the South Vietnamese government struggled to resist internal guerrilla opposition by the National Liberation Front ('Vietcong'), and increasing pressure from North Vietnam, the US government supplied military 'advisors', and from 1963 sent increasing numbers of US troops. The Australian government also agreed to send troops to Vietnam. In 1965 the USA began to bomb North Vietnam.

Resistance to the US role in the war (initiated largely by pacifists from 1961) became widespread in 1965, when the first teach-ins were held, both in the USA and around the world. Opposition was especially strong in Australia, where there was resistance to the draft, and in Japan, where people feared being drawn into the war. Canadians became involved in offering refuge to U.S. draft resisters. Protests against the war in countries not directly involved often took the form of marches and confrontations outside US embassies. In the USA itself, in addition to frequent large demonstrations and student direct action against the military presence on campuses, there was also widespread draft resistance (e.g. burning draft cards) and acts of solidarity with draft resisters. Resistance also grew inside the armed forces, and led to public protest and acts of defiance, and also to desertions.

US bombing, and dropping of chemicals to defoliate the Ho Chi Minh trail, spread beyond Vietnam to Laos. Even more controversially, the USA under Nixon began in 1969 an undeclared war of bombing and military incursions against what it claimed were North Vietnamese/National Liberation Front bases in neutral Cambodia. This secret war destabilized Prince Sihanouk who was eventually ousted in a military coup. After the US Administration launched an invasion of Cambodia in spring 1970, without consulting Congress, opposition increased dramatically – about a third of colleges and universities were closed down by mass protests. At Kent State university in Ohio confrontation between the students and the National Guard led to four students being shot dead.

There is a large literature on the origins and development of the French and then American wars in Indo-China. See:

651.Charlton, Michael and Anthony Moncrieff, <u>Many Reasons Why: The American Involvement in Vietnam</u>, London, Scolar Press, 1978, pp. 250.

Based on BBC series of programmes and consisting primarily of interviews with wide range of those involved in first French and then US policy on Vietnam, and individuals prominent in opposition. Covers period 1945-1975. Chapters 7 and 8 discuss protests inside USA and the leaking by Daniel Ellsberg of <u>The Pentagon Papers</u>, which revealed in detail secret internal policy making.

652.McCarthy, Mary, <u>Vietnam</u>, Harmondsworth, Penguin Books, 1968, pp. 119.

Mary McCarthy's influential account of her visit to Vietnam, in which she argued that the US was fighting a war it could not win, and called for withdrawal.

653.Shawcross, William, <u>Side Show: Kissinger, Nixon and the Destruction of Cambodia</u>, London, Andre Deutsch, 1979; Fontana 1980, pp. 467.

Detailed analysis of the evolution of the US war on Cambodia.

654.Sheehan, Neil et al., <u>The Pentagon Papers as published by the New York Times</u>, New York, Bantam Books, 1971, pp. 677.

655.Wintle, Justin, <u>The Vietnam Wars</u>, London, Weidenfeld & Nicolson, 1991, pp. 202.

A brief history and analysis of the wars in Vietnam from the 1945 declaration of independence to the US withdrawal in 1973.

a. General

656.Arrowsmith, Pat, <u>To Asia in Peace: The Story of a Non-Violent Action Mission to Indo-China</u>, London, Sidgwick and Jackson, 1972, pp. 188.

Account by participants in British team demonstrating opposition to US war in Vietnam and its extension to Cambodia. The team planned to share the hazards of US bombing in the hope of deterring it. They were received in Cambodia (but not North Vietnam); some later demonstrated at a US base in Thailand.

657.Dumbrell, John (ed.), <u>Vietnam and the Antiwar Movement: An International Perspective</u>, Aldershot, Avebury, 1989, pp. 182.

Chapters include: 'Kent State: How the war in Vietnam became a war at home'; 'Congress and the anti-war movement'; 'US presidential campaigns in the Vietnam era'; 'Opposing the war in Vietnam – the Australian experience'; 'Vietnam war resisters in Quebec'; 'Anger and after -Britain's CND and the Vietnam war'.

658.Feinberg, Abraham L., Hanoi Diary, Ontario, Longmans, 1968, pp. 258.

Rabbi Feinberg's account of his participation in a mission to North Vietnam in 1966-67 to investigate and publicize the effects of the US bombing. The other participants in the mission were the veteran US pacifist A.J. Muste, Rev. Martin Niemoeller, incarcerated in Dachau during part of World War II for opposing Hitler, and Rt Rev Ambrose Reeves, former Bishop of Johannesburg, exiled for speaking out against apartheid.

659.Weiss, Peter and Ken Coates (eds.), Prevent the Crime of Silence. Reports from the sessions of the International War Crimes Tribunal founded by Bertrand Russell, London, Allen Lane, 1971, pp. 384.

See also: Young, An Infantile Disorder, frequent references to New Left opposition to war in US and UK, including critique in chapter 9 'Vietnam and alignment', pp. 163-88 (G.1.a.), and Prasad, War is a Crime Against Humanity: the Story of War Resisters' International, pp. 371-385, (G.3.a) which also includes in full the eloquent WRI Statement on Wars of Liberation.

b. Australia

660.Forward, R and B. Reece, Conscription in Australia, Brisbane, University of Queensland Press, 1968,

See chapter 4, 'Conscription, 1964-1968'.

661.Hammel-Greene, M.E., 'The resisters: A history of the anti-conscription movement 1964-1972' in P. King, (ed.), Australia's Vietnam, Sydney, Allen and Unwin, 1983.

662.Noone, Val, Disturbing the War: Melbourne Catholics and Vietnam, Richmond VIC, Australia Spectrum, 1993, pp. 333.

663.Summy, Ralph V., 'Militancy and the Australian peace movement 1960-67', Politics (Journal of the Australasian Studies Association), vol. 5 no 2 (November 1970).

664.York, Barry, 'Power to the young' in Verity Burgmann and Jenny Lee (eds.), Staining the Wattle: A People's History of Australia, Ringwood VIC, McPhee Gribble/ Penguin Books, 1988, pp. 228-42.

c. South Vietnam (Buddhists)

Opposition to the war within South Vietnam was dramatized in particular by Buddhist monks, but students and academics also protested.

665.Halberstam, David, The Making of a Quagmire, London, The Bodley Head, 1965, pp. 323.

Includes helpful information on the Buddhist resistance in 1963, see especially pp. 194-243, though there are some factual errors.

666.Roberts, Adam, 'Buddhism and politics in South Vietnam', World Today, vol. 21 no. 6 (June 1965), pp. 240-50.

Account of the 1963 Buddhist revolt, its origins and aftermath. See also later article by Roberts assessing the political potential of the Buddhists, 'The Buddhists, the war and the Vietcong', World Today, vol. 22 no. 5 (May 1966), pp. 214-22.

667.Thich Nhat Hanh, Lotus in a Sea of Fire, New York, Hill and Wang, 1967, pp. 128.

Puts Buddhist case.

668.Wirmark, Bo, The Buddhists in Vietnam: An Alternative View of the War – Introduction by Daniel Berrigan, Brussels, War Resisters' International, 1974, pp. 40.

d. USA

669.Bannan, John F. and Rosemary Bannan, Law, Morality and Vietnam: The Peace Militants and the Courts, Bloomington, Indiana University Press, 1974, pp. 241.

Explores the conflict between law and morality, and case for civil disobedience, with reference mainly to six well known prosecutions, including that of the Fort Hood Three (GIs who refused to be posted to Vietnam), Dr Spock and others in 1967-68 charged with conspiracy to violate draft laws, and Daniel and Philip Berrigan and five others who burnt draft files at Catonsville in 1968.

670.De Benedetti, Charles (with Charles Chatfield as assisting editor), The Antiwar Movement of the Vietnam Era, Syracuse NY, Syracuse University Press, 1990, pp. 495.

Detailed and well researched account of the movement. Includes a final chapter by Charles Chatfield analysing the strengths and weaknesses of the movement and the ways in which it influenced US policy. Concludes that anti-war activists contributed to the growth of public disaffection with the war but could not harness it, but that both Johnson and Nixon Administrations adapted their policies in response to pressure from dissenters.

671.Berrigan, Daniel, America is Hard to Find, London, S.P.C.K., 1973, pp. 191.

Poems, articles and letters from prison by Catholic radical priest who, with his brother Philip, was among the most persistent critics of the Vietnam war and American militarism, and pioneered the direct action 'Plowshares' campaigns in the USA.

672.Boardman, Elizabeth Jelinek, The Phoenix Trip: Notes on a Quaker Mission to Haiphong, Burnsville NC, Celo Press, 1985, pp. 174.

Diary of a participant in this defiance of the US prohibition on taking supplies to the Democratic Republic of Vietnam.

673.Boyle, Richard, The Flower of the Dragon: The Breakdown of the US Army in Vietnam, San Francisco CA, Ramparts Press, 1972, pp. 283.

Traces the growth of disillusionment with the war amongst American GIs and the increasingly militant opposition to it within the US forces.

674.Chatfield, Charles, 'Ironies of protest: Interpreting the American anti-Vietnam war movement' in Guido Gruenewald and Peter Van den Dungen (eds.), <u>Twentieth Century Peace Movements</u>, Lewiston NY, Edwin Mellen Press, 1995, pp. 198-208.

Argues that the radical left never had a cohesive centre and that when the movement appeared at its most confrontational, its liberal wing was working more effectively within the political system. Suggests the movement became associated with social and cultural iconoclasm, which appealed to section of the middle classes, but the broader public eventually opposed both the war and the antiwar protest, because 'both seemed to threaten the established social order'.

675.Ferber, Michael and Staughton Lynd, <u>The Resistance</u>, Boston, Beacon Press, 1971, pp. 300.

Chronicles the history of the radical wing engaged in collective burning of draft cards and other acts of defiance. Suggests that few thought draft resistance would affect the operational ability to prosecute the war, but activists did believe in its political impact. Cites columnist Walter Lippmann, who concluded that this was the first 20th century American war 'when it was fashionable not to go to war and entirely acceptable to avoid it'.

676.Foner, Philip S., <u>American Labor and the Indochina War: The Growth of Union Opposition</u>, New York, International Publishers, 1971, pp. 126. (New version entitled <u>US Labor and the Vietnam War</u> issued 1989.)

Traces the emergence of (belated) trade union opposition from a November 1967 conference in Chicago, attended by 523 trade unionists from 38 states and 63 international unions, which established the trade union division of the peace organization SANE. Includes a chapter on Labour-Student alliances.

677.Halstead, Fred, <u>Out Now! A Participant's Account of the American Movement Against the Vietnam War</u>, New York, Monad Press, 1978, pp. 759.

Traces the rise of the anti-Vietnam war movement, including accounts of the ideological and institutional rivalries between organizations, and covers all the major demonstrations and civil disobedience actions from the Students for a Democratic Society March on Washington in 1965 to US withdrawal from Vietnam in 1973.

678.Kasinsky, Renee Goldsmith, <u>Refugees from Militarism: Draft Age Americans in Canada</u>, New Brunswick NJ, Transaction Books, 1976, pp. 301.

Study of the lives and problems of draft resisters in Canada.

679.Lifton, Robert Jay, <u>Home from the War: Vietnam Veterans, Neither Victims Nor Executioners</u>, London, Wildwood Press, 1974, pp. 474.

Study by a psychiatrist of plight of anti-war Vietnam veterans. Includes accounts of some of their campaigning activities to expose the nature of the war and demand US withdrawal.

680. Lynd, Alice, We Won't Go: Personal Accounts of War Objectors, Boston, Beacon Press, 1988, pp. 332.

Deals with conscientious objection in US during the Vietnam war, 1961-1975.

681. Menashe, Louis and Ronald Radosh, Teach-ins, U.S.A.: Reports, Opinions, Documents, New York, Praeger, 1967, pp. 349.

Records how the Teach-In movement began modestly in a mid-West campus in 1965 but spread across the country, engaging many students and professors, and released a vast quantity of material about the Vietnam war.

682. Powers, Thomas, The War at Home: Vietnam and the American People, 1964-1968, Boston MA, G.K. Hall, 1984, pp. 348.

Argues that every kind of opposition to the war had some effect, but in general those methods that cost the most in a personal sense worked best. However, these sacrifices had most impact the first time or two, before the public came to accept and then ignore them. Concludes that opposition to the war did not cause its failure, but forced the government to recognize the failure.

683. Simons, Donald L., I Refuse: Memories of a Vietnam War Objector, Trenton NJ, Broken Rifle Press, 1997, pp. 184.

A personal account which includes a brief summary of the course of the war and statistics on the scale of draft resistance and desertion.

684. Small, Melvin, Covering Dissent: The Media and the Anti-Vietnam War Movement, New Brunswick NJ, Rutgers University Press, 1994, pp. 228.

685. Small, Melvin, Johnson, Nixon and the Doves, New Brunswick NJ and London, Rutgers University Press, 1988, pp. 319.

Focus on the presidents and their relationship with the Vietnam anti-war movements between 1961 and 1975.

686. Taylor, Clyde, Vietnam and Black America, New York, Anchor Books, 1993, pp. 335.

Includes essays, articles and poems by black opponents of the war, including Martin Luther King, James Baldwin, and (in a section 'The Black Soldier') extracts from the diaries of black GIs and the Statement of Aims of 'GIs United Against the War in Vietnam'. Taylor notes how the advice to African Americans from some leaders to 'prove themselves worthy' by taking part in the war in Vietnam became increasingly discredited.

687. Unseem, Michael, Conscription, Protest and Social Conflict: The Life and Death of a Draft Resistance Movement, New York, John Wiley, 1973, pp. 329.

A history and critical assessment of 'The Resistance' (to the draft) during the Vietnam war. The author argues that it failed to reach the necessary size to affect the viability of the draft, partly because it had little appeal to working class youth.

See also: Sale, SDS (G.1.e).

3. Peace Movements Since 1945

This section covers a wide range of campaigns against war, weapons and bases. It focuses particularly on protest in the West or countries allied to the West, but some issues such as nuclear testing have prompted opposition in the affected region (especially the Pacific). Other wars, such as those which broke up Yugoslavia, have prompted groups within the combatant countries to protest.

This section does *not* include the autonomous peace campaigns which began to emerge in the Soviet bloc in the 1980s (see Section C); resistance to war and internal repression in South Africa, or Israeli resistance to service in the Occupied Territories (see Section D) – although these may be referred to in some wideranging surveys of conscientious objection under G.3.b.ii.

a. General: National and Transnational Movements

688. Brock, Peter and Nigel Young, Pacifism in the Twentieth Century, Syracuse NY, Syracuse University Press, 1999, pp. 434. Revised and updated version of Peter Brock, Twentieth Century Pacifism, 1970, Van Nostrand Reinhold.

History of opposition to war drawing primarily on US and British experience, but including material on Gandhi and the later Gandhian movement, assessments of the position of conscientious objectors in many parts of the world, and references to transnational organizations, e.g. the War Resisters' International. Although the focus is on pacifism, the book includes material on the role of pacifists in the nuclear disarmament and anti-Vietnam War movements.

689. Bussey, Gertrude and Margaret Tims, Pioneers for Peace: Women's International League for Peace and Freedom 1915-1965, London, WILPF British Section, 1980, pp. 255.

History of first 50 years of transnational body campaigning against war and for disarmament, which opposed NATO and nuclear weapons, was active (especially in the US) in resisting the Vietnam War and promotes social justice and reconciliation.

690. Carter, April, Peace Movements: International Protest and World Politics Since 1945, London, Longman, 1992, pp. 283.

Particular focus on European and North American movements against nuclear weapons in the 1950s-60s and 1980s and East European responses in the 1980s. But other nuclear disarmament protests, peace campaigns on other issues and nonviolent initiatives in other parts of the world are indicated more briefly.

691. Flessati, Valerie, Pax: The History of a Catholic Peace Society in Britain 1936-1971, University of Bradford, PhD Thesis, 1991, pp. 535 (in 2 vols).

Detailed historical study of both Pax and the Catholic element in the British peace movement. Pax from the outset opposed war under modern conditions as contrary to traditional just war teaching, a stance underlined by the development of nuclear weapons. Influenced Catholic thinking about modern war and the decision of the Second Vatican Council to recognize the right to conscientious objection and to call upon states to make provision for it.

692.Gress, David, <u>Peace and Survival: West Germany, the Peace Movement and European Security</u>, Stanford CA, Hoover Institution Press, 1985, pp. 266.

693.Howorth, Jolyon and Patricia Chilton (eds.), <u>Defence and Dissent in Contemporary France</u>, London, Croom Helm, 1984, pp. 264.

Part 1 covers France's defence policy since 1945 – including the wars in Indo-China and Algeria, and De Gaulle's decision (supported by the major political parties) to develop a French nuclear bomb. Part 2 focuses on anti-nuclear critiques and movements in the 1980s, including a military critique of French defence policy by Admiral Sanguinetti and Claude Bourdet on the 'The rebirth of the peace movement'.

694.Locke, Elsie, <u>Peace People – A History of Peace Activity in New Zealand</u>, Christchurch and Melbourne, Hazard Press, 1992, pp. 335.

Chronicles peace activities in New Zealand from Maori time and early colonial settlement to the anti-Vietnam war movement and anti-nuclear campaigns of the 1960s and 1970s. Includes accounts of the direct action protests against French nuclear tests in 1972.

695.Meaden, Bernadette, <u>Protesting for Peace</u>, Glasgow, Wild Goose Publications, 1999, pp. 151.

Sympathetic coverage of a wide range of campaigns in Britain – Greenham Common, Trident Ploughshares, the arms trade, British troops in Northern Ireland, US bases, the 'peace tax', and opposition to the (first) Gulf War.

696.<u>Pacific Women Speak-Out for Independence and Denuclearisation</u>, Christchurch, Women's International Legaue for Peace and Freedom, 1998, pp. 80.

Indigenous women from Australia, Aotearoa (New Zealand), Belau, Bougainville, East Timor, Ka Pa'aina (Hawaii), the Marshall Islands, Te Ao Maohi (French Polynesia) and West Papua (Irian Jaya) condemn imperialism, war, 'nuclear imperialism' (in the form of nuclear tests) and military bases in the hope 'that when people around the world learn what is happening in the Pacific they will be inspired to stand beside them and to act'. The book is a contribution to the Hague Appeal for Peace, 1999.

697.Peace, Roger C., <u>A Just and Lasting Peace: The US Peace Movement from the Cold War to Desert Storm</u>, Chicago IL, The Noble Press, 1991, pp. 345.

Peace, a writer/activist, documents the growth of the peace and justice movement in the US, with particular focus on the 1980s. Areas covered include anti-nuclear campaigning and campaigns for justice in Latin America. Discusses also debates and controversies within the movement.

698.Prasad, Devi, <u>War is a Crime Against Humanity: The Story of War Resisters' International</u>, London, War Resisters' International, 2005, pp. 560.

A history of the first 50 plus years of the organization (1921-1973).

699.Taylor, Richard and Nigel Young (eds.), <u>Campaigns for Peace: British Peace Movements in the Twentieth Century</u>, Manchester, Manchester University Press, 1987, pp. 308.

Collection of analytical and descriptive essays spanning period from late 19th century to 1980s, but the main focus is on post-World War II movement against nuclear weapons. Michael Randle assesses 'Nonviolent direct action in the 1950s and 1960s', pp. 131-61.

Much of the information about peace protest and nonviolent direct action is to be found in movement newsletters or journals, though some of these are transient. Long-running peace periodicals are:

Peace News, London, which has transnational interests but particularly covers Britain; The Nonviolent Activist (since 1984) and Fellowship in the USA. The Bulletin of the Atomic Scientists, although primarily a socially concerned journal covering scientific and strategic issues, has carried articles on peace campaigns. Peace and Change (published by Sage) is an academic journal which examines peace campaigns and activity.

b. Pacifist Protest, Conscientious Objection and Draft Resistance

Conscientious objection to taking part in or supporting war has for a long time been associated in the west with particular religious beliefs. Since the Reformation protestant groups such as the Quakers, Anabaptists, Mennonites and Dukhobors have consistently refused military service. In past centuries some emigrated from Europe or Russia to North America to avoid conscription.

In the 20th century, although religious objectors to military service, such as Jehovah's Witnesses, have played a heroic role in resisting enforced military service in dictatorships, and a small but significant Catholic pacifist movement has also developed, there has been a growth of individual conscientious objection based on humanist beliefs. There have also been significant movements based on socialist or anarchist objections to capitalist wars, and major campaigns against participation in wars viewed as imperialist, racist, aggressive, illegal under international law or in any other way unjust. Many western states, especially since the end of the cold war, no longer require general conscription, but reservists or serving soldiers have also sometimes refused to take part in a particular war – as for example in the 1991 Gulf War.

Liberal democratic states have increasingly recognized the right to be a conscientious objector (CO) – and this has been reflected by many intergovernmental bodies, including the UN Human Rights Commission – and gradually extended the definition of conscience beyond religious beliefs. But militant resisters have rejected recognition of the state's right to demand alternative civilian service, and have committed themselves to total resistance. Open draft resistance has often occurred alongside draft evasion – many young US citizens crossed the border into Canada during the Vietnam War – and desertion from the forces. One important role for organized peace groups, nationally and transnationally, has been to provide legal information, advice and support.

Refusing military service is limited to those of military age and until very recently has been limited to young men, but some have also seen conscientious refusal to pay taxes for war as a relevant form of protest. Moreover, in national campaigns against particular wars, prominent individuals have encouraged defiance of the draft or even desertion by signing subversive manifestoes, or have taken direct action at recruitment offices. Some examples of conscientious objection and draft resistance have been covered in sections above, see for example C (where antimilitarist opposition to Communist regimes has been included), D (South Africa and Israel), and G.2 (Movement Against the Vietnam War).

There is a large literature on pacifism, much of it not directly relevant here. Selective references dealing with pacifist beliefs, with transnational and national organizations and campaigns against conscription, with the experiences of COs and draft resisters, and analyses of the legal position are listed below. We also include a couple of references to just war theory, influential in opposition to many wars, but critical of pure pacifism.

i. Pacifist and Nonviolent Thought

700.American Friends Service Committee, <u>Speak Truth to Power: A Quaker Search for an Alternative to Violence</u>, Philadelphia PA, AFSC, 1955, pp. 71.

Manifesto outlining a nonviolent approach to international politics and social change. Influenced the thinking of radical direct actionists in the US and Britain.

701.Ceadel, Martin, <u>Thinking about Peace and War</u>, Oxford, Oxford University Press, 1987, pp. 222.

A frequently cited analysis and classification of different ways of thinking about war, which examines 5 'ideal types' of 'militarism', 'crusading', 'defencism', 'pacific-ism' (representing many ideological and organizational strands within peace movements), and 'pacifism'.

702.Childress, James F., <u>Moral Responsibility in Conflicts: Essays on Nonviolence, War and Conflict</u>, Baton Rouge, Louisiana State University Press, 1982, pp. 224.

Includes chapters on conscientious objection and Reinhold Niebuhr on violent and nonviolent methods.

703.Hentoff, Nat (ed.), <u>The Essays of A.J. Muste</u>, New York, Simon and Schuster, 1967, pp. 515.

Essays on revolution, nonviolence and pacifism by a key figure on US radical/pacifist left, from 1905 to 1966, commenting in later essays on conscientious objection, opposition to French nuclear tests in Africa, the Civil Rights movement and the opposition to the Vietnam War.

704.Mayer, Peter (ed.), <u>The Pacifist Conscience</u>, Harmondsworth, Penguin, 1966, pp. 447.

Collection of writings on war, pacifism and nonviolence from 500 BC to 1960 AD, but emphasis on more modern figures, such as William Lloyd Garrison, Thoreau, Tolstoy, Gandhi, Simone Weil and Albert Camus. Includes also Martin Buber's criticism of Gandhi for advocating nonviolent resistance by Jews to Hitler, and Reinhold Niebuhr's reasons for leaving the (pacifist) Fellowship of Reconciliation.

705.Merton, Thomas, <u>The Nonviolent Alternative</u>, ed. Gordon C. Zahn, New York, Farrar Strauss Giroux, 1980, pp. 270.

Collection of essays by well-know Catholic thinker on war, peace and nonviolence.

706.Teichman, Jenny, <u>Pacifism and the Just War: A Study in Applied Philosophy</u>, Oxford, Blackwell, 1986, pp. 138.

Discussion of pacifist theory and major objections to it from a just war perspective.

707.Unnithan, T.K.N. and Yogendra Singh, <u>Traditions of Nonviolence</u>, New Delhi and London, Arnold-Heinemann, 1973, pp. 317.

Examines nonviolent traditions in Hindu, Chinese, Islamic and Judeo-Christian thought.

708.Walzer, Michael, <u>Just and Unjust Wars: A Moral Argument with Historical Illustrations</u>, Harmondsworth, Penguin, 1980, pp. 359.

Highly regarded interpretation of just war theory. See also his earlier essays on war and disobedience, including an essay on conscientious objection in: <u>Obligations: Essays on Disobedience, War and Citizenship</u>, Cambridge MA, Harvard University Press, 1970, pp. 244.

ii. Conscientious Resistance and Legal Frameworks

709.Amnesty International, <u>Out of the Margins: The Right to Conscientious Objection to Military Service in Europe</u>, London, Amnesty, 1997, pp. 61.

Surveys provisions for conscientious objection to military service, and expresses particular concern in relation to treatment of COs in some countries. Recommends the release of all COs in prison, that all member states of EU and Council of Europe re-examine their legislation regarding conscientious objection, and that the EU include in the criteria for membership the recognition of conscientious objection and provisions for alternative service 'of non-punitive length'.

710.Biesemans, Sam, <u>The Right to Conscientious Objection and the European Parliament</u>, Brussels, European Board for Conscientious Objection, 1995, pp. 109.

Urges incorporation of right to conscientious objection in national constitutions, and the European Convention of Human Rights and Fundamental Freedoms.

711.Blatt, Martin, Uri Davis and Paul Kleinbaum (eds.), <u>Dissent and Ideology in Israel: Resistance to the Draft, 1948-1973</u>, London, Ithaca Press for Housmans Bookshop, WRI, Middle East Research Group (MERAG) and Lansbury House Trust Fund, 1975, pp. 194.

Accounts by Israeli conscientious objectors of their experience and the reasons for their stance. Editors relate these to a critique of Zionism.

712.Braithwaite, Constance, with Geoffrey Braithwaite, <u>Conscientious Objection to Compulsions Under the Law</u>, York, William Sessions, 1995, pp. 421.

History of conscientious objection to compliance with various legal provisions involving compulsion of citizens, including taking of oaths, vaccination and religious education. Chapter on ethical and political problems related to conscientious objections takes the form of imaginary dialogue between author and a critic of her thesis.

713.Brock, Peter, 'These Strange Criminals': An Anthology of Prison Memoirs by Conscientious Objectors from the Great War to the Cold War, Toronto, University of Toronto Press, 2004, pp. 505.

Anthology of prison memoirs by conscientious objectors from World War I to the Cold War. Contributions from Britain, Canada, New Zealand and the USA.

714.Evans, Cecil, The Claims of Conscience: Quakers and Conscientious Objection to Taxation for Military Purposes, London, Quaker Home Service, 1966, pp. 51.

715.Fifth International Conference on War Tax Resistance and Peace Tax Campaigns and Founding Assembly of Conscience and Peace Tax International: Hondarribia, September 16-19 1994, Pamplona-Irunea, Asamblea de Objecion Fiscal de Navarra, 1994, pp. 111.

Text of contributions, workshop reports and summaries of discussions. Conscience and Peace Tax International was established in Brussels as a non-profit association under Belgian law.

716.Flynn, Eileen P, My Country Right or Wrong: Selective Conscientious Objection in the Nuclear Age, Chicago, Loyola University Press, 1985, pp. 98.

Discusses varieties of conscientious objection, from pacifist objection to all wars, selective objection to particular wars considered unjust and objection to indiscriminate and, most notably, nuclear warfare. Includes a discussion of just war principles.

717.Horeman, Bart and Marc Stolwijk, Refusing to Bear Arms: A World Survey of Conscription and Conscientious Objection to Military Service, War Resisters International, 1998, pp. 310. (Ringbinder format for ease of update.) Foreword Devi Prasad.

The most authoritative country by country survey of the position on conscription and conscientious objection in all member states of the UN, following the same formula in each case and setting out legal possibilities for avoiding military service. Historical overview of the evolution of conscription and conscientious objection appended to many country reports. There are also often additional sections on forced recruitment by non-governmental armed groups. Each report is dated. The online version includes April 2005 updates on most of the countries in the Council of Europe, see http:// www.wri-irg.org/co/rtba/index.html

718.Moskos, Charles C and John Whiteclay Chambers II (eds.), The New Conscientious Objection: From Sacred to Secular Resistance, New York and Oxford, Oxford University Press, 1993, pp. 286.

Section 1 suggests 'the secularisation of conscience and modern individualism have been the driving force' in the rise of conscientious objection. Section 2 looks at the historical record in the USA. Section 3 has articles on France, the Federal Republic of

Germany, Denmark, Norway, Switzerland, the former Communist states in Eastern Europe, Israel and South Africa.

(NB chapter on South Africa listed under D.I.1.a.).

719.Pentikainen, Merja (ed.), <u>The Right to Refuse Military Orders</u>, Geneva, International Peace Bureau in collaboration with International Association of Lawyers Against Nuclear Arms, Peace Union of Finland and Finnish Lawyers for Peace and Survival, 1994, pp. 110.

Contributions on various forms of refusal – to do military service, to fire at one's own people, to participate in torture, or to accept orders relating to nuclear weapons – together with summaries of relevant international law.

720.Quaker Council for European Affairs, <u>Conscientious Objection to Military Service in Europe</u>, Report for the Council of Europe, Parliamentary Assembly, Legal Affairs Committee, 1984, pp. 99.

Sets out the legal provision for COs in all the European states at that date. Notes the importance of resolutions in support of making provisions for COs adopted by the Council of Europe in 1967, the UN in 1978 and the European Parliament in 1983.

721.Quaker Peace and Service, <u>Taxes for Peace Not War: 6th International Conference on Peace Tax Campaigns and War Tax Resistance</u>, London, Quaker Peace and Service, 1997, pp. 51.

Assesses the impact of peace tax campaigns in the area of peacemaking and considers their possible future influence.

722.Rohr, John A, <u>Prophets Without Honor: Public Policy and the Selective Conscientious Objector</u>, Nashville and New York, Abingdon Press, 1971, pp. 191.

Examines lack of a constitutional right or political tolerance for selective refusal to take part in particular wars.

723.Schlissel, Lillian, <u>Conscience in America: A Documentary History of Conscientious Objection in America, 1757-1967</u>, New York, E.P. Dutton, 1968, pp. 444.

Documents and statements on conscientious objection, later sections cover COs in two world wars and Vietnam, and case for tax resistance.

724.War Resisters' International and Green Alternative European Link, <u>Refusing War Preparations: Conscientious Objection and Non-cooperation: International Seminar Brussels, 76-10 February 1981</u>, London, War Resisters' International and Brussels, Green Alternatives European Link, 1987, pp. 95.

Contributors from six European countries and the US look at non-cooperation in relation to different aspects of militarism. Emphasis of seminar is on 'collective non-cooperation … people acting together to frustrate militarism'. Includes text of Bart de Ligt's Anti-War Plan first presented in 1934 to WRI (also published in De Ligt, <u>Conquest of Violence</u> – A.1.).

See also: Brock and Young, <u>Pacifism in the Twentieth Century</u> (G.3.a.); Muste, A.J., 'Of holy disobedience', in Hentoff (ed.), <u>Essays of A.J. Muste</u>, pp. 355-77, on case for total resistance to conscription as opposed to alternative civilian service (G.3.b.1).

c. Opposition to Nuclear Weapons since the 1950s

After 1945 the invention of nuclear weapons created a new peril, dramatized by Hiroshima and Nagasaki, that gradually aroused widespread public concern. This concern was exacerbated from the mid-1950s by growing awareness of the dangers to health and the environment caused by the testing of nuclear bombs in the atmosphere.

But development of atomic and then hydrogen bombs, and later of nuclear missiles, was also a product of the arms race between the United States and the Soviet Union, and the deep distrust generated by the cold war. Once both sides had nuclear weapons, developing strategic doctrines of the necessity of deterrence made opposition to US (or British) weapons more politically sensitive. The fact that the Soviet Union mobilized a worldwide 'peace campaign' against nuclear weapons in the early 1950s also meant that in the most frigid period of the cold war western peace protests were almost automatically seen by governments and the media as pro-Soviet. (How far these campaigns, which undoubtedly drew in many non-Communists concerned about the dangers of nuclear war, should be seen as part of the overall peace movement is disputed.)

A strong explicitly nonaligned movement against nuclear weapons, linked in Britain to the Campaign for Nuclear Disarmament (CND), did not therefore develop until 1957/58. The 'first wave' of the nuclear disarmament movement in the late 1950s and early 1960s resulted in mass marches and a wide variety of nonviolent direct action protests against nuclear testing sites, nuclear bases and installations and government buildings. In some cases (as in West Germany) protest originated on the organized left, in others popular protest impacted on trade unions and leftist political parties, leading for example to a unilateralist resolution being passed by the British Labour Party Conference in 1960. The debate also spread to the churches and raised the question whether nuclear weapons were compatible with the doctrine of just war. The 1963 Partial Test Ban Treaty, signed initially by the USA, Soviet Union and Britain, could be interpreted as a success for the movement, and the USA and USSR began to engage more seriously in a series of arms control negotiations.

By the late 1960s many campaigners had turned their energies to opposing the Vietnam War. During the 1970s environmental protests came to the fore, though concern about nuclear energy sometimes linked up with opposition to nuclear weapons. A second mobilization of mass opposition to nuclear weapons was sparked by US proposals to deploy the neutron bomb and by the NATO decision to deploy cruise and Pershing II missiles – Intermediate Nuclear Forces (INF) – in Western Europe. The campaigns of the 1980s had greater transnational reach, involved many more people than the 'first wave' of the movement, and influenced the policy of some local councils and regions. The role of the European Nuclear Disarmament (END) campaign in promoting a dialogue between western peace campaigners and East European and Soviet dissidents also opened up a new dimension.

The use of nonviolent direct action was even more widespread in the 1980s than in the 1950s/60s, and less controversial within the movement. There were, for example, many sitdowns and peace camps at bases. There was also widespread transnational cooperation, for example at the peace camp at the Comiso missile base in Sicily. The legality of nuclear weapons under international law was frequently raised in the courts. Some of the most militant actions, for example at the Greenham Common cruise missile base, are also associated with radical feminism and have been listed under the Feminist Movement, section G.4.

Although the nuclear disarmament movement has lost momentum since the break-up of the Soviet Union and the end of the cold war, the dangers from nuclear weapons and proliferation ensure that campaigning continues. There are still frequent nonviolent direct action demonstrations in Britain, for example at nuclear bases and installations.

There is a large literature on the nuclear disarmament movement. The titles below include assessments from a range of ideological perspectives, but many of them have been chosen because they give some prominence to forms of direct action and civil disobedience.

i. Theoretical Debates about Nuclear Weapons

There is an immense literature on strategic thinking about nuclear weapons since the late 1950s, as theories of deterrence and arms control evolved and as missile deployments and strategic rationales altered over time. The titles selected here focus on moral, political and strategic arguments which influenced campaigners. But a well-regarded survey of official nuclear policies is: Mandelbaum, Michael, The Nuclear Question: The United States and Nuclear Weapons 1946-1976, Cambridge, Cambridge University Press, 1979.

725.Boulton, David (ed.), Voices from the Crowd: Against the H-Bomb, London, Peter Owen, 1964, pp. 185.

Collection of essays, many by leading writers and thinkers of the period, including Albert Schweitzer, Bertrand Russell, J.B. Priestley, Herbert Read and Michael Foot. Includes first hand account of six anti-nuclear campaigners charged under the Official Secrets Act for their part in organizing direct action at a USAF base.

726.Church of England, Board of Social Responsibility, The Church and the Bomb: Nuclear Weapons and Christian Conscience. The Report of the Working Party under the Chairmanship of the Bishop of Salisbury, London, Hodder and Stoughton, 1982, pp. 190.

Influential report which concluded that Just War principles forbid the use of nuclear weapons, and recommended that the UK should renounce its independent nuclear deterrent, followed by a phased withdrawal from other forms of reliance on nuclear weapons including, ultimately, the presence of US air and submarine bases.

727.Holroyd, Fred (ed.), Thinking about Nuclear Weapons: Analyses and Prescriptions, London, Croom Helm in association with the Open University, 1985, pp. 409.

Covers a range of perspectives on nuclear weapons. Includes influential McGeorge Bundy/Kennan/McNamara/Smith article 'Nuclear weapons and the Atlantic Alliance', Foreign Affairs, vol. 60, 1982, arguing that NATO should not use nuclear weapons in response to a conventional attack. Also includes section from the Alternative Defence Commission report on 'The rationale for rejecting nuclear weapons', as well as an extract from Edward P. Thompson's 1980 pamphlet Protest and Survive (see below).

728.Schell, Jonathan, The Abolition, London, Picador in association with Jonathan Cape, 1984, pp. 170.

Definition of the nuclear predicament and radical proposals for the abolition of all nuclear weapons.

729.Stein, Walter (ed.), Nuclear Weapons and Christian Conscience, London, Merlin Press, 1961 and 1981, pp. 163. With foreword by Archbishop Roberts.

Essays by six leading Catholic thinkers on the moral issues raised by nuclear weapons. Had considerable influence in Christian and wider circles. The 1981 edition has a postscript by Anthony Kenny on Counterforce and Countervalue nuclear doctrines.

730.Thompson, Edward P., Protest and Survive, Campaign for Nuclear Disarmament and Bertrand Russell Peace Foundation, 1980, pp. 33.

This polemic, whose title was prompted by government civil defence advice 'Protect and Survive', provided considerable impetus to the rejuvenated nuclear disarmament movement of the 1980s, and the launch of the European Nuclear Disarmament (END) campaign in which Thompson played a leading role.

731.Urquhart, Clara (ed.), A Matter of Life, London, Jonathan Cape, 1963, pp. 256.

A collection of brief essays or speeches by eminent proponents of peace or nonviolence on dangers facing the world and role of civil disobedience. Contributors include Martin Buber, Danilo Dolci, Erich Fromm, Kenneth Kaunda, Jawaharlal Nehru and Albert Schweitzer. There are essays by founding members of the Committee of 100: Bertrand Russell, Michael Scott and Robert Bolt.

732.US Bishops, The Challenge of Peace: God's Promise and our Response: The US Bishops' Pastoral Letter on War and Peace in the Nuclear Age, London, CTS/SPCK, 1983, pp. 34.

Influential Catholic document. Argues that 'a justifiable use of force must be both discriminatory and proportionate' and that 'certain aspects of both US and Soviet strategies fail both tests'. Urged greater consideration of nonviolent means of resistance whilst upholding the right of governments to conscript (with provision for general or selective objection).

ii. Comparative and General Studies

733.Evangelista, Matthew, Unarmed Forces: The Transnational Movement to End the Cold War, Ithaca NY, Columbia University Press, 1999, pp. 406.

Well documented examination of the role of transnational civil movements in contributing to arms control and the ending of the Cold War. Includes assessment of the Pugwash Conference which brought together scientists from East and West, and also the wider anti-war movement.

734.Kaltefleiter, Werner and Robert L. Pfaltzgraff (eds.), <u>Peace Movements in Europe and the United States</u>, London, Croom Helm, 1985, pp. 211.

Essays arising out of May 1984 conference at the Christian-Albrechts University, Kiel, on peace movements in Sweden, Norway, the Netherlands, West Germany, France, Italy, Britain and the US.

Focus is on the anti-nuclear movements of the 1980s, though some contributors sketch the earlier history of movements in their countries.

735.Laqueur, Walter and Robert Edwards Hunter (eds.), <u>European Peace Movements and the Future of the Western Alliance</u>, New Brunswick, Transaction Books in association with the Center for Strategic and International Studies, Georgetown University, Washington DC, 1985, pp. 450.

Generally critical contributions on the peace movements of the 1980s in various European countries and their impact on the Western alliance. Includes chapter on the US peace movement of the 1980s.

736.Rochon, Thomas R., <u>Mobilizing for Peace</u>, Princeton NJ, Princeton University Press, 1988, pp. 232.

Wide ranging analysis of West European anti-missile/nuclear disarmament campaigns 1979-1986, incorporating discussion of social movement theory and the wider political context. Focuses particularly on Britain, the Netherlands, West Germany and France. It includes great deal of information on organizations, campaigns and types of action, as well as many useful sources and references.

737.Wittner, Lawrence S., <u>The Struggle Against the Bomb</u>, vol. 1.

<u>One World or None: A History of the World Nuclear Disarmament Movement Through 1953</u>, Stanford CA, Stanford University Press, 1993, pp. 456.

Covers responses to the Bomb from 1945-1953, including by scientists and churches, but with emphasis on the Soviet-initiated protests under the World Peace Council.

738.Wittner, Lawrence S., vol. 2. <u>Resisting the Bomb: A History of the World Nuclear Disarmament Movement 1954-1970</u>, vol. 2, Stanford CA, Stanford University Press, 1997, pp. 641.

Extensive and thoroughly researched history of campaigns and governments responses, including Japan, with quite a lot of material on nonviolent direct action.

739.Wittner, Lawrence, <u>Towards Nuclear Abolition: A History of the World Nuclear Disarmament Movement 1971 to the the Present</u>, vol. 3, Stanford CA, Stanford University Press, 2003, pp. 657.

Traces the development of the movement in the 1970s, the rise of a new activism in the 1980s, the 'breakthrough' of the Intermediate Range Nuclear Forces (INF)

Agreement of 1987, and the end of the cold war. While noting later more worrying trends, Wittner concludes that 'This study – like its predecessors – indicates that the nuclear arms control and disarmament measures of the modern era have resulted primarily from the efforts of a worldwide citizens' campaign, the biggest mass movement in modern history'.

iii. Studies of Particular Countries, Campaigns or Actions

740.Baxendale, Martin, <u>Cruisewatch: Civil Resistance against American Nuclear Cruise Missile Convoys in the English Countryside: 1984-1990</u>, Stroud, Silent but Deadly, c1991, pp. 41.

741.Bigelow, Albert, <u>The Voyage of the Golden Rule: An Experiment with Truth</u>, Garden City NY, Doubleday, 1959, pp. 286.

Account by former Lieutenant in the US navy of an attempt by four people to sail a ketch into the US nuclear testing zone at Eniwetok in protest against the tests. Defying an injunction, the ketch sailed 5 miles into the zone before being stopped by US navy. Their example inspired a second attempt by Earle and Barbara Reynolds (see <u>The Forbidden Voyage</u> below).

742.Bradshaw, Ross, Dennis Gould and Chris Jones, <u>From Protest to Resistance</u>, Nottingham, Mushroom, 1981, pp. 64 (<u>Peace News</u> pamphlet).

Story of the rise of direct action against nuclear weapons in the British context. Includes diary of main protest in the 1957-1966 period, and interviews with those involved.

743.Breyman Steven, <u>Why Movements Matter: The West German Peace Movement and U.S. Arms Control Policy</u>, Albany NY, State University of New York Press, 2001, pp. 359.

Charts the evolution of the movement from 1979 to deployment of missiles in Germany at the end of 1983, linking accounts of major protests in West Germany to internal political developments and US/USSR negotiations. The final chapter assesses the impact of the movement and its relation to the INF Treaty.

744.Cairns, Brendan, 'Stop the drop', in Verity Burgmann and Jenny Lee (eds.), <u>Staining the Wattle</u>, Ringwood VIC, McPhee Gribble/Penguin Books, 1988, pp. 243-53.

On the 1980s revived movement against nuclear weapons, in particular Australia's People for Nuclear Disarmament.

745.Carter, April 'The Sahara Protest Team' in Hare and Blumberg (eds.), <u>Liberation Without Violence</u>, pp. 126-56 (A.4.).

On a transnational expedition in 1959-60 attempting to prevent French nuclear tests in the Algerian Sahara.

746.Deming, Barbara, 'Earle Reynolds: Stranger in this country' in <u>Revolution and Equilibrium</u>, pp. 124-35 (A.1.).

On the transnational protests by the ship 'Everyman III' which sailed from London to Leningrad to protest against Soviet nuclear tests.

747.Driver, Christopher, <u>The Disarmers: A Study in Protest</u>, London, Hodder and Stoughton, 1964, pp. 256.

Account of the emergence of the Campaign for Nuclear Disarmament, Direct Action Committee Against Nuclear War and the Committee of 100 in Britain. Describes the main actions and internal debates within the movement.

748.Faslane Peace Camp, <u>Faslane: Diary of a Peace Camp</u>, Edinburgh, 1984, pp. 86.

Account of direct action campaign against Trident missile base in Scotland.

749.Hinton, James, <u>Protests and Visions: Peace Politics in 20th Century Britain</u>, London, Hutchinson Radius, 1989, pp. 248.

Covers pacifist and anti-war campaigning in Britain from the 'imperialist pacifism' of the Victorian period, through both World Wars to the birth of the Campaign for Nuclear Disarmament and the New Left in the 1950s and 1960s. Written from a democratic socialist perspective. Final chapters cover CND's 'second wave' in the 1980s, the Gorbachev initiatives, and the role of the European Nuclear Disarmament campaign seeking to transcend the cold war divide.

750.Hudson, Kate, <u>Now More than Ever</u>, London, Vision Paperbacks, Satin Publishers, Sheena Dewan, 2005, pp. 278.

Up to date account of British nuclear disarmament movement since the 1950s by chair of CND, giving some weight to direct action.

751.Jezer, Marty, <u>Where Do We Go From Here? Tactics and Strategies for the Peace Movement</u>, New York, A.J. Muste Institute, 1984, pp. 74.

Answers by range of peace activists to questions about the future of the movement, including whether it should focus on the arms race or more broadly on US foreign policy, its relationship to electoral politics, the role of civil disobedience and issues related to feminist separatism.

752.McCrea, Frances B. and Gerald E. Markle, <u>Minutes to Midnight: Nuclear Weapons Protest in America 1950s-80s</u>, Newbury Park CA, Sage, 1989, pp. 200.

753.McTaggart, David and Robert Hunter, <u>Greenpeace III: The Journey into the Bomb</u>, London, Collins, 1978, pp. 372.

Leading Greenpeace activists recount how their boat succeeded in sailing into the French nuclear testing zone near Mururoa Atoll in 1971, forcing the French government to halt one of its planned nuclear tests.

754.Mitcalfe, Barry, <u>Boy Roel: Voyage to Nowhere</u>, Auckland, New Zealand, Alister Taylor, 1972, pp. 154.

Diary of events aboard Boy Roel, one of the fleet of four ships, including Greenpeace III, which attempted to sail into French nuclear testing zone near Mururoa Atoll in 1972.

755.Muste, A.J. 'Africa against the Bomb' in Hentoff (ed.), Essays of A.J. Muste, pp. 394-409 (G.3.b.1.).

On attempts by transnational team to enter French Sahara testing area from Ghana.

756.Reynolds, Earle, The Forbidden Voyage, Westport CT, Greenwood Press, 1975, pp. 281.

Earle and Barbara Reynolds lived in Hiroshima, where he was studying effects of atomic radiation, from 1951-1954. In 1958, whilst cruising on their yacht the Phoenix of Hiroshima, they heard about the arrest of Bigelow's Golden Rule protesting against US testing (see above) and later that year sailed 65 nautical miles inside the Bikini Atoll testing zone.

757.Robie, David, Eyes of Fire: The Last Voyage of the Rainbow Warrior, Philadelphia PA, New Society Publishers, [1986] 2005 2nd edition. pp. 180.

Account of final voyage of Greenpeace ship the Rainbow Warrior, trying to sail into French nuclear testing area near Mururoa Atoll, before it was blown up by French secret service agents in Auckland Harbour July 1985. See also: Sunday Times Insight Team, Rainbow Warrior: The French Attempt to Sink Greenpeace, London, 1986, pp. 302.

758.Robson, Bridget Mary, What Part did Nonviolence Play in the British Peace Movement 1979-1985?, MA Dissertation, Bradford, 1992, pp. 89.

Recounts debates surrounding the use of direct action and civil disobedience in anti-nuclear campaigns, noting the influence of New Left politics and feminism and the rise of nonviolence training, affinity groups and peace camps in the 1980s. Demonstrates that direct action was initiated at the grassroots level but in time accepted by CND leadership.

759.Sawyer, Steve, 'Rainbow Warrior: Nuclear war in the Pacific', Third World Quarterly, vol. 8 no. 4 (October 1986), pp. 1325-36.

Examines sinking of Rainbow Warrior, commenting on New Zealand's reactions and the heightened awareness of the dangers of nuclear testing in the Pacific.

760.Simpson, Tony, No Bunkers Here: A Successful Nonviolent Action in a Welsh Community, Merthyr Tydfil, Nottingham and Mid-Glamorgan CND and Peace News, 1982, pp. 47.

Account of direct action campaign against the building of a nuclear-blast-proof bunker.

761.Solnit, Rebecca, Savage Dreams: A Journey into the Hidden Wars of the American West, San Francisco Sierra Club Books, 1994, pp. 401.

Autobiographical account of radical campaigning activities against nuclear tests in Nevada. Author argues that policy of testing nuclear weapons in the American West is rooted in 19th century attitudes and policies towards native American peoples.

762.Taylor, Richard, Against the Bomb: The British Peace Movement 1958-1965, Oxford, Clarendon, 1988, pp. 368.

Well researched account of the first phase of the nuclear disarmament campaign in Britain, analysed and critiqued from a New Left/Marxist perspective.

763.Thompson, Ben, <u>Comiso</u>, London, Merlin Press jointly with END, 1982, pp. 17.

Account of transnational direct action against nuclear missile base in Sicily.

764.Zelter, Angie, <u>Trident on Trial: The Case of People's Disarmament</u>, Edinburgh, Luath Press, 2001, pp. 312.

Presents the legal case against nuclear weapons and for people's 'direct disarmament' actions against UK Trident missiles, and includes personal accounts by activists in Trident Ploughshares.

See also: Epstein, <u>Political Protest and Cultural Revolution</u>, chapter 4, 'the Livermore Action Group: Direct action and the arms race' on protests against test launching of MX missile in California (A.1.).

d. Campaigns against Specific Wars or Acts of Aggression (excluding Vietnam)

Opposition to particular wars or acts of aggression has been much wider than draft resistance. We include here references to a range of national and transnational protests against contentious wars since 1945 (other than Vietnam), including France's war in Algeria (1954-62) and the 1991 Gulf War. These protests include transporting medical or other aid to the civilians under attack, trying to deter attack by being present in areas likely to be bombed, and blockades of airfields, aircraft or troop trains.

The wars and acts of aggression evoking protest have been very varied. But since Vietnam it can be argued that wars involving major Western states have significantly new characteristics. See: Shaw, Martin, <u>The New Western Way of War: Risk Transfer and its Crisis in Iraq</u>, Cambridge, Polity, 2005, pp. 183.

Shaw, an expert on the sociology of war, argues that this new warfare focuses on containing the risks to the lives of Western soldiers in order to minimize political and electoral difficulties for governments, and transfers the risk to civilians whose killing is explained away as 'accidental'.

The US-led war on Iraq in early 2003 prompted major demonstrations across much of the world and some direct action protests. Since then the continuing crisis within Iraq and US military actions and abuse of prisoners' rights has prompted growing opposition from soldiers, reservists and their families. These protests are frequently covered in the mainstream press as well as the peace movement media, but have not yet been systematically documented, apart from a book focused on the Stop the War Coalition in Britain – Murray, Andrew and Lindsey German, <u>Stop the War</u>, London, Bookmarks, 2005, pp. 271. So this section focuses on earlier wars.

765.Burrowes, Robert, 'The Persian Gulf War and the Gulf Peace Team', in Moser-Puangsawan and Weber (eds.), <u>Nonviolent Intervention Across Borders</u>, pp. 305-16 (A.1.).

Attempt by a transnational team from the west to deter US-led war on Iraq – over 70 people set up camp in war zone, until evacuated by the Iraqi authorities 10 days after the beginning of air strikes.

766.Carter, April and Michael Randle, Support Czechoslovakia, London, Housmans, 1968, pp. 64.

Account of four transnational teams going to Warsaw Pact capitals to protest against the 1968 Warsaw Pact Invasion of Czecholoslovakia.

767.Coulson, Meg, 'Looking behind the violent break-up of Yugoslavia', Feminist Review, no. 45 (1993), pp. 86-101.

Reviews post-1945 history of Yugoslavia and the causes of its breakdown. But notes emerging feminist, peace and ecological movement in the 1980s and the role of women in the ongoing opposition to war, including the role of Serbian women demonstrating early in the war on Croatia for the return of their husbands and sons.

768.Evans, Martin, The Memory of Resistance: French Opposition to the Algerian War (1954-1962), Oxford, Berg, 1997, pp. 250.

Focuses on French who actively supported the Algerian guerrilla movement the FLN, including references to the September 1960 '121 Manifesto', in which intellectuals asserted the right to refuse to take up arms in the war. Not a history of opposition to the war, but an oral history focusing on motivations for resistance, which are of general interest. See also: Martin Evans, 'French resistance and the Algerian War', History Today, vol. 41 (July 1991), pp. 43-49.

769.Kronlid, Lotta, Andrea Needham, Joanna Wilson and Angie Zelter, Seeds of Hope: East Timor Ploughshares: Women Disarming for Life and Justice, London, Seeds of Hope, 1996, pp. 59.

Account by four women who 'disarmed' a BAE Hawk fighter-bomber plane bound for Indonesia at the time of its war against East Timor. In July 1997 a Liverpool Crown Court acquitted the four, accepting that their action aimed to prevent a crime.

770.'Operation Omega' in Hare and Blumberg (eds.), Liberation Without Violence, pp. 196-206 (A.4.).

After the 1971 East Bengali (Bangladeshi) movement for independence was suppressed by the Pakistan army, and war broke out between India and Pakistan, a transnational team tried, with some success, to take relief supplies into East Bengal. Their aim was both to protest against Pakistani army repression and to provide practical aid to refugees fleeing from the army. At the same time North American activists blocked arms supplies to Pakistan (see Taylor below).

771.Mladjenovic, Lepa and Vera Litricin, 'Belgrade Feminists 1992: Separation, guilt and identity crisis', Feminist Review, no. 45 (1993), pp. 113-19.

Reviews development of Yugoslav feminism from 1978 to early 1990s, including SOS Hotline for Women and Children Victims of Violence. Notes the strains created by the Serbian war against Croatia, and rising nationalism, but also notes how Belgrade feminists created Women in Black in 1991 and held vigils against war in Croatia and later Bosnia. See also: Women in Black, <u>Compilation of Information on Crimes of War Against Women in Ex-Yugoslavia – Actions and Initiatives in Their Defence</u>, Belgrade, Women in Black, 1993.

772.Paley, Grace,'Something about the peace movement: Something about the people's right not to know' in Victoria Brittain (ed.), <u>The Gulf Between Us: The Gulf War and Beyond</u>, London, Virago Press, 1991, pp. 61-76.

Wide ranging commentary on the US-based opposition to the 1991 Gulf War, including references to soldiers refusing to support the war pp. 64-5 and 70-1.

773.Schweitzer, Christine, 'Mir Sada: The story of a nonviolent intervention that failed', in Moser-Puangsawan and Weber (eds.), <u>Nonviolent Intervention Across Borders</u>, pp. 269-76 (A.1.).

Attempt in 1993 to set up a transnational peace caravan in Sarajevo during the war in Bosnia.

774.Talbott, John, <u>The War Without a Name: France in Algeria 1954-1962</u>, New York, Alfred Knopf, 1980, pp. 305.

Clear account of the politics surrounding the war of liberation and the French responses. Chapter 5 'Against torture' describes resignation in protest by General de Bollardiere and criticisms by reservists, as well as opposition from intellectuals. Chapter 8 'Barricades and manifestos' covers French settler intransigence as well as draft resistance and desertions, the 121 Manifesto and the repressive response by the French government, and the Jeanson FLN-support network. Chapter 9 examines the generals' putsch in 1961 and notes response to it both by the left and De Gaulle.

775.Taylor, Richard K., <u>Blockade: A Guide to Nonviolent Intervention</u>, Maryknoll NY, Orbis Books, 1977, pp. 175.

Account of how a nonviolent fleet of canoes and kayaks blocked Pakistani shipping at East Coast ports of the US to oppose US support for Pakistan's repression in East Bengal. Part 2 is a manual for direct action.

776.Walker, Charles C.'The Delhi to Peking Friendship March', <u>Friends Journal</u>, vol. 9 no. 23 (1963), pp. 517-18.

Attempt to challenge hostility between India and China in the wake of the 1962 border war – the Chinese authorities refused to allow the marchers in. (See also Carter, <u>Peace Movements</u>, pp. 245-47 (G.3.a.).

See also on opposition to 1991 Gulf War: Bhatia, Dreze and Kelly, <u>War and Peace in the Gulf</u>, and Burrowes, 'The Persion Gulf War and the Gulf Peace Team (A.4.); Carter, <u>Peace Movements</u>, pp. 249-52; Meaden, <u>Protesting for Peace</u>, and Peace, <u>A Just and Lasting Peace</u>, (G.3.a.).

e. Protests Against Militarism

Peace campaigners have also engaged in many activities which do not fall within either the categories of conscientious objection/draft resistance or opposition to nuclear weapons or particular wars. Much of this activity involves education and publicity or meetings, petitions and lobbying. But there is also a wide range of direct action, for example resistance to the siting or extension of military bases or firing ranges. A transnational movement against the arms trade includes both publicizing the extent and nature of the trade and regular demonstrations and blockades at arms fairs. In Britain the Campaign Against the Arms Trade publishes details of protests in <u>CAAT News</u>.

777. Caldecott, Leonie, 'At the foot of the mountain: The Shibokusa women of Mount Fuji', in Lynne Jones (ed.), <u>Keeping the Peace</u>, pp. 98-107 (see F.4.c.).

Account of prolonged struggle to recover agricultural land occupied by US forces in 1945 and later retained by Japanese armed forces.

778. Deming, Barbara, 'San Francisco to Moscow: Why they walk' and 'San Francisco to Moscow: Why the Russians let them in' in <u>Revolution and Equilibrium</u>, pp. 51-59 and 60- 72 (see A.1.).

Articles originally published in the <u>Nation</u> July 15 and December 23 1961.

779. Lyttle, Brad, <u>You Come with Naked Hands: The Story of the San Francisco to Moscow March for Peace</u>, Raymond NH, Greenleaf Books, 1966, pp. 246.

Participant's account of march for disarmament organized by the Committee for Nonviolent Action. After marching across the USA the participants walked in Britain, Belgium and West Germany (they were debarred from entering France). But they were allowed to enter the Soviet bloc to travel through parts of the GDR, Poland and the USSR.

780. Packard, George R., <u>Protest in Tokyo: The Security Treaty Crisis of 1960</u>, Princeton NJ, Princeton University Press, 1966, pp. 423.

Includes coverage of petitions, strikes and demonstrations of May-June 1960 with emphasis on role of Zengakuren student organization.

781. Rawlinson, Roger, <u>Larzac: A Nonviolent Campaign of the 70s in Southern France</u>, York, William Sessions, 1996, pp. 202.

Story of the successful ten-year struggle of French farmers in Larzac to protect their land from military encroachment. The Gandhian pacifists at the Community of the Arch, and industrial and professional unions played a role in the struggle. An earlier account is: Rawlinson, <u>Larzac: A Victory for Nonviolence</u>, London, Quaker Peace and Service, 1983, pp. 43.

782. Waldman, Sidney R., Susan Richards and Charles C. Walker, <u>The Edgewood Arsenal and Fort Detrick Projects: an Exchange Analysis</u>, Haverford PA, Center for Nonviolent Conflict Resolution, c. 1967, pp. 67.

'Exchange analysis' between organizers of two protests against Chemical and Biological Weapons (CBW) weapons production, the first a 21 month campaign at Fort Detrick from January 1960, the second planting a tree inside the base.

783.Walker, Charles C. 'Culebra: Nonviolent action and the US Navy', in Hare and Blumberg (eds.), Liberation Without Violence, pp. 178-95 (A.4.).

Resistance to the use of Puerto Rican island as a US Navy bombing and gunnery range. Recounts direct action by Puerto Ricans and development of transnational action involving US Quakers to build chapel on the island.

784.Waugh, Michael H.M., Peace Camping: History of British Peace Camps from the 1930s, Eastleigh, Compositions by Carn, 1998, pp. 374.

Detailed description (with photos) of camps from 1930s through to Aldermaston picket late 1950s and Greenham Common and beyond.

See also: Rawlinson, ' The battle of Larzac' in Hare and Blumberg (eds.), Liberation Without Violence, pp. 58-72. (A.4.); Routledge, Terrains of Resistance, pp. 39-73 on 1980s resistance in Orissa, India, to Baliapal missile testing range (G.a).

4. Feminist Protest since the 1960s

The first wave of feminist protest in the late 19th and early 20th centuries is closely associated in Britain with mass demonstrations and the direct action of the suffragettes – some of their tactics, such as chaining themselves to railings, have been taken up by recent activists. But direct action has been much less central to the second wave of feminism launched in the late 1960s. This is true of both Britain and other western countries. The beginning of the movement did include eye-catching protests in the USA and Britain against beauty contests and products, and there have been demonstrations (sometimes including forms of direct action) to challenge restrictions on abortion, tolerance of rape, and promotion of pornography in a number of countries.

But the political strand of the movement focused primarily on political lobbying, sometimes supplemented by marches and rallies to demonstrate popular support, or using the courts to achieve new legislation to promote equality. See, for example, Jan Mercer (ed.), The Other Half: Women in Australian Society, Ringwood, VIC, Penguin, 1975; Monica Threlfall, 'The Women's Movement in Spain', New Left Review, no. 151 (May/June 1985), pp. 44-73 on post-Franco development of feminist movement and legislative results, and Joyce Gelb, 'Feminism and political action' in R.J. Dalton and M. Kuechler (eds.), Challenging the Political Order: New Social and Political Movements in Western Democracies, Cambridge, Polity, 1990, pp. 137-56, comparing the US, British and Swedish movements.

Direct action by middle class women involved brief symbolic protests to highlight particular issues, but during the 1960s and early 1970s there were also significant signs of militancy among working class women in Britain, which included a number of strikes, some supported by socialist feminists. The bitter miners' strike of 1984-85 also mobilized women in the pit villages to come out in active support. This was not a claim for women's rights but a significant expression of political activism in male-dominated communities. In the USA agitation for women's rights was more exclusively middle class (although in practice some of these rights, such as the right to abortion, had enormous significance for poor women).

Although many feminist pressure groups sprang up in the 1970s (and pre-existing ones were revivified), women's liberation was also a social movement, which grew partially out of the New Left but criticized male chauvinism on the left. Marxist and/or radical feminists were influential in the movements in many countries (see Vicky Randall, Women and Politics, Basingstoke, Macmillan, 1982; Chapter 5 'The Politics of the Women's Movement', pp. 138-68).

Radical feminism therefore encouraged positive feminist experiments in communal organization, to complement protest, on issues such as male violence: for example rape counselling centres and refuges for battered women. These could be interpreted as a form of constructive programme in the context of resistance. But in practice they were rather a complement to pressure for legislative and institutional reform (for example of police attitudes to rape).

Second wave feminism's roots in the radicalism of the 1960 was reflected in its emphasis on internal consciousness raising and challenging dominant cultural and theoretical constructions of femininity. A new feminist publishing arose, heralded by polemical and widely read books by authors such as Andrea Dworkin, Eva Figes, Shulamith Firestone, Betty Friedan, Germaine Greer, Kate Millet and Juliet Mitchell, and developed into a sustained theoretical critique of many academic disciplines.

Radical feminism was also associated with a strong commitment to an anti-hierarchical mode of organization. These feminist views influenced many major environmentalist direct action campaigns in the west in the 1970s and campaigns against nuclear weapons in the 1980s (see Barbara Epstein, Political Protest and Cultural Revolution (A.1.)).

Feminism has always been a transnational movement, although the forms and priorities of campaigning have differed considerably between countries and different areas of the world. The feminist movement in the west has since the 1980s been diffused in abstruse theoretical debates, and lost momentum among younger generations, partly because of the (partial) successes of the 1970s and 1980s. But in other parts of the world women's groups are often struggling for the most basic of rights. Opposition to violence against women is a major transnational issue, emphasized at the 1992 UN Conference in Beijing.

Wide-ranging theoretical issues and some specific information about particular campaigns can be found in a range of feminist periodicals, such as:

Signs (see for example vol. 17 no. 2 (1992), pp. 393-434, for section on 'Feminisms in Latin America'), Women's Studies International Forum (see Ahmed, Leila, 'Feminism and feminist movements in the Middle East: a preliminary exploration', vol. 5 (1982), pp. 153-68), and Feminist Review.

In the 21st century the economic exploitation of women's labour has become a focal point for campaigning around the world, including the west. But this issue is subsumed in the wider global movement against corporate power and neoliberal ideology (see G.7).

Feminism is naturally focused primarily on the rights of women in all spheres of social and political life. But there has since the rise of feminism in the 19th century been a close link between feminist activists and peace movements. In the 1980s feminist direct action for peace, symbolized by the camp at the Greenham Common missile base, provided a committed and militant wing to the revived movement against nuclear weapons.

a. Protest for Women's Rights

785.Bouchier, David, <u>The Feminist Challenge: The Movement for Women's Liberation in Britain and the USA</u>, London, Macmillan, 1983, pp. 252.

Traces the course of the feminist movement from its beginnings at a meeting in Seneca Falls, USA, in 1848, through the campaign for voting rights in the early years of the 20th century to the re-emergence of radical feminism in the 1960s and 1970s

786.Cliff, Tony, <u>Class Struggle and Women's Liberation: 1640 to the Present Day</u>, London, Bookmarks, 1984, pp. 271.

Sweeping historical and transnational survey from a socialist standpoint, noting industrial action by working women and criticizing class base and focus of second wave American and British feminism.

787.Coote, Anna and Beatrix Campbell, <u>Sweet Freedom: The Struggle for Women's Liberation in Britain</u>, London, Pan Books, 1982, pp. 258.

Study of British movement since 1960s, legislative changes and political developments in areas central to women: work, the family, sex and culture. Chapter 1, pp. 9-47 charts the evolution of the movement in terms of key protests, campaigns and organization, including some examples of nonviolent action.

788.Duchen, Claire, <u>Feminism in France from May 1968 to Mitterand</u>, London, Routledge, 1986, pp. 165.

Chapter 1 'Beginnings' examines role of women in May 1968 and the emergence of the Mouvement de Liberation des Femmes in 1970, laying of a wreath on the tomb of the unknown soldier to commemorate his wife (leading to arrest), support for women strikers (e.g. a hat factory in Troyes) and the 5th April 1971 Manifesto by 343 prominent women who had resorted to illegal abortions. Later chapters explore ideological divisions within the movement, a range of theoretical issues and the relationship of feminists to socialist government in France.

789.Freeman, Jo, <u>The Politics of Women's Liberation</u>, New York, Longman, 1975, pp. 268.

Examines the evolution of second wave feminism in the USA from the early protests.

790.Wilson, Elizabeth, <u>What Is To Be Done About Violence Against Women?</u>, Harmondsworth, Penguin, 1983, pp. 256.

Chapter 8 'Feminists fight back' (pp. 169-224) covers the protests in Britain against male violence, and also the constructive organizational responses and the campaigns for legal change and challenges to prevailing attitudes.

b. Women's Strikes

791.Alexander, Sally, 'The Nightcleaners' campaign' in Sandra Allen, Lee Sanders and Jan Wallis (eds.), <u>Conditions of Illusion</u>, London, Feminist Books, 1974, pp. 309-25. See also 'Striking progress' a list of strikes in which women involved 1973-74, pp. 332-48.

792.Dromey, Jack, <u>Grunwick: The Workers' Story</u>, London, Lawrence and Wishart, 1978, pp. 207.

793.Miller, Jill, <u>You Can't Kill the Spirit: Women in a Welsh Mining Village</u>, London, Women's Press, 1986, pp. 142.

794.Rogaly, Joe, <u>Grunwick</u>, Harmondsworth, Penguin, 1977, pp. 199.

Account of the 1976-77 strike by non-unionized Asian women workers in a film processing company, which generated support from the wider labour and socialist movement, many of whom joined the picket line.

795.Stead, Jean, <u>Never the Same Again: Women and the Miners' Strike</u>, London, Women's Press, 1987, pp. 177.

See also: Coote and Campbell, <u>Sweet Freedom</u>, p.18 on ground-breaking strike for equal pay by women workers at Ford, Dagenham, 1968 (G.4.a); Loach, Loretta, 'We'll be here right to the end...and after: Women in the miners' strike', in Benyon (ed.), <u>Digging Deeper: Issues in the Miners' Strike</u>, chapter 9, (F.4).

c. Feminist Direct Action for Peace

Theoretical issues raised by the links between radical feminism and peace activity are explored in: Feminism and Nonviolence Study Group, <u>Piecing it Together: Feminism and Nonviolence</u>, London, Feminism and Nonviolence Study Group, War Resisters' International, 1983, pp. 58; and Strange, Penny, <u>It'll Make a Man of You</u>, London, Peace News, 1983, pp. 30. For a more extended discussion see: Sara Ruddick, <u>Maternal Thinking: Towards a Politics of Peace</u>, London, The Women's Press, 1989, pp. 297.

796.Cook, Alice and Gwyn Kirk, <u>Greenham Women Everywhere</u>, London, Pluto Press, 1983, pp. 127.

797.Eglin, Jospehine, 'Women and peace: from the Suffragists to the Greenham Women' in Richard Taylor and Nigel Young (eds.), <u>Campaigns for Peace: British Peace Movements in the Twentieth Century</u>, Manchester, Manchester University Press, 1987, pp. 221-59.

798.Harford, Barbara and Sarah Hopkins (eds.), <u>Greenham Common: Women at the Wire</u>, London, The Women's Press, 1984, pp. 171.

799.Jones, Lynne (ed.), <u>Keeping the Peace</u>, London, The Women's Press, 1983, pp. 162.

Gives transnational examples of women's peace activism.

800.Liddington, Jill, <u>The Long Road to Greenham: Feminism and Anti-Militarism in Britain since 1820</u>, London, Virago, 1989, pp. 341.

Parts 1 and 2 examine the historical evolution of feminist peace activity (much of it constitutional), but Part 3 'Liberation and Peace Camps (1970-88)' covers recent militant campaigns.

801.Roseneil, Sasha, <u>Disarming Patriarchy: Feminism and Political Action at Greenham</u>, Buckingham, Open University Press, 1995, pp. 225.

This PhD thesis is a detailed account of the history and everyday life at Greenham, based on participation in the peace camp and 35 interviews with other women. More recently Roseneil has explored life-style and lesbian issues connected with the camp: <u>Common Women, Uncommon Practices: The Queer Feminism of Greenham</u>, London, Cassell, 2000.

See also Epstein, <u>Political Protest and Cultural Revolution</u>, esp. pp. 160-68 which briefly describe Women's Pentagon Action and Seneca Peace Camp in USA (A.1.).

5. Green Campaigns since the 1970s

The most dynamic social movements in the later 1970s tended to be environmental campaigns, which mounted some major direct action protests against nuclear power. By the 1980s environmental groups like Greenpeace were also taking direct action against nuclear tests. In the west green protests often overlapped with feminist and disarmament concerns, and developed new styles of informal democratic organization for mass demonstrations. Green activism against logging, dams, motorways, supermarkets, toxic dumps and other environmental hazards continued into the 1980s and 1990s, and uprooting genetically modified crops became widespread in the early 2000s. Green protests now often overlap with the concerns and targets of the global social justice movement. There is also often an overlap between indigenous people's resistance to multinationals and environmental concerns.

Green activists have taken up nonviolent direct action with daring and imagination, greatly extending the range of tactics used. Some greens have also used forms of sabotage (ecotage), raising questions about the limits of nonviolence. But, alongside direct action, environmental campaigners have also developed sophisticated lobbying techniques, some have moved towards closer cooperation with corporations and governments and others have developed green political parties to fight local, national and (where relevant) EU elections. As in many movements, greens are divided over strategy, so moderate ('realistic') approaches are opposed by the more radical groups. The ideological range stretches from 'deep ecologists' to conservatives protecting local neighbourhoods. Greens campaign for biodiversity, e.g. Greenpeace resistance to whaling, but are divided about other animal rights protests.

Warnings and analyses of possible environmental disaster by scientists have become increasingly common since the ground-breaking book by Rachel Carson, <u>Silent Spring</u>, 1962. Green theorists and activists have also developed new interpretations of economics – exploring sustainable development, political thought, philosophy and spirituality. These literatures are not covered here, but one book relevant here is:

802.Kelly, Petra, <u>Thinking Green! Essays on Environmentalism, Feminism and Nonviolence</u>, Berkeley CA, Parallax Press, 1994, pp. 167.

Includes essays on creating an ecological economy, women and power, the arms race and nonviolent social defence.

Relevant periodicals: <u>The Ecologist</u> is a useful source of information on green issues and campaigns. Environmental concerns and campaigns are covered by a number of movement journals such as <u>New Internationalist</u>, <u>Peace News</u>, <u>Schnews</u> and <u>Resurgence</u>.

a. General Studies and Transnational Protest

803.Bahro, Rudolf, <u>Building the Green Movement</u>, Philadelphia PA, New Society Publishers, 1986, pp. 219.

Collection of writings (from November 1982 to June 1985) by former East German dissident and radical ecologist. Covers issues such as North-South relations, the peace movement and the crucial role of communes in rebuilding an ecologically sound society. Includes his statement on resigning from the German Greens, claiming that they 'have identified themselves – critically – with the industrial system and its administration'.

804.Brown, Michael and John May, <u>The Greenpeace Story</u>, London, Dorling Kindersley, 1989, pp. 160.

Covers voyages to challenge nuclear testing, at Amchitka Island, Alaska and Mururoa Atoll; but also the voyages protesting against nuclear waste disposal and pollution and to protect marine mammals.

805.Dalton, Russell, <u>The Green Rainbow: Environmental Groups in Western Europe</u>, New Haven, Yale University Press, 1994, pp. 305.

Examines development of Green movement in Western democracies. Argues that environmental interest groups are important new participants in the contemporary political process and that, if the movement is politically successful 'it may at least partially reshape the style and structure of democratic processes in these countries'.

806.Flam, Helena (ed.), <u>States and Anti-Nuclear Movements</u>, Edinburgh, Edinburgh University Press, 1994, pp. 427.

Deals with the anti-nuclear power movements and government responses to them and their demands in eight West European states – Austria, Britain, France, Italy, the Netherlands Norway, Sweden and West Germany.

807.Hart, Lindsay, 'In defence of radical direct action: Reflections on civil disobedience, sabotage and nonviolence', in Jan Parkis and James Bowen (eds.), <u>Twenty-First Century Anarchism: Unorthodox Ideas for a New Millennium</u>, London, Cassell, 1997, pp. 41-59.

Defends new forms of radical direct action, including 'ecotage', arguing that violence should be measured by harm inflicted not use of physical force.

808.Hunter, Robert, The Greenpeace Chronicle, London, Pan Books, 1980, pp. 448. (Published in US as Warriors of the Rainbow: A Chronicle of the Greenpeace Movement, New York, Rinehart and Winston, 1978.)

The story of Greenpeace from its emergence in the early 1970s to the time of the book's publication. Autobiographical account by a founder member of Greenpeace International.

809.McCormick, John, The Global Environmental Movement: Reclaiming Paradise, London, Belhaven, 1989, pp. 259; (US title Reclaiming Paradise: The Global Environmental Movement, Bloomington IN, Indiana University Press, 1989.)

Despite its title, this is not primarily about protest, but the international/state context in which protest occurs, stressing the UN and international agreements.

810.Rootes, Christopher (ed.), Environmental Movements: Local, National and Global, London, Cass, 1999, pp. 1999.

Primary emphasis on sociological analysis of how environmental movements change, with statistics on participation in them. Chapters on Germany, Spain and Southern Europe and the USA. Derek Wall writes on 'Mobilizing Earth First!' in Britain. Jeff Haynes, 'Power, politics and environmental movements in the Third World' (pp. 222-42) includes specific references to the Chipko, Narmada and Ogoniland movements, as well as other forms of environmental action in Kenya and the role of the WTO.

811.Taylor, Bron Raymond (ed.), Ecological Resistance Movements: The Global Emergence of Radical and Popular Environmentalism, Albany NY, State University of New York Press, 1995, pp. 422.

Collection examining range of grassroots groups with different long term aims and backgrounds in all parts of the world, their impacts and prospects. (Some individual chapters also listed below.)

812.Wapner, Paul, Environmental Activism and World Civic Politics New York, State University of New York Press, 1996, pp. 238.

Analysis of roles of different types of transnational organizations and their impact on environmental 'discourse'. Chapter 3 is specifically on Greenpeace, direct action and changing attitudes.

813.Weyler, Rex, Greenpeace: An Insider's Account, Rodale, Pan Macmillan, 2004, pp. 600.

By a founder of Greenpeace International focusing on 1970s.

See also: McTaggart and Hunter, Greenpeace III, Mitcalf, Boy Roel, Robie, Eyes of Fire on Greenpeace opposition to French nuclear tests; and Solnit, Savage Dreams (resisting US nuclear tests) (G.3.b.) Relevant titles also appear under G.7.c.

b. Country Studies

814.Akula, Vikram, 'Grassroots environmental resistance in India', in Taylor (ed.), Ecological Resistance Movements, pp. 127-45 (G.5.a.).

Discusses early resistance in 19th and early 20th centuries and contemporary campaigns against destruction of forests, dams, pollution and over-fishing of seas, and mining. Akula also describes Jharkand separatist 'tribal' struggle to own their historic land and promote sustainable use of resources.

815.Connors, Libby and Drew Hutton, A History of the Australian Environmental Movement, Cambridge, Cambridge University Press, 1999, pp. 324.

Survey of the movement from early concerns about conservation through the 'second wave' 1945-72, and the campaigns of 1973-83 up to the subsequent professionalization of the movement. Chapter 4 'Taking to the streets' covers 'green bans' and the anti-uranium campaigns; Chapter 5 'Taking to the bush' looks at direct action on a number of issues, culminating in the 1982 blockade of the Franklin Dam; and Chapter 6 'Fighting for wilderness' assesses further protests around Australia. Chapter 8 considers the role of the Green Party.

816.Doyle, Timothy, 'Direct action in environmental conflict in Australia: a re-examination of non-violent action', Regional Journal of Social Issues, vol. 28 (1994), pp. 1-13.

817.Gould, Kenneth, Allan Schnaiberg and Adam Weinberg, Local Environmental Struggles: Citizen Activism in the Treadmill of Production, Cambridge, Cambridge University Press, 1996, pp. 239.

A study of community power and regional planning on the environment, based on US case studies.

818.Hayes, Graeme, Environmental Protest and the State in France, Basingstoke, Palgrave, 2002, pp. 246.

819.Seel, Benjamin, Matthew Patterson and Brian Doherty, (eds.), Direct Action in British Environmentalism, London, Routledge, 2000, pp. 223.

Useful collection of essays, including a survey of British environmentalism 1988-97 in the changing political context, assessments of different types of environmental activity and role of the media. Brian Doherty,'Manufactured vulnerability: protest camp tactics' looks at evolution of nonviolent direct action tactics and transnational influences. There is some discussion of the incidence of violence and media (mis)perceptions.

820.Shiva, Vandana, with J. Bandyopadhay et. al., Ecology and the Politics of Survival, London, Sage Publications (and Tokyo, UN University Press), 1991, pp. 365.

Analysis by expert on issues of ecology, development and role of women in conflicts over natural resources in India, includes references to Appiko protests to save forests and satyagraha against mining. She has also published: Staying Alive: Women, Ecology and Development, London, Zed Press, 1988.

c. Campaigns Against Nuclear Power

821.Gyorgy, Anna and friends, <u>No Nukes: Everyone's Guide to Nuclear Power</u>, Cambridge MA, South End Press, 1979, pp. 478.

Includes large section on the transnational movement against nuclear power.

822.Joppke, Christian, <u>Mobilizing Against Nuclear Energy: A Comparison of Germany and the United States</u>, Berkeley, University of California Press, 1993, pp. 307.

823.Nelkin, Dorothy and Michael Pollak, <u>The Atom Besieged: Antinuclear Movements in France and Germany</u>, Cambridge Mass, MIT Press, 1982, pp. 235.

Examines the political contexts, nature of the movements against nuclear power and their tactics, and government responses, in the 1970s.

824.Newnham, Tom, <u>Peace Squadron: The Sharp End of Nuclear Protest in New Zealand</u>, Auckland, Graphic Publications, 1986, pp. 60.

Account of 'nuclear-free-zone' protesters who blocked nuclear-powered vessels from entering port with ships, boats and canoes.

825.Price, Jerome, <u>The Antinuclear Movement</u>, Boston MA, Twayne Publishers, 1982, pp. 207. (revised edition 1989).

General analysis of evolution of movement and groups and organizations involved. Chapter 4 examines direct action groups and their protests.

826.Touraine, Alain, <u>Anti-nuclear Protest: The Opposition to Nuclear Energy in France</u>, Cambridge, Cambridge University Press, 1983, pp. 202. Translation and abridgement of <u>La prophetie anti-nucleaire</u>,

See also: Epstein, <u>Political Protest and Cultural Revolution</u>, chapter 2 'The Clamshell Alliance', p. 58-91 (A.1.) and Flam (ed.), <u>States and Antinuclear Movements</u> (G.5.a.).

d. Campaigns Against Deforestation

827.Ramachandra, Guha, <u>The Unquiet Woods: Ecological Change and Peasant Resistance in the Himalayas</u>, Berkeley, University of California Press, 1989; expanded edition with Oxford University Press, 2000, pp. 244.

Emphazises local roots of movement, including development of 'non-secessionist regionalism' in Uttarakhand. The epilogue, written in 1998, adds historical perspective to the movement's achievements and reports on-going struggles. Seeks to offer 'corrective' to romanticized western and ecofeminist interpretations.

828.Weber, Thomas, <u>Hugging the Trees: The Story of the Chipko Movement</u>, New Delhi, Penguin, 1981 and 1989, pp. 175.

Traces development of the 'tree hugging' movement to protect Himalayan forests, stresses the importance of the Gandhian legacy in the strategy and tactics of the movement, discusses the role of women and profiles the leading men.

e. Campaigns Against Dams

829.Hirsch, Philip, 'The politics of environment: Opposition and legitimacy', in Hewison (ed.) Political Change in Thailand. pp. 179-194 (D.II.6).

Examines growing significance of environmental movement in Thailand since the success in stopping proposed dam in 1988.

830.Jumbala, Prudhisan and Maneerat Mitprasat, 'Non-governmental development organisations: Empowerment and the environment', in Hewison (ed.), Political Change in Thailand, pp. 195-216 (D.II.6.).

Examines two case studies in Thailand of Raindrops Association encouraging villagers to resuscitate the natural environment, and the opposition to planned Kaeng Krung Dam.

831.Palit, Chitaroopa, 'Monsoon risings: Megadam resistance in the Narmada valley', New Left Review, II no. 21 (May/June 2003), pp. 80-100.

Anti-dam resistance persuaded the World Bank to withdraw from funding one of the dams, but did not change Indian government policy.

See also: Connors and Hutton, History of the Australian Environmental Movement, chapter 5 on resistance to Franklin dam (G.5.b.).

f. Campaigns Against Mining and Pollution

832.Beynon, Huw, Andrew Cox and Ray Hudson, Digging up Trouble: The Environment, Protest and Opencast Mining, London, Rivers Oram, 1999, pp. 288.

General analysis of impact of opencast (strip) mining which spread in Britain in the 1980s. Chapter 7 'Changing patterns of protest' (pp. 167-206) looks at the collaboration between the National Union of Miners, Miners' Support Groups and environmental groups to oppose mines creating pollution, and turn from conventional protest to direct action.

833.Broadbent, Jeffrey, Environmental Politics in Japan: Networks of Power and Protest, Cambridge, Cambridge University Press, 1998, pp. 418.

Examines dilemma of growth versus environmentalism, and how Japan has resolved it, with focus on how anti-pollution protests 1960s-1973 changed government policy, using the movement in one prefecture as case study.

834.McKean, Margaret A., Environmental Protest and Citizen Politics, Berkeley CA, University of California Press, 1981, pp. 291.

Study of 'citizens' movements' against industrial pollution.

835.Strangio, Paul No Toxic Dump: a Triumph for Grassroots Democracy and Environmental Justice, Annandale, NSW, Pluto Press, 2001, pp. 217.

An Australian case study.

836.Szasz, Andrew, <u>Ecopopulism: Toxic Waste and the Movement for Environmental Justice</u>, Minneapolis, University of Minnesota Press, 1994, pp. 216.

g. Campaigns Against Roads, Airports, Redevelopment etc.

837.Apter, David E. and Nagayo Sawa, <u>Against the State: Politics and Social Protest in Japan</u>, Cambridge MA, Harvard University Press, 1984, pp. 271.

Protest by agricultural community against loss of land for airport.

838.Burgmann, Verity and M. Burgmann, <u>Green Bans, Red Union: Environmentalism and the the New South Wales Builders' Labourers Federation</u>, Sydney, University of New South Wales Press, 1998.

On the initiation of 'green bans' – work bans by unions to prevent redevelopment of working class neighbourhoods and destruction of historic buildings and urban green spaces in Sydney. Between 1971 and 1974 42 separate bans were imposed and linked unionists with middle class conservationists. See also Jack Mundey, <u>Green Bans and Beyond</u>, Sydney, Angus and Robertson, 1981.

839.Doherty, Brian, 'Paving the way: The rise of direct action against British road building', <u>Political Studies</u>, 47, 1999, pp. 275-91.

840.Merrick (full name), <u>Battle for the Trees: Three Months of Responsible Ancestry</u>, Leeds, Godhaven Ink, 1996, pp. 132.

Account of 3 months struggle against Newbury bypass.

841.Wall, Derek, <u>Earth First! and the Anti-Roads Movement</u>, London, Routledge, 1999, pp. 219.

6. Campaigns for Indigenous Rights since the 1960s

Indigenous campaigns in the west since the 1960s have often relied primarily on conventional liberal campaigning methods such as lobbying, petitions, rallies and marches. Resort to the courts has often been important. But indigenous peoples have also used forms of direct action such as strikes, blockades and occupying land, both in earlier stages of resistance and as part of the rise in militancy since the 1970s. They have occasionally resorted to violence, for example after militant Native Americans took over the village of Wounded Knee.

This section focuses on four western countries where indigenous peoples have campaigned vigorously for their rights. For an overview of the political position of indigenous peoples in three of them – Canada, New Zealand and the USA – see:

842.Fleras, Augie and Jean Leonard Elliot, <u>The Nations Within</u>, Oxford, Oxford University Press, 1992.

Significant campaigns by indigenous people in the South are listed in other sections. For resistance to mining, logging, dams, etc. see sections G.7.c.i and G.5. Many of these campaigns have included nonviolent direct action; some have included appeals to the courts or lobbying by transnational supporting groups; others have included resort to guerrilla tactics (usually on a minor scale). In Latin America, where indigenous peoples are often a substantial proportion of the population, they are also often at the forefront of campaigns of resistance to corporations and IMF-inspired economic policies (for example the Zapatisatas). (See G.7.a., G.7.b.ii and iii; G.7.c.i and ii; and G.7.e.)

a. Australia

843.Bennett, Scott, <u>Aborigines and Political Power</u>, Sydney NSW, Allen and Unwin, 1989, pp. 167.

General analysis, includes some reference to protest.

844.Chesterman, John and Galligan, Brian, <u>Citizens Without Rights: Aborigines and Australian Citizenship</u>, Cambridge, Cambridge University Press, 1997, Chapter 7, 'From Civil to Indigenous Rights' includes some details of protest.

845.Grenfell, Damian, 'Environmentalism, State Power and "National Interests"', in James Goodman (ed.), <u>Protest and Globalisation</u>, pp. 111-15 (see G.7.a.).

Covers 'Stop Jabiluka' campaign by Aborigines and environmentalists against uranium mining in Kakadu National Park.

846.Mandle, W.F., <u>Going It Alone: Australia's National Identity in the Twentieth Century</u>, Ringwood, VIC., Penguin, 1980.

Chapter on 'Donald Macleod and Australia's Aboriginal Problem' pp. 174-89 covers Pilbara strike and Pindan movement of late 1940s.

847.Read, Peter, <u>Charles Perkins: A Biography</u>, Melbourne VIC, Penguin, 2001, pp. 392.

Perkins has been one of the leading activists for Aboriginal rights. The freedom rides against discrimination in New South Wales and Perkins' role in leading them are described in some detail.

See also: Burgmann, <u>Power and Protest</u>, chapter 1 'Black movement, white stubborness', on land occupations, freedom rides, black power and tent embassy (G.a.).

b. Canada

Substantial political progress has been made in Canada through constitutional tactics and lobbying – the Inuit now have an autonomous territory, Nunavut. But there have also been direct action protests.

848.Gedicks, A. L. 'International native resistance to the new resource wars' in Bron Raymond Taylor (ed.), <u>Ecological Resistance Movements</u>, pp. 89-108 (G.5.a.).

Covers resistance by Cree and Inuit, supported by Kayapo Indians in Brazil and transnational green groups, to major hydro-electric project in Quebec.

849.Robertson, Heather, <u>Reservations Are for Indians</u>, Toronto, James Lewis and Samuel, 1970, pp. 303.

Includes material on protest march and a 'drink-in' in 1960s.

c. New Zealand

850.Hazelhurst, Kayleen M., <u>Political Expression and Ethnicity: Statecraft and Mobilization in the Maori World</u>, Westport CT, Praeger, 1993, pp. 222.

Includes information on demonstrations; chapter 6 covers the Mana Motukhake protest group.

851.Walker, Ranginui, <u>Ka Whawhai Tonu Motu: Struggle Without End</u>, Auckland NZ, Penguin Books, 1990, pp. 334.

History of the Maori, including resistance to white occupation in nineteenth century; chapters 11-12 cover recent political protest, for example to protect land and fishing rights, and other forms of political activism.

d. USA

852.Cohen, Fay G., <u>Treaties on Trial: The Continuing Controversy over Northwest Indian Fishing Rights</u>, Seattle, University of Washington Press, 1986, pp. 229.

Covers protest 'fish-ins'.

853.Deloria, Vine, Jr. <u>Behind the Trail of Broken Treaties: An American Indian Declaration of Independence</u>, Austin TX,University of Texas Press, 1985, pp. 296.

Covers developing activism in 1960s, protest caravan of 1972 and site occupations, including Wounded Knee.

854.Schragg, James L. 'Report from Wounded Knee', in Hare and Blumberg (eds.), <u>Liberation Without Violence</u>, pp. 117-24. (A.1.).

855.Smith, Paul Chaat and Robert Allen Warner, <u>Like a Hurricane: The Indian Movement from Alcatraz to Wounded Knee</u>, New York, New Press, 1996, pp. 343.

856.Steiner, Stan, <u>The New Indians</u>, New York, Harper and Row, 1968, pp. 220.

7. Global Justice Movement Against Global Neoliberalism and Multinational Corporations

Since the demonstrations at Seattle in December 1999 a growing number of books have been published both by participants in the global justice movement and by mainstream publishers. There is also a lively theoretical debate between proponents and critics of neoliberalism, which is not covered here. Well known critics of neoliberalism include Benjamin Barber, Walden Bello, Alex Callinicos, Susan George, Naomi Klein and George Monbiot. For a critique of aspects of neoliberal policies from former World Bank chief economist see:

857.Stiglitz, Jospeh, <u>Globalization and its Discontents</u>, London, Allen Lane, The Penguin Press, 2002, pp. 282.

A great strength of the movement is that it has brought together many from other social movements, who see their own goals threatened by neoliberal economic policies. The global justice movement also embraces the struggles of many indigenous peoples, and exploited workers and poor communities round the world. Although the focus is on social justice, the World Social Forum, and its European branch, the European Social Forum, which provide a policy platform for all participating groups, have also been important for the coordination of protests against the 2003 Iraq war. But diversity of movements entails diversity of ideologies and attitudes to nonviolence. For counter summit protests, there is an agreement on tactical 'diversity', which means respecting nonviolent actions but not imposing an overall nonviolent discipline.

Periodicals which support the global justice movement and supply information about both neoliberal policies and protests against them are:

<u>New Internationalist</u> (monthly), <u>Red Pepper</u> (monthly), <u>Schnews</u> (www.schnews.org.uk) and <u>New Left Review</u> (bi-monthly). For advocacy of neoliberalism and critical but informative perspectives on protests see the weekly <u>Economist</u>.

a. General

858.Bircham, Emma and Charlton, John (eds.), <u>Anti-Capitalism: A Guide to the Movement</u>, London, Bookmarks Publications, 2000, pp. 407.

Collection of brief articles on key issues, protest by regions, key actors, and assessments by activists within 'anti-globalization' movement.

859.Crossley, N., 'Global anti-corporate struggle: A preliminary analysis', <u>British Journal of Sociology</u>, vol. 53 no. 4 (2002), pp. 667-91.

A preliminary sociological analysis of the 'recent wave of anti-corporate protest' seeking to outline framework and highlight important themes.

860.<u>Development</u>, Issue on 'The Movement of Movements', vol. 48 no. 2 (June 2005), pp. 1-121.

Analysis of Social Forum processes, the nature of the global justice movement and the Zapatista experience. Includes list of key networks and individuals. NB <u>Development</u>, vol. 47 no. 3 (2004) is on 'Corporate Social Responsibility'.

861.George, Susan, <u>Another World Is Possible If...</u>, London, Verso, 2004, pp. 268.

Committed political and economic analysis of the injustice and dangers of neoliberal globalization by a leading thinker and activist in the global justice movement. Includes a brief discussion of campaigns (Jubilee 2000, opposition to the Multilateral Agreement on Investment, summit protests) and ends with a chapter on why the movement should be nonviolent.

862.Goodman, James (ed.), <u>Protest and Globalisation: Prospects for Transnational Solidarity</u>, Annandale NSW, Pluto Press, 2002, pp. 276.

863.Graeber, David, 'The new anarchists', New Left Review, II no. 13 (Jan/Feb 2002), pp. 61-73.

864.Klein, Naomi, Fences and Windows: Dispatches from the Front Lines of the Globalization Debate, London, Flamingo, 2002, pp. 267.

Collection of articles documenting 'anti-globalization' protests at economic summits, developments in global neoliberal policies, attempts to prevent protest and comments on movements.

865.Klein, Naomi No Logo, London, Flamingo, 2001, pp. 490.

Now a classic analysis of the role of brands and sources of leverage on corporations, including extensive information on a range of campaigns, many including direct action. See also: Klein, Naomi, 'Reclaiming the commons', New Left Review, II no 9 (May/ June 2001), pp. 81-9.

866.Monbiot, George, Anticapitalism: A Guide to the Movement, London, Bookmarks, 2001, pp. 416.

867.Newell, Peter, 'Campaigning for Corporate Change: Global citizen action on the environment,' in Edwards and Gaventa (eds.), Global Citizen Action, pp. 189-201 (G.b.).

868.Notes from Nowhere (ed.), We Are Everywhere, London, Verso, 2003, pp. 521.

Extensive collection of brief articles on campaigns around the world using differing tactics and approaches.

869.Prokosh, Mike and Laura Raymond, The Global Activist's Manual: Local Ways to Change the World, New York, Thunder Mouth's Press/Nation Books, 2002, pp. 324.

Accounts of campaigns illustrating movement building and different types of action. Final section on 'practical tips' and list of organizations.

870.Sellers, John, 'Raising a Ruckus', New Left Review, II no 10 (July/Aug 2001), pp. 71-85.

On evolution of Ruckus out of Greenpeace.

871.Solnit, David (ed.), Globalize Liberation: How to Uproot the System and Build a Better World, San Francisco, City Lights, 2004, pp. 451.

Thirty three essays, mainly by US-based activists, on the new radicalism and direct action in the global justice movement.

872. Starhawk, Webs of Power: Notes from the Global Uprising, Gabriola Island, BC, New Society Publishers, 2003.

Part 1, The author, an activist and ecofeminist, chronicles the global justice movement from Seattle to Genoa. Part 2 explores the future of the movement and debates between advocates of violent and nonviolent tactics.

873. Starr, Amory, <u>Naming the Enemy: Anti-Corporate Movements Confront Globalization</u>, London, Zed Books, 1999, pp. 268.

Early analysis which both documents and theorizes the growing transnational resistance to multinationals and neoliberal globalization.

874. Welton, Neva and Linda Wolf (eds.), <u>Global Uprising: Confronting the Tyrannies of the 21st Century</u>, Gabriola Island BC, New Society Publishers, 2001, pp. 273.

See also: Kingsnorth, <u>One No, Many Yeses</u>, a personal account of a range of important campaigns against neoliberal globalization seen at first hand (F.1.).

b. Resistance to International Economic Organizations

i. Opposing Global Summits

875. Epstein, Barbara 'Not your parents' protest', <u>Dissent</u>, vol. 47 (Spring 2000), pp 8-11.

On Seattle.

876. Neale. Jonathan, <u>You Are G8, We Are 6 Billion: The Truth Behind the Genoa Protests</u>, London, Vision Paperbacks, 2002, pp. 275.

877. Morse, David, 'Beyond the myths of Seattle', <u>Dissent</u>, vol. 48 (Summer 2001), pp. 39-43.

See also: Klein, <u>Fences and Windows</u>, pp. 3-13 (Seattle), pp. 34-36 (Prague); Sellers, 'Raising a Ruckus', on role of Ruckus at Seattle (G.7.a.).

ii. Opposing IMF Policies and Privatization

Argentina

878. Lopez Levy, Marcella, <u>We Are Millions: Neo-Liberalism and New Forms of Political Action in Argentina</u>, London, Latin American Bureau, 2004, pp. 142.

Examines popular response to collapse of Argentine economy in December 2001, including banging pots and pans, mass marches and assemblies, development of 'piqueteros', neighbourhood assemblies, and workers taking over and running failed businesses.

879. McCabe, Patrice, 'Argentina's new forms of resistance' in Solnit (ed.), <u>Globalize Liberation</u> (G.7.a.), pp. 339-46.

On 'piqueteros', December 2001 demonstrations and the popular assemblies.

880. Rock, David, 'Racking Argentina', <u>New Left Review</u>, II no. 17 (September/October 2002), pp. 55-86.

Analyses background and causes of the meltdown of the economy in 2001, considering Argentina's role in the world economy and the impact of neoliberal policies.

881.Whitney, Jennifer and John Jordan, 'Que se Vayan Todos: Argentina's popular rebellion' in Solnit (ed.), <u>Globalize Liberation</u> (G.7.a.), pp. 313-38.

Bolivia

882.Crabtree, John, <u>Patterns of Protest: Politics and Social Movements in Bolivia</u>, London, Latin American Bureau, 2005, pp. 118.

Analysis of October 2003 predominantly nonviolent rebellion which toppled the President, who had privatized large sections of the economy. The book also examines earlier protests, for example against water privatization in Cochabamba.

883.Dunkerley, James and Rolando Morales, 'The crisis in Bolivia', <u>New Left Review</u>, no, 155 (January/February 1986), pp. 86-106.

Examines the introduction of a neoliberal economic policy, and the initial worker resistance.

884.Schultz, Jim, 'The water is ours, dammit!', in Notes from Nowhere (ed.), <u>We Are Everywhere</u>, pp. 264-71.

On successful resistance to privatization of water (Bechtel company) in Cochabamba in early 2000.

Ecuador

885.Sawyer, Suzana, <u>Crude Chronicles: Indigenous Politics, Multinational Oil and Neoliberalism in Ecuador</u>, Durham NC, Duke University Press, 2004, pp. 294.

Against the backdrop of mounting government attempts to privatize and liberalize the national economy, Sawyer shows how neoliberal reforms led to a crisis of governance, accountability and representation that spurred one of 20th century Latin America's strongest indigenous movements. An example of engaged anthropological research.

South Africa

886.Desai, Ashwin, <u>We Are the Poors: Community Struggles in Post-Apartheid South Africa</u>, New York, Monthly Review Press, 2002, pp. 153.

On resistance to neoliberal policies and privatization in the townships, strikes, and the Durban Social Forum.

887.Mayekiso, Mzwanele, <u>Township Politics: Civic Struggles in the New South Africa</u>, New York, Monthly Review Press, 1996, pp. 288.

888.Ngwane, Trevor, 'Sparks in the township', <u>New Left Review</u>, II no. 22 (July/Aug 2003), pp. 37-56.

See also: Kingsnorth, <u>One No, Many Yeses</u>, pp. 89-123 (F.1.).

iii. Opposing the World Bank

889.Brown, L.David, and Jonathan Fox, <u>The Struggle for Accountability: NGOs, Social Movements, and the World Bank</u>, Cambridge MA, MIT Press, 1998, pp. 570. See also: Brown, L. David and Jonathan Fox, 'Transnational civil society coalitions and the World Bank: Lesson from project and policy influence campaigns' in Edwards and Gaventa (eds.), <u>Global Citizen Action</u>, pp. 43-58 (G.a.).

890.Keck, Margaret E. and Kathryn Sikkink, <u>Activists Beyond Borders: Advocacy Networks in International Politics</u>, Ithaca NY, Cornell University Press, 1998, pp. 228.

Focuses on opposition to World Bank loans to projects affecting indigenous peoples pp. 135-47.

See also: Palit, 'Monsoon risings' on Narmada dam protests and change of Bank policy (G.5.e).

c. Resistance to Multinational Corporations

i. Logging, Mining, etc.

891.Evans, Geoff, James Goodman and Nina Lansbury (eds.), <u>Moving Mountains: Communities Confront Mining and Globalisation</u>, London, Zed Books, 2002, pp. 284.

Discusses role of corporations and governments in different parts of the world. Chapters 8-12 focus on resistance in Bougainville, the Philippines and Australia – Chapter 12 (pp. 195-206) covers the resistance to the Jabiluka uranium mine by the local Aboriginal people supported by environmentalists.

892.Gedicks, Al, <u>The New Resource Wars: Native and Environmental Struggles against Multinational Corporations</u>, Boston MA, South End Press, 1993, pp. 270.

Examines struggles by the Ojibwa Indians against mining and over land tenure and the role of multinationals in Wisconsin.

See also: Keck and Sikkink, <u>Activists Beyond Borders</u>, pp. 150-60 on campaign against deforestation in Sarawak by Dayaks, who barricaded logging roads (G.7.b.iii).

ii. Oil Companies

893.Cooper, Joshua, 'The Ogoni struggle for human rights and a civil society in Nigeria' in Zunes et al (eds.), <u>Nonviolent Social Movements</u>, pp. 189-202 (A.1.).

Account of one of the best known and documented campaigns against oil drilling which damages the local environment and communty, by the Ogoni people of Nigeria.

894.Hunt, Timothy J., <u>The Politics of Bones: Dr Owens Wiwa and the Struggle for Nigeria's Oil</u>, Toronto, McClelland and Stewart, 2005, pp. 400.

Focuses on the brother of executed leader of the Ogoni movement, Kenule Sarowiwa, and his efforts to carry on the campaign.

895.Obi, Cyril I, 'Globalization and local resistance: The case of Shell versus the Ogoni' in Gills, Barry K. (ed.), Globalization and the Politics of Resistance, Basingstoke, Macmillan, 2000; Palgrave (paperback) 2001, pp. 280-94.

896.Yearley, Steve and John Forrester, 'Shell, a target for global campaigning?' in Cohen and Rai (eds), Global Social Movements, pp. 134-45 (G.b.).

See also Carter, Direct Action and Democracy Today, pp. 129-33. (A.1.); Howard Clark, 'An obstacle to "progress"', on the campaign by U'wa people in Colombia to prevent oil drilling, Peace News (Dec 2002-Feb 2003), pp. 12-13 (D.IV. Introduction, Colombia); and Sawyer, Crude Chronicles on Ecuador (G.7.b.ii).

iii. Sweatshops

897.Hale, Angela and Linda M. Shaw, 'Women workers and the promise of ethical trade in the globalised garment industry: A serious beginning?' in Peter Waterman and Jane Wills (eds.), Place, Space and the New Labour Internationalism, Oxford, Blackwell, 2001, pp. 206-26.

Discusses company codes of conduct introduced in response to ethical trade boycotts in west of products made with sweatshop labour, and analyses the global economic conditions undercutting such codes and the right to union organization.

898.Johns R. and L. Vural, 'Class, geography and the consumerist turn: UNITE and the stop sweatshops campaign', Economic Geography, vol. 74 (2000), pp. 252-71.

899.Ross, Andrew (ed,), No Sweat: Fashion, Free Trade and the Rights of Garment Workers, New York, Verso, 1997, pp. 256.

900.Young, Iris, 'From guilt to solidarity: Sweatshops and political responsibility', Dissent, (Winter 2003), pp. 39-44.

On US movement.

See also: Klein, No Logo, pp. 405-10 (G.7.a.).

iv. McDonald's

901.Vidal, John, McLibel: Burger Culture on Trial, Basingstoke, Macmillan, 1997, pp. 354.

Detailed account of the trial of two members of London Greenpeace, who refused to withdraw a leaflet denouncing McDonald's.

d. Resistance by Small Farmers

902.Bove, Jose, 'A farmers' international?', New Left Review, II no 12 (Nov/Dec 2001), pp. 89-101.

Bove on resisting McDonald's, the Confederation Paysanne and the farmers' international, Via Campesina.

e. Zapatistas and Other Indigenous Resistance in Mexico

The Zapatistas, an armed movement to protect Mayan agriculture and culture from destruction by neoliberal policies, has increasingly relied on nonviolent methods and transnational solidarity and has become a symbol for the global justice movement. But there are other significant indigenous campaigns in Mexico and a wider resistance to elite policies. See: Latin American Perspectives: A Journal of Capitalism and Socialism, vol. 32, no. 4 (July 2005) which focuses on Mexico.

903.Harvey, Neil, 'Globalisation and resistance in post-cold war Mexico: Difference, citizenship and biodiversity conflicts in Chiapas', Third World Quarterly, vol. 22, no. 6 (2001), pp. 1045-1061.

Discusses Zapatistas and other indigenous organizations to show how resistance relates to struggle for collective rights and more inclusive form of democracy.

904, Holloway, John and Eloina Pelaez (eds), Zapatista! Reinventing Revolution in Mexico, London, Pluto, 1998, pp. 216. See also his exposition of Zapatismo: Holloway, John, Change the World Without Taking Power: The Meaning of Revolution Today, London Pluto, 2nd edition 2005, pp. 288.

905.Marcos, Subcommandante 'Punch card and hourglass', Interview with Gabriel Garcia Marquez and Roberto Pombo, New Left Review, II no. 9 (May/June 2001), pp. 69-80.

906.Nash, June, 'The war of peace: Indigenous women's struggles for justice in Chiapas, Mexico' in Susan Eva Eckstein and Timothy Wickham Crowley (eds.), What is Justice? Whose Justice? Fighting for Fairness in Latin America, Berkeley, University of California Press, 2003, pp. 285-312.

907.Olesen, Thomas, International Zapatismo: The Construction of Solidarity in the Age of Globalization, London, Zed Books, 2005, pp. 256.

See also: Kingsnorth, One No, Many Yeses, pp. 3-45 (F.5.), Klein,'Rebellion in Chiapas', Fences and Windows, pp. 208-23, and Marentes, Cynthia P., 'No borders: In community with the indigenous peoples of Chiapas' in Welton and Wolf (eds.), Global Uprising, pp. 144-9, and Reinke, Leanne, 'Utopia in Chiapas? Questioning disembodied politics', in Goodman (ed) Protest and Globalisation, pp. 75-87 (G.7.a.).

H. Bibliographies, Websites and Library Resources

a. Bibliographies

908. Carter, April, <u>Mahatma Gandhi: A Selected Bibliography</u>, Westport, CT, Greenwood Press, 1995, pp. 169.

Includes a summary biography, pp. 1-28 and detailed chronology. Special emphasis on links to campaigning groups in west and some coverage of literature on nonviolent theory. 472 items.

909. Carter, April, David Hoggett and Adam Roberts, <u>Nonviolent Action: A Selected Bibliography</u>, London, Housmans, 1970 and Haverford Penn, Center for Nonviolent Conflict Resolution 1970, pp. 84. Revised and enlarged edition of 1966 <u>Non-Violent Action: A Selected Bibliography</u>, pp. 48.

Covers theory of nonviolent action, including classic works, discussion of methods and case studies, plus sections on organizing for nonviolent action, civilian defence, and nonviolent social order.

910. <u>Gandhi: A Bibliography</u>, A holdings list of books and journals by and about Mohandas K. Gandhi in the Commonweal Collection, University of Bradford, Commonweal Collection and Gandhi Foundation, 1995, pp. 50.

Includes all aspects of Gandhi's life and thought – for example his constructive programme and views on economics, education, Indian politics and religion – as well as satyagraha.

911. Indian Council of Social Science Research, <u>Mohandas Karamchand Gandhi: A Bibliography</u>, New Delhi, Orient Longman, 1974, pp. 379. Introduced by R.R., Diwakar. Covers books in English up to 1972, 1095 items.

912. McCarthy, Ronald M. and Gene Sharp, <u>Nonviolent Action: A Research Guide</u>, New York, Garland, 1997, pp. 720 (hardback). An Albert Einstein Institution publication.

An exhaustive, annotated, bibliography, very strong on earlier history of nonviolent action, but also including many recent nonviolent campaigns up to the mid-1990s. Part I covers cases of nonviolent struggle, Part II the methods and dynamics of nonviolent action and theories of conflict, power and violence. NB the index is seriously flawed (a correct version is available on the Albert Einstein Institution website), but it is possible to trace campaigns through the List of Contents.

913. Pandiri, Ananda M., <u>A Comprehensive, Annotated Bibliography on Mahatma Gandhi</u>, Vol. 1 Westport CT, Greenwood Press, 1995, pp. 424. Foreword by Dennis Dalton.

This volume covers biographies, works by Gandhi and bibliographical sources in English.

914.Randle, Michael and Gene Sharp, 'Annotated Bibliography on Training for Non-Violent Action and Civilian-Based Defence', UNESCO Yearbook on Peace and Conflict Studies 1981, Westport CT, Greenwood Press and Paris, UNESCO, 1981, pp. 63-180.

Includes an introductory essay by Michael Randle on training and another by Gene Sharp on civilian-based defence.

b. Websites

Information about almost every issue is now available on the Web, and most campaigning groups and research centres now have their own web page which can be found via Google or another search engine. This section mentions some important sites that are likely to be maintained. It does not include web addresses mentioned elsewhere in the bibliography, and for web sites on preparation for nonviolent action, readers are referred to Section I.

The Albert Einstein Institution: http://www.aeinstein.org/

This institution founded by Gene Sharp provides extensive well researched information on nonviolent action around the world.

Center for Global Nonviolence, Hawaii, has a web page that includes on-line publications such as Islam and Nonviolence, and Buddhism and Nonviolence. http://www.globalnonviolence.org

European Social Forum: http://www.fse-esf.org/ This is the European branch of the World Social Forum: http://forumsocialmundial.org.br/

The WSF since 2001 and the ESF since 2002 have aimed to be an open meeting place for those opposed to neoliberalism.

International Center on Nonviolent Conflict: http://www.nonviolent-conflict.org/ website includes information on resources: books, articles, TV documentaries, related organizations, etc.

The Nonviolence Web: http://www.nonviolence.org/

Founded by Martin Kelley in 1995. Includes introductory material on nonviolence, direct action, news on peace movement and anti-war activities, and an archives section.

Peacemakers Trust: http://www.peacemakers.ca/

Includes materials on conflict, conflict resolution, reconciliation, and nonviolent direct action. Selected bibliography on nonviolence and nonviolent direct action available.

Peace News: http://www.peacenews.info/

Back copies are becoming available on the web. Since the 1950s Peace News has been particularly concerned to cover nonviolent direct action and has run (usually brief) reports on actions round the world (but especially in Britain). Whilst its primary focus is on opposing war and militarism, the paper has covered green, feminist, human rights and many other forms of radical protest. At the time this bibliography went to press, the Peace News Archives on line were available from December 1994 on, but earlier issues will eventually be accessible.

Program on Nonviolent Sanctions, http://www.wcfia.harvard.edu/ponsacs/ Navigate via 'seminars' to 'Transforming Struggle' for material based on seminars at Harvard in 1992.

Also available in printed form as: Transforming Struggle: Strategy and the Global Experience of Nonviolent Direct Action, Cambridge MA, Centre for International Affairs, Harvard University, 1992, (but not easily found in British libraries).

The War Resisters' International web page www.wri-irg.org includes a number of articles on nonviolent action under 'programme/nonviolence' including all the texts in Brian Martin and others, Nonviolent Struggle and Social Defence, Shelley Anderson and Janet Larmore (eds) (A.1.) and from WRI's 2001 study conference in Orissa, 'Nonviolence and Social Empowerment', see: Ney, Chris (ed.), Nonviolence and Social Empowerment (WRI 2001-2005). Available at: http://www.wri-irg.org/nonviolence/nvse-index.html

Nonviolent Tools and Philosophy is a distance learning course directed by Jorgen Johansen in the context of the Transcend Peace University: http://www.transcend.org/tpu/

Some individual nonviolent researchers have websites listing all their relevant publications. See for example:

Brian Martin, University of Wollongong, New South Wales, Australia http://www.uow.edu.au/arts/sts/bmartin/pubs/peace.html

Gene Sharp website: www.genesharp.com/ Due to come into operation circa 2006. Will house electronic copies of most of Sharp's publications as well as some work by others on nonviolent action.

c. MA and PhD Theses

There are unpublished theses on Gandhi, nonviolence or specific campaigns, which may be a useful source for those doing detailed research and with access to university libraries. They can be accessed at the library of the university concerned or through Inter-University library loan. Registers of PhD theses are available and are now on the internet. An illustrative selection of theses from the Bradford School of Peace Studies is listed below.

Garcia-Duran, Mauricio, To What Extent is There a Peace Movement in Colombia? An Assessment of the Country's Peace Mobilization 1978-2003, PhD Thesis

Overy, Bob, Gandhi as a Political Organiser: An Analysis of Local and National Campaigns in India 1915-1922, PhD Thesis, pp. 373.

MA Dissertations

Baird, Adam D.S., Peace Activism and Nonviolence: Dilemmas for Colombian Civil Society Organisations, 2004, pp. 102.

Garavaglia, Paola, The Potential Relevance of Non-violence Training Towards Empowerment, 2000, pp. 69.

Watson, John Francis, The Role of Violence and Nonviolence in the Liberation of South Africa, 1996, pp. 150.

(Some Bradford theses on the peace movement have also been cited in relevant sections.)

A few additional relevant PhD theses from other universities are:

Holzer, Boris, Transnational Subpolitics and Corporate Discourse. A Study of Environmental Protest and the Royal Dutch/Shell Group, University of London, 2001.

Mills, A.J., Workers Occupations, 1971-1975: A Socio-historical analysis of the development and spread of sit-ins, work-ins and worker co-operatives in Britain, University of Durham, 1982.

Wills, John, The Diablo Canyon, California: An Environmental History, University of Bristol, 2000, on nuclear protest and the Sierra Club.

d. Library Sources and Archives

i. Britain

The Commonweal Collection, J.B. Priestley Library, University of Bradford has focused on Gandhi and Gandhianism, nonviolence, peace studies and social movements of the past 50 years. It has 11,000 books and a valuable collection of relevant periodicals, 150 current, as well as a growing number of archives.

The Fraser Nuclear Disarmament Collection, also at the J.B. Priestley Library, University of Bradford, has archives from the campaigns of 1980s.

The London School of Economics holds some peace movement archives.

The Imperial War Museum has for some time been collecting materials on peace campaigns and conscientious objection, including taped interviews with activists.

ii. Netherlands

The International Institute for Social History, Amsterdam, has an extensive archive on social activism, including the archive of the War Resisters' International.

iii. USA

The Hoover Institution of War, Revolution and Peace (Stanford, California) is one of the major repositories for relevant archives, including materials on the European nuclear disarmament campaigns of the 1980s.

The Swarthmore College Peace Collection (Swarthmore, Pennsylvania) keeps the archives of many American peace organizations and will become the repository of Gene Sharp's papers on nonviolent action.

I. Preparation and Training for Nonviolent Action

Movements that expect their nonviolent actions to be met with violence generally pay attention to how to prepare themselves for that reaction. However, nonviolence training has come to involve much more than that – a range of activities embracing personal empowerment, group formation, campaign planning, strategy development, and preparation and evaluation of actions. This section focuses strictly on preparation for action.

Nevertheless the dividing lines between preparation for action and nonviolence as a way of life are by no means clear. A quality such as self-discipline, for Gandhi, was something best instilled by daily participation in constructive programme activities. – constructive work was, he said, the best training for satyagraha (nonviolent direct action). Rather than self-discipline, today's activists are more likely to emphasize the element of empowerment necessary for action. Again, however, they treat this not as a quality simply to be switched on during a particular event but as something that touches on attitudes underpinning everyday behaviour.

Many materials used in nonviolence training overlap with other forms of workshops – conflict transformation, pedagogy of the oppressed (Paolo Freire), theatre of the oppressed (Agosto Boal), nonviolent communication (Marshall Rosenberg), or the Alternatives to Violence programmes on institutional and domestic violence. Nonviolent action training has evolved according to what people have found useful and practical. Therefore workshop leaders have been eclectic in choosing and developing methods, using whatever works in their experience and culture, be it from the world of human potential workshops, of religious or spiritual practices, of business management options analysis or be it from other forms of campaigning.

Without going back to any of these sources, this section narrowly addresses preparation for nonviolent action. It omits technical 'how-tos' (such as on fence-scaling, making tripods, ways to lock on to objects, coping with tear gas) as well as briefings on the legal consequences of actions. For bibliographies on training, see:

915. Nonviolence International, <u>Annotated Bibliography of Nonviolent Action Training</u>.

A large but somewhat dated bibliography available on the website: <u>http://www.nonviolenceinternational.net/</u> It includes reports and evaluations of nonviolent action training workshops in all continents as well as handbooks produced for particular actions or campaigns. See also Randle, Michael and Gene Sharp, 'Annotated Bibliography on Training for Nonviolent Action and Civilian-Based Defence' (H a).

916.Beck, Sanderson, <u>Nonviolent Action Handbook</u>, Goleta, California: World Peace Communications, 2002, pp. 95. introductory texts, copies available from World Peace Communications, 495 Whitman St. #A, Goleta, CA 93117, USA and on their website: <u>www.san.beck.org/worldpeacebooks.org/News.html</u>

917.Clark, Howard, Sheryl Crown, Angela McKee and Hugh MacPherson, <u>Preparing for Nonviolent Direct Action</u>, London, Peace News/CND, 1984, pp. 80. A small book written for and by activists in the 1980s British nuclear disarmament movement, placing nonviolent direct action in a wider strategic framework, urging a small group approach to organizing nvda, describing a range of tools and exercises, and offering short success stories. Fanny Tribble's cartoons provide a humorous commentary on the text.

918.Coover, Virginia, Ellen Deacon, Charles Esser and Christopher Moore, <u>Resource Manual for a Living Revolution</u>, Philadelphia, New Society Publishers, first edition 1977, latest 1985, pp. 351. Familiarly known as the 'Monster Manual', this was *the* source book for English-speaking nonviolence trainers in the 1970s and 1980s. Produced collectively within the US Movement for a New Society, the Resource Manual aimed to be comprehensive – dealing with theory, working in groups, developing communities of support. personal growth, consciousness raising, training and education, organizing for change. Offers a host of exercises and other tools for preparing and evaluating nonviolent action, plus a section on practical skills (cooking, sign making, legal support).

919.Desai, Narayan, <u>Handbook for Satyagrahis: A Manual for Volunteers of Total Revolution</u>, New Delhi, Gandhi Peace Foundation, 1980. pp. 57. The founder of the Institute for Total Revolution outlines a Gandhian approach to nonviolence training.

920.Fisher, Simon, Dekha Ibrahim Abdi, Jawed Ludin, Richard Williams, Steve Smith and Sue Williams, <u>Working with Conflict: Skills and Strategies for Action</u>, London, Zed, 2000, pp. 185. Includes exercises and advice on active nonviolence.

921.Francis, Diana, <u>People, Peace and Power: Conflict Transformation in Action</u>, London, Pluto 2002, pp. 264. In addition to reflecting on her experiences as a workshop facilitator, Francis includes various tools and exercises. Puts people power and active nonviolence firmly at the centre of conflict transformation.

922.<u>Genetix Snowball Handbook for Action: A Guide to Safely Removing Genetically Modified Plants from Release Sites in Britain</u> (1998), http://www.fraw.org.uk/gs/handbook.html. A detailed guide to the issues and methods of this 'campaign of nonviolent civil responsibility'

923.Greenpeace, <u>Nonviolent Direct Action</u>. Advice sheets on planning actions, running a nonviolent direct action workshop and nvda and the law from: www.greenpeace.org.au/getactive/happen/nvda.html

924.Herngren, Per, <u>Paths of Resistance: The Practice of Civil Disobedience</u>, Philadelphia, New Society Publishers, 1993, pp. 214. Reflections and practical advice on civil disobedience by Swedish Ploughshares activist covering, amongst other things, nonviolence, affinity groups, accountability and overcoming fear.

925.Hunter, Daniel and George Lakey, <u>Opening Space for Democracy: Training Manual for Third-Party Nonviolent Intervention</u>, Philadelphia, Training for Change, 1501 Cherry St. Philadelphia PA 19102-1477 USA, 2004, pp. 634. Devised as a training resource for the Nonviolent Peace Force, this manual contains hundreds of training activities, with special emphasis on team-building and defending human rights. It includes over 60 handouts, an integrated 23-day curriculum, and many tips for trainers. Much of the book can be downloaded from www.trainingforchange.org.

926.Jelfs, Martin and Sandy Merritt, <u>Manual for Action</u>, London, Action Resource Group, 1982, pp. 81 – a shorter and more readable version of a mimeographed manual produced by Martin Jelfs after the early 1970s wave of British nonviolence training. Descriptions of various tools and exercises.

927.Lakey, George and Martin Oppenheimer, <u>Manual for Direct Action</u>, Chicago: Quadrangle Books, 1965, pp. 137. Produced during the US Civil Rights Movement. Foreword by Bayard Rustin.

928.Macy, Joanna, <u>Despair and Personal Power in the Nuclear Age</u>, Gabriola Island, BC: New Society Publishers, 1983, pp. 178. Includes 47 group exercises to 'ignite creative responses to the nuclear threat'.

929.Moyer, Bill (with JoAnn McAllister, Mary Lou Finley, and Steven Soifer), <u>Doing Democracy: The MAP Model for Organizing Social Movements</u>, Gabriola Island: New Society Publishers, 2001, pp. 228. From his central insight that some movements could not recognize when they were succeeding, Bill Moyer constructed his model MAP – Movement Action Plan – as a tool of strategic analysis for nonviolent movements. The book includes case studies of five US movements: civil rights, anti-nuclear energy, gay and lesbian, breast cancer, and anti-globalisation.

930.Nonviolence Training Project, <u>Nonviolence Trainers Resource Manual</u>, Melbourne, May 1995, pp. 211 – printed version available from Pt'chang Nonviolence Training Project, PO Box 2172MDC, Fitzroy VIC 3065, Australia or downloadable as pdf from: http://www.nonviolence.org.au/downloads/trainers_resource_manual_may05.pdf Wide-ranging manual with sections on Defining nonviolence, Power and conflict, Learning from other movements, Strategic Frameworks, Nonviolence and communication, Working in groups and Preparing for nonviolent action. Also includes case studies of action campaigns and a variety of sample agendas.

931.Olson, Theodore and Lynne Shivers, <u>Training for Nonviolent Action</u> London, War Resisters' International, 1970, pp. 42.

932.Rose, Chris, <u>How to Win Campaigns: 100 Steps to Success</u>. London, Earthscan, 2005, pp. 231). Tips from an environmental campaigner and communications consultant who has worked for Greenpeace, among other organisations.

933.Schutt, Randy, <u>Papers on Nonviolent Action and Cooperative Decision-Making</u>, www.vernalproject.org/RPapers/shtml, a nonviolence trainer's sample agendas and workshop notes dealing with Preparing for Nonviolent Action, Nonviolent Action Strategic Planning, Cooperative Decision-Making and Interpersonal Behaviour.

934.Starhawk, <u>Truth or Dare: Encounters with Power, Authority and Mystery</u>, New York: Harper Collins, 1990, pp. 370. Based in Starhawk's experience in 1980s peace movement affinity groups, this exploration of eco-feminist spirituality proposes an understanding of power along three axes – power-over, power-within and power-with. The book includes many 'exercises, rituals and meditations for individuals and groups' on themes connected with empowerment, group functioning, preparing for action, and recovering from violence. Starhawk's web page includes a section on resources for trainers developed by herself and others, including sample short and long agendas used in the anti-globalization movement and a wide range of advice sheets. See: http://www.starhawk.org/

935. Trident Ploughshares, <u>Tri-Denting It Handbook</u> (3rd edn 2001), http://www.trident.ploughshares.org/article1068/ has sections arguing the illegality of nuclear weapons before introducing the campaign and its action philosophy and suggesting how to prepare for action.

936. <u>Turning the Tide</u> – A British Quaker project which offers information sheets on various elements of preparing for nonviolent action. Current titles: <u>Planning a Campaign</u>, <u>Nonviolence and Active Nonviolence</u>, <u>Power</u>, <u>How Change Happens</u>, and <u>Consensus Decision-Making</u>. It also publishes <u>Making Waves, A Newsletter</u> available at www.turning-the-tide.org/infoSheets and from <u>Turning the Tide</u>, Quaker Peace & Social Witness, Friends House, 173 Euston Road, London NW1 2BJ

937. UHC collective, <u>NVDA Toolbox</u> – http://www.uhc-collective.org.uk/knowledge/toolbox/ Produced and distributed as a CD for the anti-Gulf War demonstrations of 2003. Compiled from diverse sources – from the peace to anti-motorway movements. Material ranges from meetings and organizing to particular methods, including 'how-tos' on techniques such as tripods and tunneling, and legal information.

938. War Resisters League, <u>Handbook for Nonviolent Action,</u> New York: War Resisters League, Donnelly/Colt Graphix, 1989, reprinted 1991, 1995, 1999, pp. 36. Designed as a tool for learning about different aspects of nonviolent civil disobedience actions, this draws on the handbooks produced for some of the major US civil disobedience actions of the 1970s and 1980s, and covers every stage of action preparation from planning a campaign to evaluation. Most of it can be downloaded as part of ACT UP New York's Manual for Civil Disobedience: http://www.actupny.org/documents//

See also:

Sharp, Gene, <u>Waging Nonviolent Struggle: 20th Century Practice and 21st Century</u> Potential (A. 1.) which includes an appendix (pp. 525-541) on 'Preparing a Strategic Estimate for a Nonviolent Struggle' based on Robert Helvey's work. A checklist of questions for such a strategic estimate appears as an appendix in Helvey's <u>On Strategic Nonviolent Conflict: Thinking about Fundamentals,</u> (A.1.).

Taylor, Richard K., <u>Blockade: A Guide to Nonviolent Intervention</u> (G.3.d.) Part 2 is a manual for direct action.

The Ruckus Society web page: www.ruckus.org/ Offers manuals on <u>Action Planning</u> and <u>Media</u> among other topics, plus numerous links to other web pages.

The Seeds for Change Network – http://www.seedsforchange.org.uk/ – offers a variety of workshops from practical organising skills (computers, fund-raising) to action preparation. Although their own writing does not use the term nonviolence, their web page includes material on nonviolence reproduced from Turning the Tide.

Index to Bibliography

Author Index by Item Numbers

A

Abdi, Dekha Ibrahim 920

Abernathy, Ralph 526

Abrahimian, Ervand 486

Ackerman, Peter 1, 2, 423

Aczel, Tamas 173

Agbodeka, Francis 100

Aiello, Pat 291

Akiner, Shirin 286

Akula, Vikram 814

Albert, David H. 487

Albert, Peter J 527

Alexander, Robert J. 458

Alexander, Sally 791

Ali, Tariq 345

Allen, Bruce 157

Allen, Sandra 791

Alport, Baron Charles James MacCall 89

Alternative Defence Commission 58

Alvarez, Sinia E. 629

Alvez, Maria Helena Moreira 451

American Friends Service Committee 435, 700

Amnesty International 228, 709

Ananaba, Wogu 110

Anarchy 614

Anderson, Jervis 528

Anderson, Shelley 22

Antal, Dan 219

Antoine, Charles 452

Apter, David E. 837

Arendt, Hannah 3

Arillo, Cecilio T. 350

Aronson, Geoffrey 490

Arnold, Guy 104

Arriagada, Gennaro 463

Arrowsmith, Pat 656

Arroyo, Gloria Macapagel 363

Arthur, Paul 564

Ascherson, Neal 207

Ash, Timothy Garton 124, 206, 424

Asher, Sarah Beth 37

Asia Monitor Resource Center 274

Association of Polish Students in Exile 200

'Athenian' 411

Aung San Suu Kyi 333, 334

Austin, Dennis 101

Awad, Mubarak R. 491

B

Bagguley, Paul 618, 619

Bahro, Rudolf 158, 803

Bailey, Ron 615

Baker, Colin 92

Balfour, Sebastian 417

Bandyopadhay, J. 820

Bannan, John F. 669

Bannan, Rosemary 669

Bar-On, Mordechai 507

Barnett, Robert 286

Bashirey, Hossein 488

Bastian, Gert 291

Baxendale, Martin 740

Beck, Sanderson 916

Becker, Jasper 115

Becker, Jill 644

Bedau, Hugo 4

Beer, Michael A. 335

Bello, Walden 351, 352

De Benedetti, Charles 670

Benewick, Robert 5

Bennett, George 105

Bennett, Jana 444

Bennett, Scott 843

Benson, Mary 294

Bernhard, Michael H. 196

Berrigan, Daniel 671

Bethell, Nicholas 197

Beynon, Huw 605, 832

Bhatia, Bela 75

Bhutto, Benazir 346

Biesemans, Sam 710

Bigelow, Albert 741

Biko, Steve 295

Bircham, Emma 858

Bitar, Sergio 459

Blackburn, Robin 637

Blatt, Martin 711

De Blaye, Edouard 418

Bleiker, Roland 6, 159

Blincoe, Nicholas 73

Blumberg, Herbert H. 14, 77, 745, 770, 854

Boardman, Elizabeth F. 74

Boardman, Elizabeth Jelinek 672

Bondurant, Joan V. 38

Boots, Wilson T. 445

Boserup, Anders 59

Bouchier, David 785

Boulton, David 725

Bourdeaux, Michael 225

Bouvard, Marguerite Guzman 440

Bove, Jose 902

Bowen, James 807

Boyle, Richard 673

Bradshaw, Ross 742

Braithwaite, Constance 712

Branch, Taylor 529, 530

Branford, Sue 583, 584

Brant, Stefan 154

Bregman, Ahron 492

Breyman, Steven 743

Brierley, John 520, 627

Brill, Harry 623

Brinkley, Douglas 531

Broadbent, Jeffrey 833

Brock, Peter 688, 713

Broers, Laurence 404

Bromke, Adam 198

Brown, Archie 241

Brown, Carolyn A. 111

Brown, Cynthia 464

Brown, Judith M. 39, 40, 41

Brown, L. David 889

Brown, Michael 804

Browne, Michael 226

Brumberg, Abraham 199

Buckland, Patrick 560

Buckle, Catherine 322

Buckley, Kevin 471

Bugajski, Janusz 116

Bukovsky, Vladimir 227

Bulletin of Peace Proposals 60

Bunster, Ximena 465

Burgess, Guy 35

Burgess, Heidi 35

Burgmann, Verity 628, 664,744,838

Burke, Patrick 125

Burrowes, Robert 61, 765

Bussey, Gertrude 689

C

Cairns, Brendan 744

Caldecott, Leonie 777

Calderon, Ricardo Arias 472

Callahan, William A. 375

Callinicos, Alex 296, 606

Camara, Helder 454

Campbell, Bextrix 787

Carbado, Devon W. 532

Carmichael, Stokeley 533

Carr, Raymon 419

Carson, Clayborne 534, 535

Carter, April 7, 248, 690, 745, 766, 908,909

Carvalho de Jesus, Mario 453

Case, Clarence Marsh 8

Catholic Institute for International Relations 316

Caute, David 636

Ceadel, Martin 701

Chamberlain, Chris 625

Chambers, John Whiteclay 321, 718

Chan, Stephen 323

Charlton, John 858

Charlton, Michael 651

Chatfield, Charles 42, 78, 670, 674

Chatterjee, Kiron 622

Chavkin, Samuel 466

Chazan, Naomi 508

Cheng Tun-jen 369

Cherrington, Ruth 269

Chesterman, John 844

Childress, James F. 702

Chilton, Patricia 693

Chou Yangsun 370

Church of England 726

Clark, Donald N. 338

Clark, Howard 317, 399, 917

Clayton, Anthony 106

Cliff, Tony 786

Clogg, Richard 412

Clemens, Walter C. Jr. 133

Clutton Brock, Guy 93

Coad, Malcolm 441

Coates, Ken 595, 659

Cock, Jacklyn 318, 319

Cockburn, Alexander 637

Cohen, Fay G. 852

Cohen, Carl 9

Cohen, Jonathan 405

Cohen, Lenard J. 391

Cohen, R.S. 251

Cohen, Robin 632

Cohen, Stephen F. 229

Committee to Defend Czechoslovak Socialists 145

Cone, James H. 536

Connors, Libby 815

Cook, Alice 796

Cooney, Robert 10

Cooper, Joshua 893

Coote, Anna 787

Coover, Virginia 918

Copley, Anton 43

Cortright, David 353

Cotton, James 339

Coulson, Meg 767

Cox, Andrew 832

Cox, Robert 441

Coy, Patrick G. 78

Crabtree, John 446, 882

Crampton, Richard 114

Crawford, Vicki L. 537

Croan, Melvin 153

Cross, Eddie 324

Crossley, N. 859

Crow, Ralph E. 482

Crown, Sheryl 917

Curry, Jane Leftwich 117

D

Dajani, Souad 493, 494

Dalai Lama 287, 288

Dalton, Dennis 44

Dalton, Russell J. 626, 805

David, Nathaniel 460
Davis, Uri 509, 711
Day, Mark 599
Deacon, Ellen 918
Della Porta, Donatella 633
Deloria, Vine Jr. 853
D'Emilio, John 538
Deming, Barbara 11, 746, 778
Desai, Ashwin 886
Desai, Narayan 919
Deutsch, Yvonne 511
Deutsch, Richard 576
Development 860
Devlin, Bernadette 565
Djilas, Milovan 249
Doder, Dusko 250
Doherty, Brian 819, 839
Dolci, Danilo 593
Donnet, Pierre-Antoine 289
Doolin, Dennis 260
Doyle, Timothy 816
Drake, Paul 467
Dreze, Jean 75
Drezov, Kyril 403
Driver, Christopher 747
Dromey, Jack 792
Duchen, Claire 788
Duke, Michael S. 270
Dumbrell, John 657
Dunkerley, James 447, 883
Dunne, John Gregory 600
Duvall, Jack 1, 423
Dyker, David M. 401

E
Ebert, Theodore 155
Eckstein, Susan Eva 906
Economist 410
Edwards, Michael 634, 867, 889
Eglin, Josephine 797
Eglitis, Olgerts 134

Eguren, Enrique 78
Eisenmann, Roberto 473
Elliot, Jean Leonard 842
Elliott, Iain 425
El-Tahiri, Jihan 492
Elwood, Douglas J. 354
Epstein, Barbara 12, 875
Erickson, Kenneth P. 455
Escobar, Arturo 629
Esser, Charles 918
Evangelista, Matthew 733
Evans, Cecil 714
Evans, Geoff 891
Evans, Gwynfor 518, 519
Evans, Martin 768

F
Fairbanks, Charles H. 406
Fang Lizhi 271
Fannin, Anne 577
Farmer, James 539
Farrell, Michael 566
Faslane Peace Camp 748
Feinberg, Abraham L. 658
Feit, Edward 297
Fejto, Francois 191
Feldman, Herbert 347
Fenton, James 355
Ferber, Michael 675
de Figueiredo, Antonio 382
Fink, Christina 336
Finkelstein, Norman 495
Finley, Mary Lou 929
Fischer, Louis 45
Fisera, Vladimir 139
Fisher, Jo 442
Fisher, Simon 920
Fisk, Robert 575
Flam, Helena 806
Flessati, Valerie 691

Fleras, Augie 842
Flynn, Eileen P. 716
Foner, Philip S. 676
Forman, James 540
Forrester, John 896
Forward, R. 660
Fox, Jonathan 889
Francis, Diana 921
Fraser, Ronald 638
Freeman, Jo 789
Fullbrook, Mary 160
Furlong, William L. 474
Fusi, Juan Pablo 419

G
Galligan, Brian 844
Galtung, Johan 62, 496
Gamarra, Edouardo 449
Gandhi, Mohandas K. 46, 47, 910
Garrow, David J. 541
Gaventa, John 634, 867, 889
Gedicks, A.L. 848, 892
'Genetix Snowball' 922
George, Susan 861
Gern, Christiane 166
Giddings, Paula 542
Gills, Barry K. 893
Giron, Father Andres 590
Gittleman, Zvi 247
Glenny, Misha 386
Glock, Oriel 583
Gokay, Bulent 403
Golan, Galia 140, 141
Goodman, David S.G. 264
Goodman, Geoffrey 607
Goodman, James 862, 891
Gorbachev, Mikhail 242
Gorbanevskaya, Natalia 230
Gott, Richard 439
Gould, Denis 742
Gould, Kenneth 817

Graeber, David 863
Graham-Yool, Andrew 443
Grant, Philip 482
Green, Peter 201
Greenpeace 923
Greenwood, J. 596
Gregg, Richard B.13
Grenfell, Damian 845
Gress, David 692
Griffin-Nolan, Ed. 76
Grix, Jonathan 161
Grunberg, Danielle 239
Gruenewald, Guido 674
Grunfeld, A. Tom 290
Guillermo, Lora 448
Gyorgy, Anna 821

H

Habermas, Jurgen 127
Haggard, Stephen 369
Hain, Peter 313
Halberstam, David 665
Hale, Angela 897
Hall, Richard 95
Hall-Cathala, David 510
Halstead, Fred 677
Hamilton, Charles V. 533
Hammel-Greene, M.E. 661
Hammond, John, L. 585
Han Dongfang 281
Han Minzhu 272
Hankiss, Elemer 181
Haraszti, Miklos 182
Hardiman, David 48
Harding, Vincent 543
Hare, A. Paul 14, 77, 745, 770, 854
Harford, Barbara 798
Harman 174, 383
Harringey Solidarity Group 620
Harrison, J. Frank 273
Hart, Lindsay 807
Harvey, Neil 903

Havel, Vaclav 15, 146
Hawkes, Nigel 128
Hayes, Graeme 818
Haynes, Viktor 231
Hazelhurst, Kayleen M. 850
He Qinglian 282
Helsinki Watch Report 118
Helvey, Robert L. 16
Hentoff, Nat 703
Herngren, Per 924
Hewison, Kevin 376, 829, 830
Hildebrandt, Rainer 156
Hinton, James 749
Hirsch, Philip 829
Hirschmann, Albert O. 162
Hiscocks, Richard 193
Hoffman, Ronald 527
Hoggett, David 909
Holloway, John 904
Holmes, Robert L. 17
Holroyd, Fred 727
Holt, Len 544
Hope, Marjorie 298
Hopkins, Sarah 798
Horeman, Bart 717
Hosking, Geoffrey 243
Howorth, Jolyon 693
Howys, Sian 520
Hudson, Kate 392, 750
Hudson, Michael C. 497
Hudson, Ray 832
Hunnius, F.C. 645
Hunt, Timothy J. 894
Hunter, Daniel 925
Hunter, F. Robert 498
Hunter, Robert 753, 808
Hunter, Robert Edwards 735
Hurley, Judith 586
Hurwitz, Deena 512
Hutt, Michael 331
Hutton, Drew 815

I

Ibrahim, Saad E. 482
Index on Censorship 265
Indian Council of Social Science Research 911
International Crisis Group 332
Ionescu, Ghita 218
Isaksson, Eva 465
Isichei, Elizabeth 113

J

Jacobs, Paul 646
Jacobson, Julius 119
Jaksic, Ivan 467
James, C.L.R. 102
Jelfs, Martin 926
Jenkins, Bruce 69
Jenkins, J. Craig 601
Jezer, Marty 751
Jiang Xueqin 283
Johns, R. 898
Johnson, Bryan 356
Jones, Chris 742
Jones, Lynne 126, 777, 799
Jones, Michael 612
Jopke, Christian 163, 822
Jordan, John 881
Jumbala, Prudhisan 830

K

Kaltefleiter, Werner 734
Kaminer, Reuven 513
Kanaan, Ramsey 621
Kaplan, John 371
Karol, K.S. 192
Karumidze, Zurab 407
Kasinski, Renee Goldsmith 678
Kaufman, Edy 479
Kaunda, Kenneth 87, 96
Kavan, Zdenek 152
Keck, Margaret E. 890
Kecskemeti, Paul 175
Keithly, David M 164
Keller, Adam 514

Kelly, Kathy 75
Kelly, Petra K. 291, 802
Kemp-Welch, A. 208
Kenedi, Janos 183
Kennedy, R. Scott 483
Kenyatta, Jomo 107
Keyes, Gene 63, 83
Khalidi, Rashid 499
Khasbulatov, Ruslan 244
Khidasheli, Tinatin 408
Kidron, Peretz 515
King, P. 661
Kingsnorth, Paul 587
Kim Chong Lim 340
Kim Dae Jung 341
Kim Shinil 342
King, Martin Luther Jr. 545,546,547,548
King, Mary 549
Kirk, Gwyn 796
Klarman, Michael J 550
Klein, Naomi 616, 864, 865
Kleinbaum, Paul 711
Klippenstein, Lawrence 120
Kluver, Alan R. 343
Koirala, Niranjan 331
Komisar, Lucy 357
Konrad, George 184, 185
Kopacsi, Sandor 176
Kopstein, Jeffrey 165
Kostovicova, D. 400
Koszegi, Ferenc 186
Krnjevic-Miskovic, Damjan de 393
Kronlid, Lotta 769
Kruegler, Christopher 2
Kuechler, Manfred 626
Kumar, M. 278
Kuntz, Philipp 396
Kuper, Leo 299
Kurtz, Lester 37
Kusin, Vladimir V. 147
Kuzio, Taras 426

L
Laan, E. 436
Lakey, George 18, 925, 927
Lamberts, Marc 275
Landau, Saul 646
Lande, Carl H. 365
Lansbury, Nina 891
Lapchick, Richard 314
Laqueur, Walter 735
Larmore, Janet 22
Lebor, Adam 394
Lee, Jenny 664, 744
Lernoux, Penny 432
Levine, Daniel 551
Levy, Jacques 602
Lewis, Flora 194
Lewis, John 552
Lewis, Paul G. 259
Liddington, Jill 800
Lieven, Anatol 135
Lifton, Robert Jay 679
Ligt, Bartelemy de 19
Link, Perry 277
Linn, Ruth 516
Lipset, Seymour Martin 647
Lipski, Jan Jozef 202
Lipski, M. 624
Litricin, Vera 771
Little, Allan 389
Littner, Bertil 337
Locke, Elsie 694
Lodge, Tom 300
Lomax, Bill 177
Long, Simon 372
Lopez, Omar Williams 470
Lopez Levy, Marcella 878
Low, P. 278
Luckhardt, Ken 301
Ludin, Jawed 920
Lustick, Ian S 500
Luthuli, Albert 302
Lynd, Alice 20, 680
Lynd, Staughton 20, 675

Lyons, Glenn 622
Lyttle, Brad 779

M
McAllister, Jo Ann 929
McAllister, Pam 21
McCabe, Saraha 608
McCabe, Patrice 879
McCann, Eamonn 567
McCarthy, John D. 433
McCarthy, Mary 652
McCarthy, Ronald M. 912
McCaughan, Michael 439
McCluskey, Conn 568
McConville, Maureen 643
McCormack, Gavan 635
McCormick, John 809
McCrea, Frances B. 752
MacFarquahar, Roderick 261
McFaul, Michael 384
McGill, Jack 598
McGuinness, Kate 29
MacIntyre, Donald 612
Mack, Andrew 59
McKean, Margaret A. 834
McKee, Angela 917
McKeown, Ciaran 578
McKittrick, David 569
MacLean, Sandra J. 325
McManus, Philip 431, 470, 480, 588, 590
McNeish, James 594
Macpherson, Fergus 97
MacPherson, Hugh 917
McPherson, William 220
MacShane, Denis 209
McTaggart, David 753
McVea, David 569
Macy, Joanna 928
Madgwick, P.J. 521
Magas, Branka 387

Mahoney, Liam 78
Makasa, Kapasa 98
Malcolm X 553
Maliqi, Shkelzen 401
Malloy, James M. 449
Mamonova, Tatyana 233
Mandela, Nelson 303, 304
Mandle, W.F. 846
Marcos, Subcommandante 905
Markovic, Mihailo 251
Martin, Brian 22, 29, 72
Matthiesen, Peter 603
Markle, Gerald E. 752
Marx, Anthony 305
Mastnak, Tomaz 259
May, John 804
Mayekiso, Mzwanele 887
Mayer, Peter 704
Mboya, Tom 108
Meaden, Bernadette 695
Medvedev, Roy 229
Medvedev, Zhores 234, 235
Meier, August 554
Meldrun, Andrew 326
Menashe, Louis 681
Menchu, Rigoberta 437
Meray, Tibor 173, 178
Mercado, Monina Allarey 358
Meredith, Martin 306
Merrick (sic) 840
Merriman, Hardy 30
Merritt, Sandy 926
Merton, Thomas 705
Mertus, Julie 402
Meyer, Matt 86
Michalowski, Helen 10
Michelson, Cherry 307
Michnik, Adam 203
Mihajlov, Mihajlo 252
Miliband, Ralph 625
Miller, Christopher A 30

Miller, Jill 793
Miller, William Robert 23
Milne, Seumas 609
Miniotaite, Grazina 136
Mitcalfe, Barry 754
Mitchell, M. 367
Mitprasat, Maneerat 830
Mladjenovic, Lepa 771
Mlynar, Zdenek 142
Mok Chiu Yu 273
Monbiot, George 866
Moncrieff, Anthony 377, 651
Moore, Barrington Jr. 49
Moore, Christopher 918
Moorhouse, Bert 625
Morales, Rolando 883
Morgan, Gerald 522
Morley, Morris A. 461
Morris, Aldon 555
Morse, David 877
Moser-Puangsuwan, Yoshua 79, 765, 773
Moskos, Charles C. 321, 718
Moyer, Bill 929
Mufson, Steven 308
Mundey, Jack 838
Murphy, John 561
Muste, A.J. 703, 755,
Mwangilwe, Goodwin B. 99
Myant, Martin 210

N
Nanda, Bal R. 50
Nash, June 450, 906
Nathan, Andrew J. 277, 370
Nathan, Lawrence 318, 320
Nba, Nina Emma 112
Neale, Jonathan 876
Needham, Andrea 769
Nelkin, Dorothy 823
New Internationalist 280

Newell, Peter 867
Newfield, Jack 648
Newnham, Tom 824
Ngwane, Trevor 888
Nkrumah, Kwame 103
Nodia, Ghia 409
Nonviolence International 915
Nonviolence Training Project 930
Noone, Val 662
Notes from Nowhere 868, 884

O
Oates, Stephen B. 556
O'Ballance, Edgar 501
Obi, Cyril I. 894
O'Brien, Conor Cruise 570
O'Connor, Fionnuala 571, 579
Odinga, Oginga 109
O'Dochartaigh, Niall 572
O'Donnell, Dalry 580
O'Dowd, Liam 562
Oksenberg, Michael 275
Olesen, Thomas 907
Olson, Theodore 80, 931
Opp, Karl-Dieter 166
Oppenheimer, Martin 927
Orkin, Mark 315
Orwell, George 51
Osmond, John 523
Overy, Bob 52, 581, 582
Oxford University Socialist Discussion Group 640
Oxhorn, P. 629

P
Packard, George R. 780
Pagnucco, Ronald 78, 433
Paisal, Sridaradhanya 378

Paley, Grace   772
Palit, Chitaroopa   831
Pandiri, Ananda M.   913
Papandreou, Andreas   413
Parekh, Bhikhu   53, 54
Paribatra, Sukhumbhand   379
Parkis, Jan   807
Parkman, Patricia   430
Pascual, Dette   359
Patterson, Matthew   819
Paulson, Joshua   30
<u>Peace News</u>   81
Peace, Roger C.   697
Peck, James   557
Pelaez, Eloina   904
Pelikan, Jiri   148
Pentikainen, Merja719
Peretz, Don   502
Perez Esquivel, Adolfo   433
Perry, Elizabeth J.   262, 284
Pervan, Ralph   253
Petras, James   461
Pfaltzgraff, Robert L.   734
Philipsen, Dirk   167
Plamenic, D.   254
Polet, Robert   211
Pollack, Maxine   116
Pollak, Michael   823
Posner, Charles   642
Potel, Jean-Yves   212
Powers, Roger S.   24
Powers, Thomas   682
Prasad, Devi   698
Pravda, Alex   247
Preston, Paul   420
Price, Jerome   825
Prins, Gwyn   151, 181
Prokosh, Mike   869
Purdie, Bob   573

Q
Quaker Council for European Affairs   720
Quaker Peace and Service   721

R
Radcliffe, Sarah   434
Radosh, Ronald   681
Rady, Martyn   221
Rai, Shirin M.   632
Raina, Peter   204
Ramachandra, Guha   827
Ramet, Pedro   168
Ramet, Sabrina P.   120, 388, 402
Randle, Michael   25, 82, 129,579,766, 914
Ranger, Terence   88, 327
Ransby, Barbara   558
Ratesh, Nestor   222
Rawlinson, Roger   781
Raymond, Laura   869
Read, Peter   847
Redaway, Peter   236
Reece, B.   660
Reeves, Ambrose   309
Reid, Anna   422
Reid, Ben   368
Remnick, David   245
Reynolds, Earle   756
Richards, Susan   782
Riese, Hans-Peter   149
Rigby, Andrew   82, 503
Roberts, Adam   65, 66, 130, 144, 666, 909
Roberts, Katherine   480
Robertson, Heather   849
Robie, David   757
Robson, Bridget Mary   758
Rocha, Jan   584
Rochon, Thomas R.   736
Rock, David   880
Rogally, Joe   794
Rogers, John   296

Rohr, John A.   722
Rolston, Bill   562
Rootes, Christopher   810
Rose, Chris   932
Rose, Richard   563
Rosenberg, Tina   213
Roseneil, Sasha   801
Ross, Andrew   899
Rotberg, Robert I.   90
Rouse, Jacqueline   537
Routledge, Paul   630
Roy, Denny   373
Rubenstein, Joshua   237
Rucht, Dietrich   626
Rudwick, Elliott   554
Rupnik, Jacques   205
Rusinow, Dennison   255

S
Saich, Tony   276
Sakharov, Andrei   238
Sale, Kirkpatrick   649
Samudavanija, Chai-Anan   380
Samuel, Raphael   610
Sanders, Lee   791
Sandford, John   169
Sanford, Victoria   436
Saunders, Jonathan   611
Savage, Donald C.   106
Saville, John   625
Sawa, Nagayo   837
Sawyer, Steve   759
Sawyer, Suzana   885
Schapiro, Leonard   121
Schell, Jonathan   26, 728
Schell, Orville   266
Schiff, Ze-ev   504
Schlabach, Gerald   431, 470, 480, 588, 590
Schlissel, Lillian   723
Schmid, Alex P.   67
Schnaiberg, Allan   817
Schock, Kurt   27
Schopflin, George   187, 188
Scholmer, Joseph   224

Schragg, James L.   854
Schultz, Jim   884
Schutt, Randy   933
Schwarz, Ronald D.   292
Schweitzer, Christine
   773
Schwenk, Richard L.
   360
Scott, James C.   28
Scott, Michael   310
Scranton, Margaret E.
   475
Seale, Patrick   643
Seegers, Annette   321
Seel, Benjamin   819
Selden, Mark   284
Sellers, John   870
Semelin, Jacques   68
Semyonova, Olga   231
Senn, Alfred Erich   137
Seymour, James D.   267
Sharoni, Simona   517
Sharp, Gene
   29,30,55,69,70,505,912,
   914
Shaw, Linda M.   897
Shawcross, William   653
Sheehan, Neil   654
Shehadi, Nazim   485
Sher, Gerson S.   256
Shiva, Vandana   820
Shivers, Lynne   931
Shorrock, Tim   344
Short, Philip   94
Shridharani, Krishnalal
   56
Sibley, Mulford Q.   31
Sikkink, Kathryn   890
Silber, Laura   389
Simons, Donald L.   683
Simons, Mike   606
Simpson, John   131, 444
Simpson, Tony   760
Singer, Daniel   214
Singh, Yogendra   707
Sithole, M.   328
Sivaraska, Sulak   381

Skilling, H. Gordon   122,
   143, 150
Slate, W.M.   650
Small. Melvin   684, 685
Smith, Alison   105
Smith, Jackie   78
Smith, Paul Chaat   855
Smith, Steve   920
Smith, Trevor   5
Smith. Warren W. Jr.
   293
Smuts, Dene   311
Sobhan, Rehman   348
Soifer, Steven   929
Solnit, David   621, 871
Solnit, Rebecca   32, 761
Spear, Thomas   85
Spooner, Mary Helen
   468
'Starhawk'   872, 934
Starr, Amory   873
Stead, Jean   239, 795
Stedile, Joao Pedro   589
Steele, Jonathan   246,
   427
Stein, Walter   729
Steiner, Stan   856
Stempel, John D.   489
Stepan, Alfred   456
Stiglitz, Jospeh   857
Stojanovic, Svetozar
   257
Stokes, Gale   132
Stolwijk, Marc   717
Stoppard, Tom   385
Strangio, Paul   835
Sullivan, Lawrence R.
   275
Summy, Ralph   71, 663
Sunday Times Insight
   Team   382, 574, 757
Sutherland, Bill   86
Syrop, Konrad   195
Szasz, Andrew   836
Szczypiorski, Andrzej
   190
Szelenyi, Ivan   185

T
Talbott, John   774
Tarrow, Sidney   633
Taylor, Bron Raymond
   811, 814, 848,
Taylor, Clyde   686
Taylor, Richard   699,
   762, 797
Taylor, Richard K.   775
Taylor, Ronald B.   604
Teichman, Jenny   706
Theodorakis, Mikis   414
Thich Nhat Hanh   667
Third World Quarterly
   330
Thomas, Ned   524
Thomas, Robert   395
Thompson, Ben   763
Thompson, Edward P.
   186, 730
Thompson, Mark   390
Thompson, Mark R.   33,
   170, 361, 396
Tims, Margaret   689
Tokes, Laszlo   223
Tokes, Rudolf L.   123,
   189, 240
Tomlinson, Mike   562
Touraine, Alain   215, 826
Tracy, James   631
Trapans, Jan Arveds   138
Trident Ploughshares,   935
True, Michael   278
Turning the Tide   936
Tutu, Desmond   312

U
UHC Collective   937
Unger, Jonathan   279
United Reformed Church
   34
Unnithan, T.K.N.   707
Unseem, Michael   687
Urban, Jan   151
Urquhart, Clara   731
Urrutia Montoya, Miguel
   591

US Bishops 732
US Fellowship of
  Reconciliation 435
US Institute of Peace
  397

V

Valenzuela, Arturo 462,
  469
Valenzuela, J. Samuel
  469
Vali, Ferenc 179
Van den Dungen, Peter
  674
Varney, Wendy 22, 72
Vejoda, Ivan 401
Vickers, Adrian 22
Vidal, John 901
Vlachos, Helen 415
Vogele, William B. 24,
  506
Volkmer, Werner 171
Voss, Peter 166
Vural, L. 898

W

Waldman, Louis 559
Waldman, Sidney R. 782
Walesa, Lech 217
Walker, Charles C. 776,
  782, 783
Walker, Rangini 851
Wall, Brenda 301
Wall, Derek 841
Waller, Michael 403
Wallis, Jan 791
Walzer, Michael 708
Wapner, Paul 812
War Resisters'
  International 724
War Resisters League
  938
Warner, Robert Allen
  855

Warriner, Doreen 592
Ward, Philip 114
Ward, Colin 617
Wasserstrom, Jeffrey N.
  285
Waterman, Peter 897
Watts, Max 353
Waugh, Michael H.M.
  784
Way, Lucan A. 428
Weber, Thomas 79, 83,
  84,765,773,828
Weeks, John 476
Wehr, Paul 35
Wei Jingshen 268
Weinberg, Adam 817
Weinstein, Martin 477,
  481
Weise, Donald 532
Weiss, Peter 659
Welles, Benjamin 421
Welton, Neva 874
Wertsch, James V. 407
Westcott, Shauna 311
Westwood, Sallie 434
Weyler, Rex 813
Wheaton, Bernard 152
White, Stephen 247
Whitehead, Lawrence
  446
Whitney, Jennifer 881
Wickham-Crowley,
  Timothy 906
Widgery, David 641
Williams, Richard 920
Williams, Sue 920
Wills, Jane 897
Wilsher, Peter 612
Wilson, Elizabeth 790
Wilson, Andrew 429
Wilson, Duncan 258
Wilson, Joanna 769
Wilson, Mary 625

Windrich, Elaine 329
Windsor, Philip 144
Winterton, Jonathan 613
Winterton, Ruth 613
Wintle, Justin 655
Wirmark, Bo 668
Wittner, Lawrence S.
  737, 738, 739
Wolf, Linda 874
Wolin, Sheldon, S. 647
Wolpert, Stanley 349
Women in Black
  (Belgrade) 398
Wood, J.R.T. 91
Woodcock, George 57
Woodhouse, C.M. 416
Woods, Barbara 537
Woods, Roger 172
Woodward, C. Vann 525
Wu Ningkun 263

Y

Ya'ari, Edud 504
Yanez Berrios, Blanca
  470
Yannopoulos, George
  412
Yearley, Steve 896
York, Barry 664
Young, James 298
Young, Nigel 639, 688,
  699, 797

Z

Zahn, Gordon C. 705
Zelter, Angie 764, 769
Zhang Liang 277
Zielonka, Jan 216
Zimbalist, Andrew 476
Zinn, Howard 36, 535
Zinner, Paul E. 180
Zirker, Daniel 457
Zunes, Stephen 37, 362,
  457, 893

Subject Index by Page Numbers

This is not an exhaustive subject index, but a guide for those wishing to check on well know theorists of nonviolence, leaders of movements, prominent dissenters, campaigns and organizations; or to look up protests in different countries and parts of the world.

A

Accompaniment, 19, 20; of Central American refugees, 11, 92

Africa, and decolonization, 22-28; resisting oppression, 60-67

African National Congress (South Africa), 60, 61, 62, 63

Albania, 30, 31

Albert Einstein Institution, 5, 10, 176

Algerian War, protests against, 138, 151, 152, 153

Allende, Salvador, 95, 96

Amnesty International, reports by, 47, 49, 91, 141

Aquino, Cory, 72, 73

Arendt, Hannah, 5, 8, 38

Argentina, resisting military dictatorship, 92-93; resisting neoliberalism, 171-71

Asia, 11, 20, 67-77

Aung San Suu Kyi, 10, 68-69

Australia, 127, 128; environmental protest, 162, 164, 165; feminism in, 155; indigenous campaigns, 166, 172; nuclear weapons protest, 148; opposing Vietnam War, 131, 133; peace protest, 138

Austria, environmental protest, 160

B

Bahro, Rudolf, 36, 160

Baliapal anti-missile campaign, 128, 155

Balkan Peace Team, 19

Baltic Republics of USSR, 50; See also Estonia, Latvia and Lithuania

Banda, Hastings, 24, 25

Belarus (dissent today) 78-79

Berlin Wall, building of, 36; fall of, 8, 33, 36-37, 78

Berrigan, Daniel and Philip, 134

Bhutto, Benazir, 71

Bhutto, Zulfikar, 71, 72

Biko, Steve, 61-62

Black Power (USA), 108, 109-10

Black Sash (South Africa), 63

Bolivia, land occupations, 119-20; resisting neoliberalism, 171; resisting repression, 93-94

Bove, Jose, 173

Brazil, land occupations, 119, 120, 121; resisting repression, 94-95

Britain, 8; COs in, 142, 178; environmental protest, 160, 161, 162, 164, 165; feminism in, 155, 157, 158, 159; nonviolence training, 181, 182; nuclear weapons protest, 137, 144, 145, 147, 148, 149, 150, 151; peace archives, 178; peace protest, 137, 138, 139; rent refusal, 125-26; student protest, 129-30. See also: Miners' Strike, Poll Tax protests

Buddhists, in Vietnam, 133-34

Bulgaria, dissent in, 29-30, 31

Burma, in 1988, 12, 67, 68-69; in 1970s, 69; boycotts of, 68, 69

Bus Boycott, Montgomery, Alabama, 108, 111

C

Camara, Helder, 95

Campaign for Nuclear Disarmament (CND), 84, 144, 149

Canada, COs in, 142; indigenous campaigns, 165, 166-67; US draft evaders in, 131, 135, 139

Central African
 Federation, resistance
 to 24-26. See also:
 Malawi, Zambia,
 Zimbabwe
Charter 77, 33, 34, 35, 38
Chavez, Cesar, 123
Chile, mothers' protest,
 92; resisting Pinochet,
 12, 96-97; truckers'
 strike 4, 95-96
China, 29; May 4th, 53,
 54; dissent (1950s-
 70s), 54-55; dissent in
 1990s, 57-58. See also:
 Tiananmen, 1989
Chipko movement, 128,
 161, 163
Christian Peacemakers
 Team, 19
Civil Rights Movement,
 Northern Ireland, 41,
 113, 114-16;
Civil Rights Movement,
 USA, 3,4,7,9,10,14,
 107-12, 116, 128, 140,
 182
Civilian defence, 3, 10,
 11, 13, 16-18, 176; and
 governments, 16
Cochabamba water
 protest, 171
Colombia, 20, 91, 177,
 178; environmental
 protest, 173; land
 occupations, 120;
 peace communities in,
 91
Comiso missile base
 protest, 145, 151
Committee of 100, 84,
 149
Congress of Racial
 Equality (CORE), 107,
 110, 112
COs and draft resistance,
 10, 139-40, 141-44;

E. Europe, 30; South
 Africa, 64. See also:
 Vietnam War,
 opposition to
Czechoslovakia, dissent
 in 30, 31, 33-34; peace
 activity in, 34;
 resistance to Soviet
 occupation, 17, 33, 34,
 152. See also: Charter
 77, Prague Spring,
 Velvet Revolution

D
Dalai Lama, 58, 59
Democracy Movement,
 see China
Denmark, COs in, 143
Djilas, Milovan, 51, 52
Dolci, Danilo, 121, 146
Dubcek, Alexander, 33,
 34, 35

E
Earth First!, 161, 165
East Germany (GDR),
 dissent in, 8, 31, 36,
 37; 1989, 13, 35-36,
 37; peace activity in,
 37; Uprising 1953, 35,
 36. See also: Berlin
 Wall, fall of
Eastern Europe in cold
 war, 78; COs in, 143;
 dialogue with nuclear
 protesters, 144; dissent
 in 10, 11, 29-31; 1989,
 3, 31-32, 36-37, 67;
 peace activity in, 137.
 See also individual
 countries
Ecuador, resisting
 neoliberalism, 171
El Salvador, 1944, 10, 89
End Conscription
 Council, 64
Environmental
 movements, 127, 128

Environmental protest, in
 China, 57; and
 corporations, 172-73,
 178; in Yugoslavia, 53.
 See also: Green
 movements, Green
 campaigns; nuclear
 energy, protests
 against
Estonia, dissent and
 resistance in, 32-33
Europe, occupied in
 World War II, 3, 10,
 17, 18. See also
 individual countries
European Nuclear
 Disarmament (END),
 144, 146, 149
European Social Forum,
 168; website, 176
Evans, Gwynfor, 106, 107
Everyman III, 148-49

F
Factory occupations, 122,
 178; Argentina, 170
Fang Lizhi, 56
Feminist movements,
 127, 156; and
 environment, 160;
 and peace, 152-53,
 156-67, 158-59; and
 strikes, 158
Feminist protest, 5, 9, 48,
 155-59;
Fiji coups 1987, 16, 17
France, COs in, 142;
 environmental protest,
 160, 162, 163;
 feminism in, 157;
 nuclear weapons
 protest, 147; peace
 movements, 138;
 student protest, 128.
 See also: Algerian
 War, French Generals,
 May Events 1968

Freedom Rides, (US) 112; (Australia) 166

French Generals' coup attempt 1961, 16, 17, 78, 153

Fuel Tax protests, 125

G

Gandhi, Mahatma, 1,2,3,5,9,10, 11, 13-16, 137, 140, 175, 176, 177, 178; and civil disobedience 7, 8; and peace brigades 20, 21; and training, 180, 181. See also: satyagraha; South Africa, Gandhi in

Gandhian influence, 21, 32, 67, 163

Gandhian movement, 137

Gandhian thought, 3, 13, 15

Genoa G8 protest, 169, 170

Georgia, dissent in Soviet era, 50; in 2003, 4, 68, 78, 80, 82-83;

Germany, East, see East Germany

Germany, West, COs in, 142-43, environmental protest, 160, 161, 163; Greens, 160; nuclear weapons protest, 144, 147, 148; peace movements, 138; student protest, 128, 129, 130

Ghana, independence struggle, 26, 28

Global Justice Movement/resisting neoliberalism, 5, 8, 12, 167-74; and environmental protest, 159, 172; resisting

IMF, 170-71; resisting World Bank, 122; summit protests, 167, 169

Golani Druze, 99-100

Golden Rule voyage, 148, 150

Gomulka, 41, 42

Gorbachev, Mikhail, 36, 50-51

Grape strike and boycott, 122, 123

Greece, resisting Colonels, 78, 84-85

Green movement/ campaigns, 5, 10, 11, 159-65. See also: Environmental protest

Greenham Common, 138, 145, 158, 159

Greenpeace, 159, 160, 161, 169, 181, 182; Greenpeace III, 149

Guatemala, 1944, 10, 89, 91; death squads, 20; land campaigns, 120; refugee accompaniment, 20, 92

Gulf Peace Team, 21, 151-52

Gulf War 1991, draft resistance, 139; opposition to, 11, 19, 138, 151, 153; training for nonviolence, 183

H

Havel, Vaclav, 10, 29, 35

Homeless campaigns, 124

Honduras, land campaigns, 120

Hungary, in 19th century, 2; dissent in, 31, 38-40; 1956, 35, 37, 38-39, 41; 1989, 33, 36, 39, 40; peace activity in 38, 40;

I

India, Gandhian campaigns in 14, 16; independence movement, 3, 10, 13, 16; environmental protest, 127-28,

Indigenous campaigns, 12, 91, 127, 128, 165-67; and environmental protest, 159, 165, 166, 172; and opposing neoliberalism, 168, 171, 174. See also: Zapatistas

Indonesia, resisting repression, 11

International Solidarity Movement, 19, 102

Intifada, First, see Palestine

Ireland, independence movement, 2

Iran, overthrow of Shah, 100-101

Iraq War 2003, opposition to, 12, 151, 168

Israel, COs and draft resistance, 141, 143; opposition to occupation of Palestine, 104-105

Italy, environmental protest, 160; nuclear weapons protest, 147; student protest, 129

J

Jabiluka, Stop, 166, 172

Japan, environmental protest, 164, 165; nuclear weapons protest, 147; opposition to Vietnam War, 131; Security Treaty protest, 154; student protest, 128, 129, 154

K

Kaohsiung protest, 75, 76
Kaunda, Kenneth, 23, 25, 26, 146
Kenya, independence struggle, 27-28
Kenyatta, Jomo, 27
King, Martin Luther Jr., 108-109, 110, 111, 112; and civil disobedience, 4, 7; and Gandhi, 10, 14; and Vietnam, 136
Konrad, George, 39
KOR (Workers' Defence Committee), 42
Korea, South, resisting repression, 67, 69-70; student resistance in 69, 70
Kosovo, under Tito, 51, 81; resistance 1980s and 1990s, 2, 4, 18, 53, 78, 79, 81-82;
Kwangju Uprising, 69, 70
Kyrgyzstan 2005, 6, 68

L

Lambrakis, Grigor, 83, 84
Land occupations, 5, 92, 119,120
Larzac, 20, 154, 155
Latin America, 11, 20; feminism in, 156; resisting military, 89-99; social movements in, 127; US campaigns for justice in, 138. See also: Land occupations
Latvia, dissent and resistance, 32-33
Lebanon 2005, 4, 100
Lithuania, dissent and resistance, 32-33
Livermore protests, 9
Luthuli, Albert, 62, 63

M

Madagascar, 60, 80
Malawi (Nyasaland), 23, 24-25
Malcolm X, 14, 108, 110, 112
Mandela, Nelson, 60, 61, 62
March on Washington 1963, 108, 109, 110
May Events 1968, France, 10, 71, 78, 130, 157
May Events 1992, Thailand, 76, 77
Medvedev, Roy, 48, 49
Medvedev, Zhores, 48, 49
Menchu, Rigoberta, 91
Mexico, movements against neoliberalism, 92, 174
Middle East, 10, 11; feminism in 156; resisting repression, 99-105
Miners' Strike (Britain), 123-24
Mongolia 1990, 6, 8, 30
Moscow coup attempt 1991, 16, 18, 50, 51
Moscow Trust Group (peace group), 49
Mothers of the Plaza de Mayo, 92, 93
Movement for Democratic Change (MDC), 65, 66
Movimento Sem Terra, 119, 120
Muste, A.J., 128, 133, 140, 150
Muste Memorial Institute, 9

N

Nagy, Imre, 37, 38, 39, 44

Narmada dam protests, 161, 164
Nepal 1990, 6, 11, 67
Netherlands, environmental protest in, 160; nuclear weapons protest, 147
New Internationalist, 160, 168
New Left, 128-31, 149
New Zealand, COs in, 142; indigenous campaigns, 165, 167; nuclear protests, 150, 163; peace protest, 138
Nicaragua, 20
Nigeria, independence struggle, 28. See also: Ogoni resistance
Nkrumah, Kwame, 26
Nonviolence training, 176, 178, 180-83
Nonviolent intervention, 3, 18-21, 132, 133, 151, 152, 153
Northern Ireland, 2, 113; Protestant Workers' Strike, 116; troops out campaign, 138. See also: Civil Rights Movement, and Peace People
Norway, in World War II, 2, 16; COs in, 143; environmental protest, 160; nuclear weapons protest, 147
Nuclear energy, protests against, 9, 144, 160, 163, 178, 182
Nuclear testing, protests against, 20, 144, 159; French tests, 138, 140, 148, 149, 150, 160; Soviet tests, 148-49; US tests, 148, 150

Nuclear weapons, protests against, 9, 128, 137, 138, 139, 144-45, 146-51; archives, 178; training for protest, 182

O

Ogoni resistance to Shell, 161, 172-73
OTPOR (Serbian students), 80, 82

P

Pacific Islands, women's peace protest, 138
Pakistan, resisting repression, 70-72
Palestine, First Intifada, 2, 101, 102-103; transnational support for, 19, 21, 102;
Palestine Centre for Nonviolence, 104
Panama, resisting repression, 97-98
Papandreou, Andreas, 84, 85
Papandreou, George, 84
Parks, Rosa, 109
Peace brigades, see Gandhi
Peace Brigades International, 19, 20, 91
Peace movements, general, 128, 137-39; archives, 178. See also: Algerian War, protests against; COs and draft resistance; Gulf War 1991, opposition to; Iraq War, opposition to; Nuclear weapons, protests against; Peace People; Vietnam War, opposition to; and

under individual countries
Peace News 20, 117, 139, 160, 176, 177
Peace People, 41, 117
Peace tax, see War tax resistance
Perez Esquivel, Adolfo, 90
Peru, 90
Philippines, environmental protest, 172; land occupations, 121; people power: 1983-86, 3, 10, 11, 13, 67, 72-74; 1991, 72, 74-75, 80
Ploughshares, East Timor, 152
Ploughshares, Trident, 138, 151, 183
Poland, Catholic Church in, 40; 1956, 33, 35; dissent and strikes 1960s-80s, 30, 31, 40, 41-44; 1989, 33, 44. See also Solidarity Movement
Poll tax protests, 125
Portugal, 1974 revolution, 73, 77, 78
Prague Spring, 33-34, 129
Praxis, 52, 53
Protestant workers strike, 4

Q

Quakers (Society of Friends), 139, 143; AFSC, 140; training, 183

R

Rainbow Warrior, 150, 161
Randolph, A. Philip, 109

Rawls, John, on civil disobedience, 7, 8
Romania, dissent in, 44-45; 1989, 12, 45; Hungarian minority in, 45; relations with USSR, 44
Ruckus (Society), 169, 183
Russell, Bertrand, 145; on civil disobedience, 8, 146; and International War Crimes Tribunal, 133
Bertrand Russell Committee, 83
Russia, in 1905, 7, 12
Rustin, Bayard, 109, 110, 111, 128

S

Saakashvili, Mikhail, 82, 83
Sakharov, Andrei, 48, 49
Sarowiwa, Kenule, 172, 173
Satyagraha, 3, 9, 14, 15, 16, 60, 67
Seabrook (Clamshell Alliance), 9
Seattle WTO protests, 167, 169, 170
Serbia, feminist protest, 152-53; resisting Milosevic: 1990s, 79, 80-81; 2000, 7, 12, 13, 80-81
SERPAJ (Service for Peace and Justice), 89, 90, 97, 99
Shanti Sena (peace brigade), 20, 21
Sharp, Gene, archives of, 179; on civilian defence, 53, 176; on Gandhi, 16; theory of, 3, 8, 10, 12,53, 177, 183

Solidarity Movement (Poland), 40-41, 43-44
Solzhenitsyn, Alexander, 46, 48, 49
South Africa, Gandhi in, 2, 13, 14, 15, 60; boycotts of, 63-64; COs and draft resistance, 64, 143; resisting apartheid, 11, 23, 60-64, 178; resisting neoliberalism, 171-72
Southern Christian Leadership Conference (SCLC), 107, 109, 111, 112
Soviet Union, 29, 30, 31, 44; Czechoslovakia invasion, 17, 33, 34, 48; dialogue with nuclear protesters, 144; dissent in, 46, 47-49, 50-51; peace activity in, 49
Soweto children's movement, 60-61, 62
Spain, feminism in, 155; environmental protest in, 161; resisting Franco, 77, 85-87
Sri Lanka, accompaniment in, 20
Student Nonviolent Coordinating Committee (SNCC), 107, 110, 111, 112
Students for a Democratic Society (SDS), 129, 130, 131, 135
Sweatshop protests, 173
Sweden, and civilian defence, 16, 17; environmental protest, 160, 161; feminism in, 155; nuclear weapons protest, 147

T
Taiwan, protests against repression, 75-76
Tanganyika, independence struggle, 22
Thailand, environmental protest, 164; resisting military rule: 1973, 76, 77; 1992, 11, 67, 76, 77
Theodorakis, Mikis, 85
Thich Nhat Hanh, 77, 134
Thompson, Edward P., 40, 146
Thoreau, Henry, on civil disobedience, 2, 7, 8, 10, 140
Tiananmen 1989, 12, 13, 55-57
Tibet, dissent in, 58-59
Tokes, Laszlo, 45
Tolstoy, Leo, 2, 10, 140
Trident, see Ploughshares, Trident
Tutu, Desmond, 63

U
Uganda, independence struggle, 22
Ukraine, dissent in Soviet era, 47, 50; 2004-5, 4, 68, 78, 87-89
United States (USA),10, 11; COs and draft resistance, 137, 142, 143; environmental protest, 9, 161, 162, 163, 164, 165, 178, 182; feminism in, 155, 157, 159; Gandhian influence in, 14; global justice protests, 169, 170, 182; indigenous campaigns, 165, 167; peace archives in, 178-79; peace campaigns in, 9, 138, 154, 155; nonviolence training in, 181, 182, 183; nuclear weapons protests, 137, 147, 149, 150, 151, 159; resistance to Vietnam War, 131, 132, 134-36; student campaigns in, 128, 129, 130-31; sweatshop protests, 173. See also: Civil Rights Movement
Uruguay, resisting repression, 98-99
USSR, see Soviet Union

V
Velvet Revolution, 33, 35
Venezuela, 2002 coup attempt, 92; land occupations, 121
Vietnam War, general opposition to, 9, 10, 128, 129, 131-36, 137, 138, 140; COs and draft resistance, 133, 135, 136, 139, 143; GIs and veterans resist, 134, 135, 136
Voices in the Wilderness, 19
Vorkuta camp strike, 1953, 46

W
Walesa, Lech, 44
War Resisters' International, 64, 67, 133, 137, 138, 143; WRL training, 183
War tax resistance, 142, 143
Wei Jingsheng, 55
Welsh nationalist protest, 106-107
Witness for Peace, 20, 92

Women in Black (Israel), 105
Women in Black (Serbia), 81, 152-53
Women's Liberation, see feminist movements
Worker occupations, see factory occupations
World Peace Brigade, 20, 21, 26
World War II, resistance in, 2, 3, 17, 18
World Social Forum, 168; website, 176

Y
Yesh Gvul (There is a Limit), 104
Yugoslavia, break-up of, 31, 79; dissent in, 31, 52, 53, 129; 1968, 52, 53, 129; nonviolent intervention in, 153; peace activity in, 53, 137, 152-53
Yushchenko, Viktor, 87, 88, 89

Z
Zambia, independence struggle, 21, 23, 24, 25-26
Zapatistas, 12, 92, 168, 174
Zimbabwe, resisting white rule, 23-24; resisting Mugabe 2000-, 60, 65-67

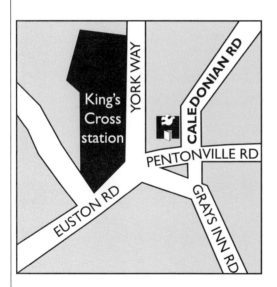